THE COMPLETE
STIR-FRY
COOKBOOK

THE COMPLETE
STIR-FRY
COOKBOOK

bay books

Curried Lobster with Capsicum, page 178

Thai Beef Salad, page 41

Quick Beef and Noodle Salad, page 46

Contents

Indian Lamb and Spinach, page 87

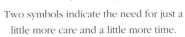

Lemon Grass Prawns, page 190

Chicken Chow Mein, page 118

Vietnamese Chicken Salad, page 142

Tempeh with Chinese Greens, page 204

Stir-fry Know-how

Once the ingredients are prepared, the secret of stir-frying is to cook quickly over high heat and keep the food moving constantly around the wok.

Stir-frying is a fast, relatively healthy way to cook food. It involves quick cooking where the food is tossed around in a wok over high heat in a minimum amount of oil (although we have also included some recipes that combine initial stir-frying of ingredients with a short simmer to produce typical Asian curries). Preparation of ingredients is essential because once you start to cook there is no time to chop anything extra or hunt through cupboards.

OILS

For stir-frying, use oils that have a high smoking point. These include canola oil and peanut oil. Olive oil may be used to add flavour to warm stir-fry salads. If you are trying to cut down on fat, use an oil spray.

INGREDIENTS

Meat and Poultry: Meat to be stir-fried needs to be from a cut which will be tender after only a short cooking time. It should be cut across the grain into strips or small pieces so that it cooks quickly and evenly. Use chicken breast or thigh. Marinating meat or chicken helps to tenderize it and allows flavours to permeate the meat. Make sure the marinade is drained well before stir-frying, otherwise the meat or chicken will tend to steam rather than fry.

Seafood: Quick cooking suits seafood perfectly. Squid, prawns and scallops need the briefest possible time in the wok until they are cooked through. Use firm-fleshed fish so it can be stir-fried without breaking up.

Vegetables: Stir-frying affects different vegetables in different ways. The intense heat caramelizes their sugar, but retains most of their vitamins and colour. Vegetables such as cauliflower,

potatoes and carrots require a slightly longer cooking time and should be cut into small pieces or thin strips, whereas peas, asparagus and mushrooms should be cooked quickly at the end. Bean sprouts, herbs and greens, such as bok choy and spinach, should be added for the final minute or so, but for no longer because they will wilt quickly.

WOKS

There are many different types of wok available. The traditional basic wok is made of carbon steel. In its modern form the wok comes made of copper, stainless steel, cast iron and non-stick materials. Buy the heaviest wok you can find as it will retain heat well without scorching. You can also buy electric woks—these are non-stick and are kept at a constant high heat by an electric element.

The shape of a wok should be wide with deep, sloping sides and a round or wide, flattish bottom. It should be about 30–35 cm (12–14 inches) in diameter as small amounts of food can be cooked easily enough in a large wok but not vice versa. Flat-bottomed woks work well on electric stovetops as they sit directly on the hotplate—a wok ring often holds the wok too far away from the heat source for successful stir-frying. Some of the more modern stovetops have a special wide gas burner for woks.

Wok lids are important as they can be used to form a seal for a couple of minutes to steam any slower cooking ingredients or greens. Many recipes will instruct you to cover the wok for a short time at the end of cooking.

If you do not have a wok, you can use a large heavy-based frying pan for stir-frying, but you will need to cook the food in smaller batches to prevent it stewing.

SEASONING THE WOK

Steel woks come with an oily film which needs to be scrubbed off with hot water and detergent before use. The wok should then be dried off and heated over high heat. When it starts to become hot, brush it with vegetable oil, remove it from the heat and wipe it dry with a paper towel (it will blacken

You can buy electric woks that are non-stick and are kept at a constant high heat by an element.

The oily film on a new wok has to be scrubbed off before use.

A wok will blacken as you season it and turn darker as you use it.

as you season it). Repeat this step several times to season the wok. As you use the wok, the seasoned layer (*wok hay*) will build up, turning darker and darker and adding flavour to the food.

A properly seasoned or a non-stick wok shouldn't be cleaned by scouring with an abrasive material like steel wool. Each time, after you have finished cooking and your wok has cooled down, simply wash it with hot water and a soft brush or cloth. Make sure you dry it throrougly over heat before storing in a dry area, otherwise it will rust. If you have a steel wok you should wipe or brush the inside with a very thin layer of oil before putting it away. This will keep it in good condition. Electric woks should also be rinsed in hot water, dried very thoroughly and coated with a thin film of oil after use.

The outside of the wok may occasionally need a good clean. Try not to used detergents—they damage the seasoning. If you do burn a stir-fry, you may need to use detergent and even a fine steel wool to clean the wok and may need to re-season.

WOK TOOLS

Utensils needed to stir-fry are minimal—a sharp knife for preparation and a wok turner or *charn*. This is a spade-like scoop, ideal for the continuous scooping and turning required. Flat spatulas also work well because they move the food around easily and follow the curvature of the wok.

Only wooden or plastic utensils should be used on non-stick woks so that the surface is not scratched.

Mesh ladles, a charn and chopsticks—ideal tools for cooking and eating stir-fries.

TEN STEPS FOR SUCCESSFUL STIR-FRYING

1 The most important thing is to have everything ready before you start to stir-fry. Arrange all the ingredients in bowls in the order you are going to cook them and measure out any liquids, pastes, sauces or cornflour that you might be adding. Once you start cooking, it is hard to stop and chop something up without overcooking whatever is already in the wok.

2 Cut all meat and vegetables into even-sized, smallish pieces. The smaller the pieces, the faster they will cook.

3 Choose vegetables which will look colourful as well as taste good with the other ingredients.

4 Heat the wok until very hot before you add the oil. When you add the oil, swirl it around to thoroughly coat the side and base of the wok. Do not start cooking until the oil is hot—the oil will start to shimmer when it is hot enough and will hiss when the first ingredients go in.

5 Drain any marinade from the ingredients before cooking and make sure all vegetables are quite dry. If any liquid hits the hot oil first, it will spit. If meat is added to the wok straight from a wet marinade, the meat will tend to steam or stew rather than fry.

6 Add the flavourings, such as ginger and garlic, first, then add the slower-cooking ingredients, followed by the faster-cooking ones. If you have too much to fit in the wok at one time, fry the meat first in batches and set it aside, otherwise it will stew. Reheat the wok between batches, adding a little more oil if necessary. Salty liquids, such as soy sauce, should be added at the end as they may draw water out of the vegetables and make them mushy.

7 Keep all the ingredients moving constantly around the wok to make sure everything cooks evenly and doesn't start to burn.

8 If an ingredient looks as if it might burn, quickly add the next ingredient to reduce the temperature of the wok.

9 If the ingredients start to look a little dry, add a splash of water.

10 Serve immediately—stir-fries don't wait for anyone!

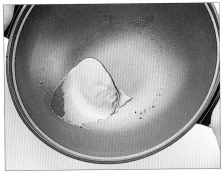

Heat the wok, add the oil and swirl it around to coat the base and side of the wok.

When the oil starts to shimmer, add the first ingredients and toss well.

Stir-fry meat in batches if there is a lot of it, to prevent it stewing.

Keep the food moving to ensure even cooking and prevent burning.

Stir-fry Ingredients

Stir-frying is a quick, easy and healthy method of cooking, which combines the best of fresh produce and exotic flavours. Most wok-cooked recipes are obviously Asian in origin, and so may require a trip to an Asian supermarket, grocer or local Chinatown. However, ingredients such as bok choy and mirin are becoming popular and are now widely available in local supermarkets.

Annatto seeds

These are small red triangular-shaped seeds with a subtle flavour and vivid colour. Used extensively in Latin American cooking, they were introduced to the Philippines by the Spanish traders. Once they have been fried in oil, the seeds are usually removed and the coloured oil is used in the dish. Annatto seeds are used by the Chinese to give their roast pork its characteristic pinkish red colouring.

Asian shallots

These are small onions with a papery reddish, purple skin, commonly used in Asian cookery. These grow in bulbs like garlic and are sold in segments that look like large cloves of garlic. They have a concentrated flavour and are easy to slice and grind. You can use red onions as a substitute—one small red onion to 4–6 shallots. French shallots are not a good substitute—the flavour is quite different.

Banana leaves

The large pliable green leaves of the banana tree are used throughout Asia as disposable plates and platters, as well as for wrapping food that is to be baked or steamed. Before use, remove the centre stalk, rinse the leaves in cold water and then blanch briefly in boiling water to soften. They are available in packets from Asian food stores if you don't have access to fresh. If they are to be used for wrapping food for cooking, foil can be used instead.

Barbecued duck pancakes

These round wrappers, made with wheat flour, are traditionally eaten as part of the Chinese meal, Peking duck, traditional to the north of the country. Crisp duck skin, raw spring onion and hoisin sauce are wrapped in the pancakes. The pancakes are sold frozen at Asian supermarkets or ask for them when you buy your barbecued duck.

Barbecued Chinese duck

These are ducks that have been spiced and glazed and then spit-roasted over a barbecue. The ducks are available from Chinese barbecue shops, which can be found in any Chinatown. You can ask the vendor to chop, shred or bone the duck for you if the recipe requires it. If you can't find barbecued duck, you could use home-roasted duck, but the flavour will not be as good (and the dish not as convenient).

Barbecued Chinese pork (*char siew*)

This is pork that has been marinated in five-spice powder, soy sauce, sugar and annatto and then spit-roasted over a barbecue. It has a strong flavour and particularly distinctive reddish-pink flesh, coloured by the annatto seeds in the marinade. The pork is available from Chinese barbecue shops, which can be found in any Chinatown. If you can't find barbecued pork, you could use home-roasted pork, but the flavour will not be as good (and the dish not as convenient).

Basil

Thai basil has a strong aroma and flavour, so don't use more than is stated in the recipe. There are three varieties most commonly used. *Bai horapha* tastes rather like anise, looks like sweet basil and is used in Thai curry dishes. *Bai manglaek* has a lemony flavour, tiny leaves and is usually sprinkled over salads. *Bai grapao* has a clove-like taste and purple-reddish tinged leaves. It doesn't store well, so buy it at the last minute. European basil can be used as a substitute for all varieties if necessary. Thai basil is often called 'holy basil' because it is grown around temples.

Bean sprouts

Used mainly in salads and as a stir-fry vegetable, soy bean sprouts are crunchy, white short sprouts. Discard any that are limp or brown. They are highly perishable so keep in the fridge and use within three days of purchase. Traditionally, the scraggly ends are removed before use.

Black beans

Salted black beans are available canned or in vacuum packs from Asian stores. They should be whole and dark and must be rinsed in cold water to get rid of their excess saltiness. Chop the beans before cooking for a more robust flavour. There are two different types of black beans—the Chinese version (which we use in this book) and the Mexican version. The Mexican ones are also known as 'turtle' beans and are often used for thick Caribbean soups.

Black fungus

This is a Chinese ingredient that is also used in some Thai dishes. It has no real flavour but is used for its chewy texture. It looks like dried black wrinkled paper but, after soaking in water for about 10 minutes, it swells and resembles wavy seaweed or jelly. Stored in its dried form it will keep indefinitely. It is also known as 'wood ear' or 'cloud ear' mushroom.

Bok choy

This popular Chinese vegetable (also known as Chinese cabbage) has fleshy white stems and dark green leaves. The whole leaf can be chopped and used for stir-frying, once the tough ends have been cut off. Baby bok choy is smaller and more tender. Shanghai bok choy has pale green stems.

Candlenuts

These large cream nuts, similar to macadamias in shape but with a drier texture, cannot be eaten raw as their oil is thought to be toxic. They are ground and used to thicken sauces and curries, and in Indonesia and Malaysia they are used to make candles, which is how they came by their name.

Chillies

Chillies make up one branch of the capsicum family (the other branch being sweet peppers). Red chillies are simply ripened green chillies, which means they are a little sweeter (just like red and green capsicums). Names of chillies vary from country to country, with growers making up new names all the time. For that reason, most recipes will simply state 1 red chilli or 1 green chilli. Dried chillies and chilli powder are also available.

Bird's eye chillies are the smallest and hottest variety of all. From 1–3 cm (1/2–1 1/4 inches) long, they are available fresh, dried or pickled in brine.

Small red chillies, approximately 5 cm (2 inches) long are the chillies used to make chilli powder and chilli flakes. They are those most commonly used in Thai cooking.

Medium chillies, 10–15 cm (4–6 inches) long, are most commonly used in Indonesian and Malaysian cooking. They are thin chillies and are hot but not overpowering, with the seeds the hottest part.

Large red and green chillies, 15–20 cm (6–8 inches) long, these thick chillies are used in Northern Thai cooking. The ripe red chillies are fiery. To avoid skin irritation, take great care when chopping or seeding chillies. Wear rubber gloves if you can, otherwise, wash your hands thoroughly in warm soapy water after chopping and before touching your face or eyes. If you like a hot curry, leave the chilli seeds in. In you prefer a milder flavour, discard the fiery seeds and membrane. Whole chillies freeze well in plastic bags and can be chopped while frozen. Some chillies are available dried and are soaked in water to soften before use.

Chinese broccoli

Chinese broccoli (*gai larn*) or Chinese kale has smooth round stems with dark green leaves and small white flowers. The stems are the part most commonly eaten.

Chinese dried mushrooms

These impart a distinct flavour to the dish and are used in Asian recipes with a Chinese influence. Store in an airtight container in a cool place and soak before use.

Choy sum

This flowering Chinese cabbage has green stems and yellow flowers. It is often confused with *gai larn* (Chinese broccoli), which is similar in appearance but has white flowers instead of yellow. The two are interchangeable in recipes.

Coriander

Also known, in its fresh form, as cilantro, coriander is the most commonly used herb in Thai cooking. The whole plant can be used—the root, stem, seeds and leaves. The seeds are roasted and then ground in a spice mill and used in curry pastes. Fresh coriander is available from greengrocers, supermarkets and Asian food stores, or in pots from nurseries.

The leaves (which look very similar to those of continental parsley) are used for their fresh, peppery flavour and as a garnish. For storage, wash and dry the fresh herbs before placing them in plastic bags in the fridge, where they will keep for 5–6 days. Dried coriander is not a suitable substitute for fresh.

Crisp-fried onion and garlic

Finely sliced garlic cloves or onions are deep-fried until crisp. They are often added to stir-fries just before serving, as a garnish. If you don't have time to make your own, you can buy them in packets. To make your own, finely slice an onion and garlic and cook over low heat in oil, stirring until crisp and golden. Drain well on paper towels and then season liberally with salt. Serve immediately so they are crisp.

Dashi

This is the basic stock of Japanese cuisine. Made with dried kelp and dried bonito (a fish), it is available packaged in ground form, as granules or in flakes—add hot water to make up to stock.

Dried lily buds

These Chinese specialities are used for their texture and subtle flavour. They have no real substitute, but could be omitted without radically altering the flavour of the dish.

Dried mandarin peel

More commonly used as a seasoning in Chinese slow-cooked dishes, you will also find these adding flavour to a couple of stir-fry dishes. Dried mandarin and tangerine peel are easily prepared at home and can be stored in an airtight container for months. Use a vegetable peeler to slice the peel thinly. Cut the strips into small pieces and carefully scrape off any remaining pith or flesh. Place the pieces in a single layer on a baking tray and dry in a preheated 180°C (350°F/Gas 4) oven for 15 minutes. Three mandarins will produce about a third of a cup of dried peel.

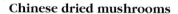

Dried shrimp

Tiny salted shrimp that have been dried in the sun, these are added to stir-fries for their strong flavour.

Eggplants (aubergines)

There are many different sizes, shapes and colours of eggplant now available. Tiny pea-sized eggplants are available in some Asian food stores and are excellent for stir-fries, although they can sometimes be a little bitter. Small long lady-finger eggplants are also used. Large European eggplants can be used, but should be cut up small for quick and even stir-frying.

Fish sauce

This brown, salty sauce with its characteristically strong fishy aroma is an important ingredient in Thai and Vietnamese cookery. It is made from small fish that have been fermented in the sun for a long time and is usually added as a seasoning at the end of cooking to balance sweetness and add saltiness. The smell from the sauce can be so off-putting that people using it for the first time may think there is something wrong with it.

Galangal

Related to ginger and quite similar looking, galangal is pinkish in colour and has a distinct peppery flavour. Use fresh galangal where possible and be careful when handling that you don't get the juice on your clothes or hands, as it stains. Dried galangal must be soaked in hot water before use. Galangal powder is also available.

Ginger

This delicious aromatic ingredient is important in Asian cooking. Fresh ginger is now readily available—buy firm, unwrinkled rhizomes and store them in a plastic bag so they don't dry out. To prepare ginger for cooking, simply remove the skin with a vegetable peeler and then either grate, finely slice or shred the ginger before stir-frying. Very young ginger may not even require peeling.

Green pawpaw

These are not a different variety, but merely underripe pawpaws. To shred the green pawpaw, peel it and slice it finely. It is sometimes blanched lightly before shredding.

Hoisin sauce

This thick reddish brown sauce, made from soy beans, sugar, spices and red rice, has a sweet spicy flavour and is popular for stir-fries. It is also used as a dipping sauce or for glazes. Available from Asian food stores and supermarkets.

Hot bean paste

Made from fermented soy beans and chilli, this sauce can be very hot and should be added very lightly.

Kaffir limes and leaves

A knobbly dark-skinned lime with a very strong lime fragrance and flavour. The leaves are finely shredded for use in stir-fries. The rind is also very pungent and is often grated for adding to dishes. The leaves are available in packets from Asian grocers.

Kecap manis

This is a thick sweet soy sauce that is widely used in Indonesian and Malaysian cooking as a seasoning or sauce. If it's not available, use soy sauce sweetened with a little soft brown sugar.

Lemon grass

This aromatic fresh herb is used in curry pastes and stir-fries, as well as myriad other Asian dishes. The stems can be up to 60 cm (2 feet) long. Trim the base, remove the tough outer layers and finely slice, chop or pound the white inner layers in a mortar and pestle or processor. For pastes, use the tender white portion just above the root. The whole stem, trimmed and washed thoroughly, can be added to dishes that are to be simmered, and then removed before serving. Dried lemon grass is available and needs soaking for half an hour before use. The flavour of fresh is superior.

Mirin

This low-alcohol rice wine, made from sake, is used in Japanese dishes. The sugar content helps to glaze food when it is cooked. Choose pure mirin as some brands are a sweet seasoning type that have corn syrup and salt added. If mirin is not available, you can use dry sherry or sweet white wine.

Miso

This thick fermented paste is made from soy beans and other ingredients, including wheat and rice. It is available in many varieties, including light brown, red, brown, yellow and white, each differing in flavour and texture.

Mushrooms

Shiitake, oyster and enoki are all types of mushroom used in Asian cookery and are all usually available fresh from supermarkets. Shiitake mushrooms, originally from Japan and Korea, have a distinctive meaty flavour. These large, dark mushrooms are now cultivated worldwide and are often found in the USA under the name *golden oak*. Often sold dried as 'winter' or 'Chinese black dried' mushrooms. Oyster mushrooms are delicately flavoured and take their name because they have a slight taste of oysters. Enoki mushrooms are also known as enokitake mushrooms. They come in clumps of long thin stems with tiny white caps and have to be gently separated before use. Available fresh and dried. Straw mushrooms, grown in straw, have globe-shaped caps and no stems. They are available in cans and have a musty flavour.

Oyster sauce

This is a Cantonese staple, found in many Thai dishes that have a Chinese influence. It is made from dried oysters and is a rich salty sauce, used for flavouring. Refrigerate after opening to prevent mould forming.

Palm sugar

This caramel-flavoured sugar is obtained from either the palmyra palm or sugar palm and is bought either in block form or in jars. The colour ranges from pale golden to very dark brown. Palm sugar is thick and crumbly and can be gently melted or grated before adding to dishes. Soft brown sugar is an adequate replacement if necessary.

Rice vinegar and seasoned rice vinegar

Rice vinegar is a mild, sweet, delicately flavoured vinegar made from rice. Seasoned rice vinegar is similar, but has sugar and salt added to it.

Seasoning sauce

This thin salty soy bean seasoning sauce is used in Asian cooking to enhance the flavour of dishes. It is also sold under the name Golden Mountain sauce.

Sesame oil

This very aromatic oil, made from roasted sesame seeds, is used in Thai recipes that have a Chinese influence. Use it sparingly, as it has quite a strong rich flavour and a little goes a long way. Rather than using it for stir-frying, you will often find a teaspoonful of it added to the cooking oil to add flavour.

Sesame and seaweed sprinkle

Seaweed is really only popular in Japan, where it is eaten as a vegetable. Wakame is the most famous variety, then kombu and nori. This combination of dried and finely chopped nori, roasted sesame seeds and salt is used as a seasoning to be sprinkled on noodle dishes after cooking.

Shoshoyu (Japanese soy sauce)

Also known as shoyu. This is much lighter and sweeter than Chinese soy sauce and not thick like kecap manis. It is naturally brewed from soya beans and grains such as wheat or barley, and so needs to be refrigerated after opening.

Shrimp paste (bagoong)

This is a paste made from shrimps or prawns that have been salted and fermented in earthenware pots. It is used as a condiment as well as an ingredient in stir-fries.

Shrimp paste, dried (blachan)

Made from prawns or shrimps that have been dried, salted and pounded into blocks, this has a pungent smell and, once opened, should be sealed in an airtight container in the fridge (the paste itself does not require refrigeration, but this will reduce the aroma). It should always be roasted (usually wrapped up in a foil parcel) or fried before adding to a recipe. Also known as belacci, terasi or kapi.

Sichuan pepper

Sichuan (Szechwan) pepper is a tiny red berry not related to ordinary peppercorns. It is aromatic and is one of the ingredients in five spice powder. Remove the black seeds and dry-fry it to bring out its full flavour before using it in cooking.

Snake beans

These are long, deep green, stringless beans that grow up to 30 cm (12 inches) long. They are cut into short lengths for stir-frying. They do not have a very strong flavour and are easy to prepare.

Soy sauce

This popular dark salty sauce of Chinese origin is made from fermented roasted soy beans, another grain (usually wheat) and brine. It is aged for up to two years before being filtered and bottled. Soy sauce is indispensable in Asian cooking and is now widely available. It should be kept in the fridge after opening.

Star anise

This dark brown star-shaped pod with its distinctive aniseed flavour is used whole to flavour curries, or ground in pastes.

Tamari

This dark, richly flavoured Japanese soy sauce is made from rice rather than wheat. It can be used as a seasoning or dipping sauce.

Tamarind

Tamarind is available in a variety of forms and this fibrous pod is used to give an acidic flavour to dishes. Most commonly found as a concentrate—a sour liquid made from the fruits of the tamarind tree. It is also available as a pulp, which must be soaked in hot water for 5 minutes, then strained before use.

Tempeh

Similar to tofu, tempeh is made from fermented soy beans. Quite firm in texture, it is suitable for most types of cooking. It is popular with vegetarians and vegans as, like tofu, when it is marinated it successfully takes on the flavour of the marinade.

Tofu (bean curd)

Silken tofu: A very soft tofu often used in soups. Take care when cooking with it or it will break up, so not usually used for stir-fries.

Silken firm tofu: Slightly firmer than silken tofu, it holds its shape a little better. More often used in soups than stir-fries.

Firm tofu: This soft tofu will hold its shape when cooking and soak up marinade flavours. Suitable for stir-frying.

Hard tofu: Rubbery and firm, this won't break up during cooking. Use for stir-frying.

Tofu tempeh: Tofu and tempeh are combined and pressed together. Use in the same way as firm tofu.

Deep-fried tofu puffs: Tofu is aerated and then deep-fried. This variety is excellent for stir-fries.

Noodles & Rice

Noodles and rice, the perfect accompaniments to stir-fries, come in an exciting array of types, colours, shapes and sizes. Some are pre-cooked and just need to be heated.

NOODLES

Fresh egg noodles
These are made from egg and wheat flour and need to be cooked in boiling water before use. Refrigerate until you are ready to use them.

Fresh rice noodles
Available thick or thin, or as a sheet or roll which can be cut to a desired width, these white rice noodles are steamed and lightly oiled before packing, and so are ready to use. They must be brought to room temperature before use, as they harden during refrigeration.

Hokkien noodles
These yellow, thick noodles are made from wheat flour and egg. They are pre-cooked and lightly oiled, so are ready to use. Refrigerate until ready to use, then roughly separate with your fingers. They can be soaked in hot water to soften up before stir-frying.

Instant noodles
Different brands of dried instant noodles are stocked in supermarkets. They are made from wheat flour and are very quick to prepare.

Rice sticks (dried)
Resembling fettuccine, these flat, translucent noodles are often used in stir-fries. They are sold packaged in bundles. Soak them in warm water before using.

Rice vermicelli (dried)
Sold packaged in blocks, these thin, translucent noodles need to be soaked in boiling water, or boiled until tender and thoroughly drained before use.

Soba noodles

A northern Japanese speciality made from buckwheat and/or wheat flour, these are eaten hot or cold. They absorb flavour well and are good with dishes that have a strongly flavoured dressing.

Udon noodles

White, round or flat Japanese wheat flour noodles, these are available either dried or fresh. They plump up to become slippery, fat noodles with a unique texture.

Noodles, from left to right, top row: fresh egg, Hokkien, dried rice sticks, soba.
Bottom row: fresh rice, instant, rice vermicelli, udon.

RICE

Basmati

With long fragrant grains which remain separate when cooked, this rice is very aromatic and complements Asian flavours well. Basmati rice is grown in India on the foothills of the Himalayas and is now popular throughout the world. Traditionally served with curries, where saffron is added to give the dish colour and flavour.

Brown rice

Brown rice has not had the bran removed and is therefore valued for its nutritional properties. Cooking is a lot slower than for white rice as it takes a considerable time for the water to break through the bran layer.

Jasmine rice

This is a long-grain, fragrant white rice used throughout Southeast Asia. It is usually steamed, or cooked using the absorption method. Jasmine rice is served as an accompaniment to all Thai meals.

Long-grain white rice

This is the rice which is chosen above all others by the Chinese—perhaps stemming from Confucius' insistence on eating the whitest rice available. It is grown in the monsoon region of Southeast Asia and is often referred to as 'water rice'. Long-grain white rice has been processed to remove the outer hull and bran, then polished until it is white and glossy.

Wild rice

Wild rice has a nutty flavour and a high protein content. These long dark brown grains come from an aquatic grass—so wild rice is not really a rice at all, but the grain of a water grass native to the great lakes of North America. Grown originally by the Chippewa Indians and harvested by hand, it is now farmed by machine. The grains have a delicious flavour and a distinguishable chewy texture. Wild rice requires thorough washing before use. It can be bought in small packets and is expensive compared to other rices. These days it is available mixed with brown rice and sold as a wild rice blend, which makes it cheaper.

Rice, from top: basmati, brown, jasmine, long-grain white, wild.

Rice on the Side

You can serve stir-fries with boiled white or saffron rice, or flavour your rice with pandan and coconut cream. Fried rice can be a side dish or a meal by itself. All recipes serve 6 generously.

BOILED RICE

If you don't have a rice cooker, you will need a large heavy-based pan that is wider than it is deep and has a tight-fitting lid. Before cooking, wash the rice in a sieve under running water until the water runs clear. For each 200 g (6¹/2 oz) rice, add 1¹/4 cups (315 ml/ 10 fl oz) water. Bring to the boil, cover tightly and cook over very low heat for 10 minutes. Remove from the heat and leave, covered, for 10 minutes. When you take off the lid, the surface of the rice should be dotted with steam holes. Fluff up the rice with a fork before serving. For fried rice it is best to cook your rice a day in advance and leave it in the fridge overnight. This allows the grains to dry and separate and prevents the rice being gluey.

SAFFRON RICE

2 cups (400 g/13 oz)
    basmati rice
25 g (1 oz) butter
3 bay leaves
¹/4 teaspoon saffron
    threads
2 cups (500 ml/16 fl oz)
    boiling vegetable stock

1 Wash the rice, then cover with cold water and soak for 30 minutes. Drain well.
2 Heat the butter in a frying pan, add the bay leaves and rice and cook, stirring, for 6 minutes, or until dry.
3 Soak the saffron in 2 tablespoons hot water for 5 minutes. Add to the rice with the stock and 1¹/2 cups (375 ml/12 fl oz) boiling water. Bring to the boil, then simmer, covered, for 12–15 minutes, or until all the water is absorbed and the rice is cooked.

NASI LEMAK (COCONUT RICE)

2 cups (400 g/13 oz) long-
    grain white rice
1 pandan leaf, tied in a knot
    (see NOTE)
³/4 cup (185 ml/6 fl oz)
    coconut cream

1 Rinse the rice under running water until the water runs clear, then transfer to a large bowl and cover with 1 litre (32 fl oz) cold water. Set aside to soak for 30 minutes and then drain well.
2 Bring 3 cups (750 ml/ 24 fl oz) water to the boil. Add the rice, pandan leaf and salt to taste. Reduce the heat and cook, covered, for 12 minutes, or until the rice is just cooked and tender.
3 Remove the rice from the heat and add the coconut cream. Stir gently to avoid breaking the grains of the rice. Cover the pan and set aside for 10 minutes or until the rice has absorbed the coconut cream. Lift out the pandan leaf and discard before serving.

NUTRITION PER SERVE
Protein 5 g; Fat 6.5 g;
Carbohydrate 54 g; Fibre 2 g;
Cholesterol 0 mg;
1240 kJ (295 cal)

NOTE: Pandan leaves, also known as pandanus or screw pine leaves, are used to wrap and flavour food. They are available in Asian grocery stores. Tying the leaf in a knot will make it easier to handle, but will also break the leaf and release the flavour.
Nasi Lemak is a Malaysian dish. The coconut is soothing for the palate and this rice is ideal for serving with spicy Malaysian and Indonesian food.

FRIED RICE WITH DRIED SHRIMP

3 tablespoons oil
1 egg, beaten with
    2 teaspoons water
2 cloves garlic, chopped
3 spring onions, chopped
1/2 cup (60 g/2 oz) dried
    shrimp, roughly
    chopped
4 cups (750 g/1 1/2 lb)
    cold cooked rice
    (see HINT)
1 tablespoon fish sauce
2 teaspoons Golden
    Mountain sauce
1 cup (30 g/1 oz) coriander
    leaves
1/4 pineapple, cut into
    pieces
1 cucumber, chopped
chilli sauce (see page 248),
    for serving

1 Heat 1 tablespoon of oil in a wok. Pour in the beaten egg and swirl the wok until the egg sets. Cut into quarters, flip each quarter and cook the other side. Remove the egg from the wok and cut it into thin strips.
2 Add the remaining oil and stir-fry the garlic, spring onions and shrimp for 2 minutes. Add the rice and stir-fry for 5 minutes over high heat until the rice is heated through.
3 Add the sauces, coriander and omelette strips to the wok and toss well. Arrange the rice on a serving platter. Mix together the pineapple and cucumber and serve as an accompaniment to the rice, with a little chilli sauce on the side.

NUTRITION PER SERVE
Protein 5.5 g; Fat 16 g;
Carbohydrate 40 g; Fibre 2 g;
Cholesterol 45 mg;
1380 kJ (330 cal)

HINT: You will need to cook 1 1/3 cups of raw rice to get 4 cupfuls. Don't forget to cook the rice the day before and leave it in the fridge overnight so the grains can dry out and separate before frying.

PINEAPPLE FRIED RICE

1 ripe pineapple
1/4 cup (60 ml/2 fl oz) oil
3 cloves garlic, chopped
1 onion, chopped
1–2 teaspoons chopped
    red chillies
150 g (5 oz) pork loin, diced
150 g (5 oz) peeled raw
    prawns
3 cups (550 g/1 lb 2 oz)
    cold cooked rice (see
    HINT)
2 tablespoons finely
    chopped Thai basil
2 tablespoons fish sauce
3 spring onions, finely
    sliced
2 tablespoons chopped
    coriander leaves
sliced red or green chillies

1 Cut the pineapple in half lengthways. Run a knife around the edge of the pineapple and then cut and scoop out the flesh. Chop into small pieces, discarding the core.
2 Heat 1 tablespoon of oil in a wok over high heat. Add the garlic, onion and chillies to the wok and cook for 1 minute. Add the pork and stir-fry for 2 minutes. Add the prawns and stir-fry for another 3 minutes. Remove all the meat from the wok and set aside. Reheat the wok and stir-fry the pineapple pieces for 3 minutes or until heated through and lightly golden and then remove from the wok.
3 Heat the remaining oil in the wok. Add the rice and stir-fry for 2 minutes. Return the pork, prawns and pineapple to the wok and stir thoroughly. Remove the wok from the heat.
4 Add the basil and fish sauce and toss well. Fill the pineapple shells with the fried rice. Scatter spring onions, coriander and chillies over the top and serve immediately.

NUTRITION PER SERVE
Protein 10 g; Fat 8 g;
Carbohydrate 20 g; Fibre 2 g;
Cholesterol 37 mg;
806 kJ (193 cal)

HINT: You will need to cook 1 cup of raw rice to get 3 cupfuls. Don't forget to cook the rice the day before and leave it in the fridge overnight so the grains can dry out and separate before frying.

Beef

BEEF WITH LEEKS AND SNOW PEAS

Preparation time: 25 minutes
Total cooking time: 15 minutes
Serves 4

oil, for cooking
375 g (12 oz) rump steak, cut into very
    thin strips
2–3 cloves garlic, finely chopped
1 stem lemon grass, white part only,
    finely chopped
1 leek, white part only, thinly sliced
2 celery sticks, thickly sliced
8 spring onions, diagonally sliced
150 g (5 oz) snow peas, halved
100 g (3½ oz) oyster mushrooms,
    halved
2 tablespoons kecap manis
2 tablespoons sweet chilli sauce
2 tablespoons lime or lemon juice
3 kaffir lime leaves, shredded (see
    HINT)
1 tablespoon fish sauce

1 Heat the wok until very hot, add
1 tablespoon of the oil and swirl it
around to coat the side. Stir-fry the
beef strips, garlic and lemon grass in
two or three batches over high heat for
2–3 minutes, or until the beef is
browned. Remove all the beef mixture
from the wok.

2 Reheat the wok, add 1 tablespoon
of the oil and stir-fry the leek, celery
and spring onion for 2 minutes. Add
the snow peas and oyster mushrooms,
and stir-fry for 1–2 minutes, or until
tender. Remove the vegetables from
the wok and set aside.

3 Add the combined kecap manis,
chilli sauce and lime or lemon juice to
the wok, and bring to the boil. Return
all the beef and vegetables to the wok
and stir-fry for 1–2 minutes, or until
the beef has just heated through and
everything is well coated with the
sauce. Toss the shredded kaffir lime
leaves through the mixture and
sprinkle with the fish sauce, to taste.
Serve at once.

NUTRITION PER SERVE
Protein 25 g; Fat 13 g; Carbohydrate 8.5 g;
Dietary Fibre 5 g; Cholesterol 65 mg;
1065 kJ (255 cal)

HINT: If kaffir lime leaves are not
available, sprinkle the stir-fry with
3 tablespoons chopped fresh basil
leaves just before serving. (If you
chop and add them earlier they tend
to turn black.)

Finely chop the white part of the lemon grass
stem, discarding the green part.

Stir-fry the beef, garlic and lemon grass until the
beef browns.

BEEF AND SPINACH

Preparation time: 20 minutes
  + 2 hours marinating
Total cooking time: 15 minutes
Serves 4

500 g (1 lb) rump or sirloin steak, cut
  into thin strips
1/4 cup (60 ml/2 fl oz) sweet chilli
  sauce
2 tablespoons soy sauce
1 clove garlic, crushed
2 teaspoons grated fresh ginger
1 tablespoon sherry

oil, for cooking
2 onions, cut into wedges
500 g (1 lb) English spinach leaves,
  shredded

1 Combine the steak with the sweet
chilli sauce, soy sauce, garlic, ginger
and sherry. Cover and refrigerate for at
least 2 hours, or overnight.
2 Drain the meat. Heat the wok until
very hot, add 1 tablespoon of the oil
and swirl it around to coat the side.
Stir-fry the meat in batches over high
heat until it is well browned, adding
more oil when necessary. Remove
from the wok and set aside.

3 Reheat the wok, add 1 tablespoon
of the oil and stir-fry the onion wedges
for 3–4 minutes, or until tender. Return
the meat to the wok.
4 Just before serving, toss the English
spinach through the beef mixture until
the spinach is just wilted. Serve
immediately.

NUTRITION PER SERVE
Protein 35 g; Fat 15 g; Carbohydrate 6.5 g;
Dietary Fibre 5 g; Cholesterol 85 mg;
1200 kJ (285 cal)

Carefully slice the rump or sirloin steak into thin
strips across the grain.

Drain all the liquid from the marinated meat, using
a sieve.

Toss the English spinach through the stir-fry until
the spinach is just wilted.

WARM CITRUS BEEF SALAD

Preparation time: 25 minutes
Total cooking time: 15 minutes
Serves 4

oil, for cooking
500 g (1 lb) rump or sirloin steak, cut into thin strips
1 onion, sliced
2 cloves garlic, crushed
1 teaspoon grated fresh ginger
1 teaspoon grated lemon rind (see HINT)
1 teaspoon grated orange rind
1 tablespoon lemon juice
1 tablespoon orange juice
100 g (3½ oz) rocket leaves
40 g (1¼ oz) snow pea sprouts
1 lemon, segmented
1 orange, segmented

1 Heat the wok until very hot, add 1 tablespoon of the oil and swirl it around to coat the side. Stir-fry the beef in batches until well browned, adding more oil when necessary. Remove all the beef from the wok and set aside.

2 Reheat the wok, add 1 tablespoon of the oil and stir-fry the onion, garlic and ginger for 3–4 minutes, or until tender. Return the meat to the wok along with the combined lemon and orange rind and juice.

3 Bring to the boil, then toss the rocket through the beef mixture and cook until the rocket is just wilted. Serve immediately on a bed of snow pea sprouts, surrounded by the lemon and orange segments.

NUTRITION PER SERVE
Protein 30 g; Fat 15 g; Carbohydrate 7 g; Dietary Fibre 3 g; Cholesterol 85 mg; 1145 kJ (275 cal)

HINT: Grate the rind you need from the lemon and orange, before peeling and segmenting them to add to the stir-fry. Collect the juice in a bowl as you segment them.

To segment the orange, cut a slice off the top and bottom to stabilize the orange.

Remove the rind and pith, following the curve of the orange.

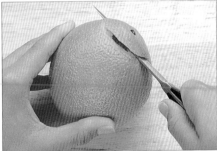

Cut out the segments by slicing between the membrane and flesh on each side.

Return the meat to the wok with the citrus rind and juice.

HONEY AND BLACK PEPPER BEEF

Preparation time: 15 minutes
Total cooking time: 10 minutes
Serves 4

oil, for cooking
500 g (1 lb) round steak, cut into thin strips
2 cloves garlic, crushed
1 onion, sliced
300 g (10 oz) sugar snap peas

2 tablespoons honey
2 teaspoons soy sauce
2 tablespoons oyster sauce
3 teaspoons cracked black pepper

1 Heat the wok until very hot, add 1 tablespoon of the oil and swirl it around to coat the side. Stir-fry the beef in batches over high heat. Remove and drain on paper towels.
2 Reheat the wok, add 1 tablespoon of the oil and stir-fry the garlic, onion and sugar snap peas until softened. Remove from the wok and set aside.

3 Add the honey, soy sauce, oyster sauce and cracked pepper to the wok. Bring to the boil, then reduce the heat and simmer for 3–4 minutes, or until the sauce thickens slightly.
4 Increase the heat, return the meat and vegetables to the wok, and toss for 2–3 minutes, or until well combined and heated through.

NUTRITION PER SERVE
Protein 30 g; Fat 15 g; Carbohydrate 20 g; Dietary Fibre 4.5 g; Cholesterol 70 mg; 1400 kJ (335 cal)

Heat the wok, then add the oil and swirl it around to coat the side of the hot wok.

Once the beef is cooked, remove it from the wok and drain on paper towels.

Add the honey, soy sauce, oyster sauce and cracked pepper and bring to the boil.

MARINATED LEMON GRASS BEEF

Preparation time: 15 minutes
  + 3–4 hours marinating
Total cooking time: 15 minutes
Serves 4

500 g (1 lb) rump steak, cut into thin
    strips
3 stems lemon grass, white part only,
    finely chopped
1 onion, finely chopped

3 cloves garlic, finely chopped
2 tablespoons fish sauce
2 teaspoons sugar
1 tablespoon oil
1/4 cup (40 g/1¼ oz) chopped
    roasted peanuts

1 Put the steak in a large glass or
ceramic bowl. Mix the lemon grass,
onion, garlic, fish sauce, sugar and oil
to make a marinade. Pour over the
meat and toss well. Cover and
refrigerate for 3–4 hours.
2 Heat the wok until very hot and stir-

fry the beef in two batches over high
heat until it is just browned. Toss
constantly to make sure the small
pieces of onion and lemon grass don't
catch on the wok and burn.
3 Return all the meat to the wok. Add
the roasted peanuts and toss quickly
until combined. Serve immediately.

NUTRITION PER SERVE
Protein 35 g; Fat 8.5 g; Carbohydrate 6 g;
Dietary Fibre 2 g; Cholesterol 85 mg;
980 kJ (235 cal)

Using a large sharp knife, cut the rump steak into thin strips.

Finely chop the lemon grass, using only the white part of the stems.

Pour the lemon grass, onion, garlic, fish sauce, sugar and oil over the meat.

BEEF WITH BLACK BEAN SAUCE

Preparation time: 20 minutes
  + 30 minutes marinating
Total cooking time: 15 minutes
Serves 4

500 g (1 lb) rump steak, cut into thin
    strips
1 tablespoon cornflour
2 tablespoons sherry
2 tablespoons soy sauce
2 teaspoons sugar
oil, for cooking
1 onion, thinly sliced
2 cloves garlic, finely chopped
1 tablespoon finely chopped fresh
    ginger
1 red capsicum, thinly sliced
90 g (3 oz) drained bamboo shoots,
    sliced
6 spring onions, diagonally sliced
2 tablespoons salted black beans,
    rinsed well and mashed

1 Put the beef in a glass or ceramic
bowl. Combine the cornflour with the
sherry, soy sauce and sugar to make a
marinade. Pour over the meat and
toss well. Cover and refrigerate for
30 minutes.
2 Drain the meat, reserving the
marinade. Heat the wok until very hot,
add 2 teaspoons of the oil and swirl it
around to coat the side. Stir-fry the
meat in two batches for 2–3 minutes,
or until browned and just cooked. Add
more oil when necessary. Remove all
the meat from the wok.
3 Reheat the wok, add 1 tablespoon
of oil and stir-fry the onion over
medium heat for 3–4 minutes, or until
softened. Stir in the garlic, ginger and
capsicum, then increase the heat to

high and cook for 2–3 minutes, or until
the capsicum is just tender.
4 Add the reserved marinade,
bamboo shoots, spring onion, black
beans and 2–3 tablespoons water to
the wok. Toss over high heat until the
ingredients are well coated and the
sauce is boiling. Return the beef to the

wok and toss until heated through.
Remove from the heat and season
well. Serve immediately.

NUTRITION PER SERVE
Protein 30 g; Fat 15 g; Carbohydrate 9 g;
Dietary Fibre 3 g; Cholesterol 85 mg;
1230 kJ (295 cal)

Drain the bamboo shoots and slice them with a
sharp knife.

Thoroughly rinse the salted black beans under
cold running water.

Add the garlic, ginger and capsicum to the
softened onion.

CORIANDER BEEF

Preparation time: 15 minutes
  + 1–2 hours marinating
Total cooking time: 15 minutes
Serves 4

500 g (1 lb) rump steak, cut into thin
  strips
4 cloves garlic, finely chopped
1 tablespoon finely chopped fresh
  ginger
1/2 cup (25 g/3/4 oz) chopped
  coriander roots, stems and leaves
1/4 cup (60 ml/2 fl oz) oil
oil, extra, for cooking

2 red onions, thinly sliced
1/2 red capsicum, thinly sliced
1/2 green capsicum, thinly sliced
1 tablespoon lime juice
1/2 cup (25 g/3/4 oz) chopped
  coriander leaves, extra

1 Place the beef strips in a glass or ceramic bowl. Add the garlic, ginger, coriander and oil. Mix together well, then cover and refrigerate for 1–2 hours.
2 Heat the wok until very hot and stir-fry the meat in three batches over high heat for 2–3 minutes, or until the meat is just cooked. Remove all the meat from the wok and keep it warm.

3 Heat 1 tablespoon oil, add the onion and cook over medium-high heat for 3–4 minutes, or until the onion is slightly softened. Add the capsicum, and cook, tossing constantly, for 3–4 minutes, or until the capsicum is slightly softened.
4 Return all the meat to the wok with the lime juice and extra coriander. Toss well, then remove from the heat and season well with salt and cracked black pepper. Serve immediately.

NUTRITION PER SERVE
Protein 30 g; Fat 25 g; Carbohydrate 5 g;
Dietary Fibre 2 g; Cholesterol 85 mg;
1620 kJ (385 cal)

Finely chop the roots, stems and leaves of the coriander.

Stir-fry the marinated meat in batches until it is just cooked.

Add the capsicum and toss constantly until it is slightly softened.

BEEF AND SHIITAKE MUSHROOMS

Preparation time: 25 minutes
   + 10 minutes soaking
Total cooking time: 15 minutes
Serves 4

6 dried shiitake mushrooms
400 g (13 oz) topside steak,
   cut into thin strips
oil, for cooking
4 cloves garlic, finely chopped
1 red chilli, finely chopped
2 onions, very thinly sliced
4 spring onions, chopped
1/2 red capsicum, thinly sliced

1/2 cup (125 ml/4 fl oz) tomato purée
2 teaspoons soft brown sugar
2 tomatoes, diced
2 teaspoons sesame oil
2 tablespoons shredded basil leaves

1 Put the dried shiitake mushrooms in a bowl and cover with boiling water. Leave to soak for 10 minutes, or until they have plumped up. Drain and thinly slice.
2 Put the steak in a bowl. Mix together 2 tablespoons of the oil, the garlic, chilli and some salt and pepper and add to the steak. Toss well.
3 Heat the wok until very hot and stir-fry the steak in two batches over high heat for 30 seconds, or until just

browned. Reheat the wok in between each batch. Remove from the wok.
4 Reheat the wok, add 2 tablespoons of the oil and stir-fry the onion, spring onion and capsicum for 3 minutes, or until golden. Add the mushrooms, tomato purée and sugar. Bring to the boil, then reduce the heat and simmer for 3 minutes. Add the beef, tomato and oil, and season. Bring to the boil, allowing the tomato to heat through. Stir in the basil. Serve immediately.

NUTRITION PER SERVE
Protein 25 g; Fat 15 g; Carbohydrate 8 g;
Dietary Fibre 3 g; Cholesterol 50 mg;
1125 kJ (270 cal)

Soak the dried shiitake mushrooms in boiling water until they plump up.

Wearing a glove to protect your hand, finely chop the chilli.

Add the chopped mushrooms and tomato purée to the onion mixture.

VEAL WITH LEMON AND OLIVES

Preparation time: 20 minutes
Total cooking time: 15 minutes
Serves 4

600 g (1 1/4 lb) veal escalopes
1–2 tablespoons plain flour
50 g (1 3/4 oz) butter
1/3 cup (80 ml/2 3/4 fl oz) lemon juice
1/3 cup (20 g/3/4 oz) finely chopped
   fresh parsley

1/2 cup (100 g/3 1/2 oz) tiny
   black olives

1 Place the veal escalopes between two pieces of plastic wrap and beat with a meat mallet or rolling pin until thin. Lightly coat the pieces of veal in the flour. Cut the veal into 2 cm (3/4 inch) wide strips.
2 Heat the wok until very hot and add half the butter. When the butter begins to sizzle, add half the veal and cook over high heat until browned and just cooked. Remove from the wok and

then cook the rest of the veal in the remaining butter.
3 Return all the veal to the wok and add the lemon juice, parsley and black olives. Stir well, scraping all the bits off the bottom of the wok, and allow the mixture to heat through for 1–2 minutes. Season with salt and pepper and serve immediately.

NUTRITION PER SERVE
Protein 35 g; Fat 15 g; Carbohydrate 6 g;
Dietary Fibre 1.5 g; Cholesterol 155 mg;
1205 kJ (290 cal)

Finely chop the parsley as close to the cooking time as possible.

Dip the escalopes of veal in the flour to coat them, then cut them into strips.

Cook the veal in the sizzling butter until it is browned and just cooked.

NASI GORENG

Preparation time: 35 minutes
Total cooking time: 25–30 minutes
Serves 4

2 eggs
oil, for cooking
3 cloves garlic, finely chopped
1 onion, finely chopped
2 red chillies, seeded and finely
    chopped
1 teaspoon dried shrimp paste
1 teaspoon coriander seeds
1/2 teaspoon sugar
200 g (6½ oz) rump steak, finely
    sliced
200 g (6½ oz) peeled raw prawns
3 cups (550 g/1 lb 2 oz) cold cooked
    rice
2 teaspoons kecap manis
1 tablespoon soy sauce
4 spring onions, finely chopped
3 tablespoons crisp-fried onions

1 Beat the eggs with a pinch of salt until foamy. Heat a frying pan and lightly brush with 1 tablespoon oil. Pour about one-quarter of the egg into the pan and cook for 1–2 minutes until the omelette sets. Flip and cook for 30 seconds. Remove from the pan and repeat with the remaining egg. When the omelettes are cold, gently roll up and shred finely.
2 Mix the garlic, onion, chilli, shrimp paste, coriander and sugar in a food processor or mortar and pestle until a paste forms.
3 Heat a wok over high heat, add 1 tablespoon of the oil and fry the paste for 1 minute or until fragrant. Add the steak and prawns and stir-fry until they change colour. Add 2 tablespoons oil and the rice. Stir-fry, breaking up any lumps, until the rice is heated through. Add the kecap manis, soy sauce and spring onion and stir-fry for another minute. Serve immediately, on a bed of lettuce and cucumber, garnished with the omelette strips and crisp-fried onions.

NUTRITION PER SERVE
Protein 20 g; Fat 23 g; Carbohydrate 44 g;
Dietary Fibre 3.5 g; Cholesterol 125 mg;
1942 kJ (465 cal)

Cook the omelette for 1–2 minutes, or until it has set. Then turn it over and cook the other side.

Process the garlic, onion, chilli, shrimp paste, coriander and sugar into a paste.

Quickly stir-fry the beef and prawns until they change colour.

Stir-fry the cooked rice, breaking up any lumps with a wooden spoon.

CALVES' LIVER WITH WINE AND PARSLEY

Preparation time: 15 minutes
Total cooking time: 20 minutes
Serves 4

600 g (1 1/4 lb) calves' liver, thinly sliced
    (ask your butcher to do this)
oil, for cooking
50 g (1 3/4 oz) butter
2 onions, thinly sliced
2 tablespoons plain flour
1/2 cup (125 ml/4 fl oz) Riesling
1 cup (30 g/1 oz) chopped parsley

1 Cut the liver into thin strips. Heat the wok until very hot, add 2 teaspoons of the oil with 10 g (1/4 oz) butter and swirl it around to coat the side. Stir-fry the onion for 3–4 minutes, or until softened. Remove from the wok.
2 Season the flour with salt and pepper and use to coat the liver. Reheat the wok, add a little more of the oil and butter, and stir-fry the floured liver in four batches until browned. Add more oil and butter to the wok if necessary. Remove all the liver from the wok.
3 Reheat the wok, then add the wine and boil until it has reduced by two-thirds. Return the onion and liver to the wok, add the parsley and toss well. Season and serve immediately.

NUTRITION PER SERVE
Protein 30 g; Fat 35 g; Carbohydrate 10 g; Dietary Fibre 1.5 g; Cholesterol 440 mg; 2025 kJ (485 cal)

Ask your butcher to thinly slice the calves' liver, then you can cut it into thin strips.

Toss the liver in the flour that has been seasoned with salt and black pepper.

Stir-fry the liver in small batches so that it fries rather than stews.

BLACK BEAN BEEF WITH NOODLES

Preparation time: 15 minutes
Total cooking time: 10 minutes
Serves 4

250 g (8 oz) instant noodles
500 g (1 lb) beef, thinly sliced
2 teaspoons sesame oil
2 cloves garlic, crushed
1 tablespoon grated fresh ginger
oil, for cooking
6 spring onions, sliced on the diagonal
1 small red capsicum, thinly sliced
125 g (4 oz) snow peas, halved on the diagonal

4 tablespoons black bean and garlic sauce (see NOTE)
2 tablespoons hoisin sauce
1/2 cup (60 g/2 oz) bean sprouts

1 Cook the noodles according to the manufacturer's directions, then drain and keep warm.
2 Place the beef, sesame oil, garlic and ginger in a bowl and mix together well. Heat the wok until very hot, add 1 tablespoon of the oil and swirl it around to coat the side. Add half the beef and stir-fry for 2–3 minutes, or until the beef is just cooked. Remove from the wok, add a little more oil and cook the rest of the beef. Remove all the beef from the wok.

3 Heat 1 tablespoon oil in the wok. Add the spring onion, capsicum and snow peas and stir-fry for 2 minutes. Return the beef to the wok and stir in the black bean and garlic sauce, hoisin sauce and 1 tablespoon water.
4 Add the noodles to the wok and toss to heat through. Serve immediately, topped with bean sprouts.

NUTRITION PER SERVE
Protein 30 g; Fat 20 g; Carbohydrate 25 g;
Dietary Fibre 5.7 g; Cholesterol 76 mg;
1751 kJ (418 cal)

NOTE: Black bean and garlic sauce is available at Asian grocery stores or good supermarkets.

Add the beef and marinade to the wok and stir-fry in two batches over high heat.

Stir-fry the spring onion, capsicum and snow peas for 2 minutes.

Add the noodles and stir to coat with the beef and vegetables.

MEE GORENG

Preparation time: 45 minutes
Total cooking time: 10 minutes
Serves 4

1 large onion, finely chopped
2 cloves garlic, finely chopped
2 red chillies, seeded and finely
    chopped
2 cm (³/₄ inch) piece fresh ginger,
    grated
oil, for cooking
350 g (11 oz) Hokkien noodles, gently
    pulled apart (see NOTE)
500 g (1 lb) peeled raw prawns
250 g (8 oz) rump steak, finely sliced
4 spring onions, chopped
1 large carrot, cut into matchsticks
2 celery sticks, cut into matchsticks
1 tablespoon kecap manis
1 tablespoon soy sauce
1 tablespoon tomato sauce

1 Combine the onion, garlic, chilli and ginger in a small food processor or mortar and pestle. Process in short bursts, or pound, until a paste forms, adding a little oil to help the grinding, if necessary.
2 Heat the wok until very hot, add 1 tablespoon of the oil and swirl it around to coat the side. Stir-fry the noodles until plump and warmed through. Remove to a serving plate; cover to keep warm.
3 Add another tablespoon of oil to the wok and stir-fry the paste until golden. Add the prawns, steak, spring onion, carrot and celery and stir-fry for 2–3 minutes. Add the kecap manis, soy and tomato sauces and season well with salt and pepper. Serve immediately over the noodles.

NUTRITION PER SERVE
Protein 43 g; Fat 17 g; Carbohydrate 14 g;
Dietary Fibre 2.5 g; Cholesterol 230 mg;
1600 kJ (380 cal)

NOTE: Hokkien noodles are thick yellow noodles that have already been cooked and are ready to use. If they are not available, you can use dried egg noodles, but they must be cooked and drained well beforehand.

Gently prise apart the Hokkien noodles before heating in the wok.

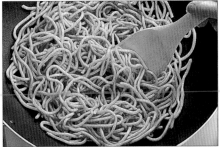
Stir-fry the noodles in the wok until they are warmed through.

Heat the oil in the wok and stir-fry the paste mixture until it is golden.

Add the kecap manis, soy and tomato sauces to the steak, prawns and vegetables.

CHILLI BEEF WITH CHINESE SPINACH

Preparation time: 30 minutes
+ 20 minutes marinating
Total cooking time: 15 minutes
Serves 3–4

500 g (1 lb) rump or fillet steak
2 tablespoons rice wine
1 tablespoon cornflour
4 tablespoons soy sauce
3 tablespoons peanut oil
250 g (8 oz) baby Chinese spinach
     with pink roots (see NOTE)
2 tablespoons salted black beans (see
     NOTE)
2 teaspoons finely chopped fresh
     ginger
2 cloves garlic, finely chopped
1 long green chilli, seeded and cut into
     fine strips
1 long red chilli, seeded and cut into
     fine strips
1 tablespoon sesame oil
1 teaspoon sugar
2 teaspoons peanut oil, extra
4 cloves garlic, finely sliced

1 Trim the meat of any excess fat and sinew and slice across the grain into thin strips (see HINT). Combine the rice wine, cornflour and 2 tablespoons of the soy sauce in a bowl. Stir in 1 tablespoon of the peanut oil. Add the beef and mix well to coat. Cover and leave to marinate in the refrigerator for 20 minutes.
2 Wash and dry the spinach. Leave the pink roots on, but trim away the straggly ends. Cut the leaves from the stems, as these will need less cooking. Rinse the black beans under cold running water, then drain and mash with the back of a spoon.

3 Drain the meat and discard the marinade. Heat 1 tablespoon of the peanut oil in a wok and cook the meat quickly over high heat, in two batches, until just browned. Do not overcook. Remove from the wok and set aside.
4 Heat the remaining peanut oil in the wok and stir-fry the ginger, garlic, chilli and black beans for 1–2 minutes. Return the beef to the wok with the sesame oil, sugar and remaining soy sauce. Stir-fry briefly until the beef is heated through. Remove from the wok, cover and set aside. Keep warm.
5 Working quickly, wipe out the wok with paper towels and heat the extra peanut oil. Add the sliced garlic and cook for about 30 seconds, until it is lightly golden.
6 Add the spinach stems and 1 tablespoon of water. Stir-fry for 30 seconds, until the spinach is bright green. Add the spinach leaves and toss until just wilted. Serve immediately with the beef.

NUTRITION PER SERVE (4)
Protein 35 g; Fat 25 g; Carbohydrate 5 g;
Dietary Fibre 3 g; Cholesterol 85 mg;
1615 kJ (385 cal)

NOTE: If Chinese spinach is unavailable, use baby English spinach instead. Salted black beans are available from Asian speciality shops. They will keep, refrigerated, in an airtight container, for up to 12 months.

HINT: To make the beef easier to slice, freeze it until it is just firm and thinly slice while it is still frozen.

VARIATION: Pork fillet is a great substitute for the beef. Trim any excess fat and sinew and cut across the grain into thin round slices.

Use a glass or ceramic bowl when marinating in an acid mixture that contains wine or citrus.

Wash and dry the spinach, then trim away the straggly ends of the roots.

Rinse the black beans under cold running water, then drain and mash them.

Stir-fry the beef in batches so that the wok doesn't overcrowd and it fries rather than stews.

Stir-fry the ginger, garlic, chilli and black beans until fragrant.

Add the spinach leaves to the wok and toss until they have wilted.

CREAMY BEEF AND EGGPLANT CURRY

Preparation time: 20 minutes
Total cooking time: 30–40 minutes
Serves 4

oil, for cooking
2–6 teaspoons red curry paste (use the recipe on page 246, or ready-made paste)
500 g (1 lb) topside steak, cut into strips
1¹/₂ cups (375 ml/12 fl oz) coconut milk
4 kaffir lime leaves
100 g (3¹/₂ oz) pea-sized eggplants or chopped eggplant
1¹/₂ tablespoons fish sauce
1¹/₂ tablespoons lime juice
2 teaspoons soft brown sugar
¹/₂ cup (15 g/¹/₂ oz) Thai basil or coriander leaves

1 Heat the wok until very hot, add 1 tablespoon of the oil and swirl it around to coat the side. Add the curry paste and stir for 1 minute over medium heat. Add the meat to the wok in batches and stir-fry for 3 minutes or until brown. Remove all the meat from the wok and set aside.
2 Add the coconut milk, kaffir lime leaves and 1 cup (250 ml/8 fl oz) water to the wok; bring to the boil and simmer for 12 minutes. Add the eggplants and cook for 5–10 minutes or until tender. Return the beef to the wok and simmer for 3 minutes.
3 Add the fish sauce, lime juice and brown sugar to the wok. Add most of the basil or coriander leaves, toss and serve immediately, sprinkled with the remaining basil or coriander leaves.

NUTRITION PER SERVE
Protein 7.5 g; Fat 13 g; Carbohydrate 3.5 g; Dietary Fibre 1 g; Cholesterol 32 mg; 653 kJ (156 cal)

Stir-fry the meat in batches for 3 minutes, or until it is brown.

Add the tiny eggplants to the wok and cook until they are tender.

Toss the fresh Thai basil or coriander leaves through the curry just before serving.

THAI BRAISED BEEF WITH SPINACH AND LEEKS

Preparation time: 10 minutes
  + 2 hours marinating
Total cooking time: 25 minutes
Serves 4

400 g (13 oz) beef fillet
2 tablespoons light soy sauce
2 tablespoons fish sauce
oil, for cooking
4 coriander roots, finely chopped
1/4 cup (15 g/1/2 oz) chopped
  coriander leaves and stems
2 teaspoons cracked black
  peppercorns
2 cloves garlic, crushed

1 tablespoon soft brown sugar
1 leek, sliced
20 English spinach leaves, stalks
  removed
3 tablespoons lime juice

1 Cut the beef into 2.5 cm (1 inch) thick pieces and place in a bowl. Place the sauces, 1 tablespoon oil, coriander, peppercorns, garlic and brown sugar in a blender and mix until smooth. Pour the marinade over the beef, cover and refrigerate for 2 hours.
2 Drain the beef, reserving the marinade. Heat the wok until very hot, add 1 tablespoon of the oil and swirl it around to coat the side. Stir-fry the beef in batches, browning well.
3 Return all the meat to the wok and add the reserved marinade and 1/2 cup (125 ml/4 fl oz) water. Reduce the heat and simmer for 8 minutes. Remove the meat and keep warm. Simmer the sauce for 10 minutes, then remove from the wok and set aside. Slice the beef into large bite-sized pieces.
4 Wipe out the wok and heat 1 tablespoon oil. Add the leek and stir-fry for 2 minutes. Add the spinach and cook for 30 seconds or until softened. Serve with the meat with the sauce poured over the top. Drizzle with lime juice and serve immediately.

NUTRITION PER SERVE
Protein 24 g; Fat 20 g; Carbohydrate 7 g;
Dietary Fibre 1.5 g; Cholesterol 67 mg;
1220 kJ (290 cal)

Place the pieces of beef in a bowl and pour the marinade over the top.

Brown the beef in batches if necessary so that you don't overcrowd the wok.

Add the spinach to the leek and toss it for about 30 seconds, or until softened.

HOT THAI BEEF CURRY

Preparation time: 20 minutes
Total cooking time: 30–35 minutes
Serves 4

oil, for cooking
1 large onion, chopped
1–2 tablespoons green curry paste
    (use the recipe on page 246 or
    ready-made paste)
500 g (1 lb) round or blade steak,
    cut into thick strips
3/4 cup (185 ml/6 fl oz) coconut milk
6 kaffir lime leaves
90 g (3 oz) pea-sized eggplants
2 tablespoons fish sauce
1 teaspoon soft brown sugar
2 teaspoons finely grated lime rind
1/2 cup (15 g/1/2 oz) coriander leaves
1/2 cup (15 g/1/2 oz) shredded basil
    leaves

1 Heat the wok until very hot, add
1 tablespoon of the oil and swirl it
around to coat the side. Add the onion
and curry paste and stir for 2 minutes
over medium heat until fragrant.
2 Add the beef in 2 batches and stir-
fry until brown. Return all the meat to
the wok. Add the coconut milk, kaffir
lime leaves and 3 tablespoons water.
Bring to the boil, reduce the heat and
simmer for 10 minutes. Add the
eggplants and cook for 10 minutes or
until tender.
3 Add the fish sauce, brown sugar
and lime rind and toss together well.
Stir in the coriander and basil leaves
just before serving.

NUTRITION PER SERVE
Protein 28 g; Fat 12 g; Carbohydrate 5 g;
Dietary Fibre 1.5 g; Cholesterol 66 mg;
1010 kJ (240 cal)

Stir the curry paste and onion over medium heat
for 2 minutes or until fragrant.

After cooking the beef for 10 minutes, add the
eggplants to the wok.

Stir in the coriander leaves and shredded basil
just before serving.

CHINESE BEEF AND SNOW PEAS

Preparation time: 10 minutes
Total cooking time: 5 minutes
Serves 4

400 g (13 oz) rump steak, finely sliced
    (see HINT)
2 tablespoons soy sauce
1/2 teaspoon grated fresh ginger
oil, for cooking
200 g (61/2 oz) snow peas, trimmed

11/2 teaspoons cornflour
1/2 cup (125 ml/4 fl oz) beef stock
1 teaspoon soy sauce, extra
1/4 teaspoon sesame oil

1 Put the meat in a glass or ceramic bowl. Mix the soy and ginger and add to the meat. Stir well. Heat the wok until very hot, add 2 tablespoons of the oil and swirl it around to coat the side. Add the beef and snow peas and stir-fry over high heat for 2 minutes, or until the meat changes colour.
2 Dissolve the cornflour in a little of

the stock. Add to the wok with the remaining stock, extra soy and oil.
3 Stir until the sauce boils and thickens. Serve immediately.

NUTRITION PER SERVE
Protein 27 g; Fat 13 g; Carbohydrate 9 g;
Dietary Fibre 3 g; Cholesterol 67 mg;
1088 kJ (260 cal)

HINT: To make the beef easier to slice, freeze it until it is just firm and thinly slice while it is still frozen.

Stir-fry the beef and snow peas over high heat until the meat browns.

Dissolve the cornflour in a little of the stock and add to the wok with the rest of the stock.

Stir the beef and snow peas until the sauce comes to the boil and thickens.

MANDARIN BEEF

Preparation time: 25 minutes
  + 15 minutes marinating
Total cooking time: 5 minutes
Serves 4

350 g (11 oz) boned rib eye steak,
    finely sliced
2 teaspoons soy sauce
2 teaspoons dry sherry
1 teaspoon chopped fresh ginger
1 teaspoon sesame oil
oil, for cooking
$1/4$ teaspoon ground white pepper
2 teaspoons finely chopped dried
    mandarin or tangerine rind
2 teaspoons soy sauce, extra
$1\frac{1}{2}$ teaspoons caster sugar
$1\frac{1}{2}$ teaspoons cornflour
4 tablespoons beef stock

1 Place the meat in a bowl. Mix the soy, sherry, ginger and sesame oil together, add to the meat and toss well. Leave to marinate for 15 minutes.
2 Heat the wok until very hot, add 1 tablespoon of the oil and swirl it around to coat the side. Add the beef and stir-fry over high heat for 2 minutes, or until the meat is browned on all sides.
3 Add the pepper, dried mandarin or tangerine rind, extra soy sauce and sugar. Stir-fry briefly.
4 Dissolve the cornflour in a little of the stock and then add the remaining stock. Pour the whole lot into the wok. Stir until the sauce boils and thickens. Serve immediately.

NUTRITION PER SERVE
Protein 20 g; Fat 8 g; Carbohydrate 9 g;
Dietary Fibre 0 g; Cholesterol 60 mg;
785 kJ (188 cal)

VARIATION: For a hotter dish, fry a whole dried chilli in the hot oil and then discard the chilli before adding the beef to the wok.

The thickened sauce is optional. You can dry-fry the marinated beef and serve with fine noodles instead of the more traditional rice.

Make a marinade from the soy sauce, sherry, ginger and sesame oil and toss over the meat.

Add the pepper, mandarin or tangerine rind, soy sauce and sugar to the meat.

Dissolve the cornflour in the stock and then add to the wok to make a sauce.

BEEF WITH OYSTER SAUCE

Preparation time: 15 minutes
Total cooking time: 5 minutes
Serves 4

1½ teaspoons cornflour
½ cup (125 ml/4 fl oz) beef stock
2 tablespoons oyster sauce
1 teaspoon finely crushed garlic
1 teaspoon caster sugar
oil, for cooking

350 g (12 oz) rump steak, finely sliced
250 g (8 oz) beans, topped and tailed,
    cut into 5 cm (2 inch) lengths
1 small red capsicum, sliced
½ cup (60 g/2 oz) bean sprouts

1 Dissolve the cornflour in a little of the stock. Mix with the remaining stock, oyster sauce, garlic and sugar and set aside.
2 Heat the wok until very hot, add 1 tablespoon of the oil and swirl it around to coat the side. Add the beef in batches and stir-fry over high heat for 2 minutes, or until it browns.
3 Add the beans and capsicum and stir-fry another minute.
4 Add the cornflour mixture to the wok and cook until the sauce boils and thickens. Stir in the bean sprouts and serve immediately.

NUTRITION PER SERVE
Protein 23 g; Fat 12 g; Carbohydrate 10 g;
Dietary Fibre 2.5 g; Cholesterol 60 mg;
1016 kJ (243 cal)

Brown the steak in batches so the wok doesn't overcrowd and reduce the temperature.

Add the beans and capsicum to the browned meat and stir-fry for 1 minute.

Add the mixture of stock and cornflour and stir until the sauce boils and thickens.

ASIAN PEPPERED BEEF

Preparation time: 10 minutes
  + 2 hours marinating
Total cooking time: 12 minutes
Serves 4

600 g (1¼ lb) skirt steak, thinly sliced
2 cloves garlic, finely chopped
2 teaspoons finely chopped fresh
   ginger
2 onions, thinly sliced
2 tablespoons Chinese rice wine
1 teaspoon sesame oil
1 tablespoon soy sauce
1 tablespoon oyster sauce

2 teaspoons sugar
1 teaspoon Sichuan peppercorns,
   crushed
1 tablespoon black peppercorns,
   crushed
2 spring onions, chopped into
   2.5 cm (1 inch) lengths
oil, for cooking

1 Place the beef strips in a large bowl. Add the garlic, ginger, onion, rice wine, sesame oil, soy sauce, oyster sauce, sugar and peppercorns, and mix together well. Cover and marinate in the refrigerator for at least 2 hours.
2 Drain, discarding any excess liquid, and stir in the spring onion.

3 Heat the wok until very hot, add 1 tablespoon of the oil and swirl it around to coat the side. Add half the beef and stir-fry for 6 minutes, or until seared and cooked to your liking. Repeat with the rest of the beef. Serve immediately.

NUTRITION PER SERVE
Protein 40 g; Fat 15 g; Carbohydrate 6 g;
Dietary Fibre 1 g; Cholesterol 117 mg;
1400 kJ (335 cal)

NOTE: The wok needs to be searing hot for this recipe. The beef is easier to thinly slice if you put it in the freezer for half an hour beforehand.

Crush the Sichuan peppercorns in a mortar and pestle to release their flavour.

Chop the spring onions into short lengths for quick and even stir-frying.

Place the beef strips in a large bowl with all the marinade ingredients.

THAI BEEF SALAD

Preparation time: 20 minutes + cooling
Total cooking time: 5 minutes
Serves 6

oil, for cooking
500 g (1 lb) beef fillet or lean rump,
    thinly sliced
2 cloves garlic, crushed
1/4 cup (15 g/1/2 oz) finely chopped
    coriander roots and stems
1 tablespoon grated palm sugar
1/3 cup (80 ml/2 3/4 fl oz) lime juice
2 tablespoons fish sauce
2 small red chillies, seeded,
    finely sliced

2 red Asian shallots, finely sliced
2 telegraph cucumbers, sliced into
    thin ribbons
1 cup (30 g/1 oz) mint leaves
1 cup (90 g/3 oz) bean sprouts
1/4 cup (30 g/1 oz) chopped roasted
    peanuts

1 Heat the wok until very hot, add
1 tablespoon of the oil and swirl it
around to coat the side. Add half the
beef and cook for 1–2 minutes, or until
medium rare. Remove from the wok
and set aside. Repeat with the rest of
the beef.
2 Place the garlic, coriander, palm
sugar, lime juice, fish sauce,
1/4 teaspoon ground white pepper and

1/4 teaspoon salt in a bowl, and stir
until all the sugar has dissolved. Add
the chilli and shallots and mix well.
3 Pour the sauce over the beef while
still hot, mix well, then cool to room
temperature.
4 In a separate bowl, toss together
the cucumber and mint leaves, and
refrigerate until required.
5 Place the cucumber and mint on a
serving platter, and top with the beef,
bean sprouts and roasted peanuts.
Serve immediately.

NUTRITION PER SERVE
Protein 22 g; Fat 13 g; Carbohydrate 7.5 g;
Dietary Fibre 2 g; Cholesterol 50 mg;
1041 kJ (248 cal)

Small red chillies are the hottest type. Remove
the seeds and white membrane, and finely slice.

Pour the sauce over the hot stir-fried beef and
leave to cool.

Toss together the cucumber and mint leaves and
leave in the fridge.

FRESH RICE NOODLES WITH BEEF

Preparation time: 10 minutes
  + 30 minutes marinating
Total cooking time: 15 minutes
Serves 4–6

2 cloves garlic, crushed
2 teaspoons chopped fresh ginger
1 tablespoon oyster sauce
2 teaspoons soy sauce
500 g (1 lb) beef, thinly sliced
oil, for cooking

1 kg (2 lb) fresh rice noodles, sliced
  into 2 cm (1 inch) strips
100 g (3¹/₂ oz) garlic chives, chopped
2¹/₂ tablespoons oyster sauce, extra
3 teaspoons soy sauce, extra
1 teaspoon sugar

1 Combine the garlic, ginger, oyster and soy sauces, add the beef and toss to coat. Cover and refrigerate for 30 minutes.
2 Heat the wok until very hot, add 1 tablespoon of the oil and swirl it around to coat the side. Add half the beef and stir-fry for 5 minutes, or until

cooked. Remove and repeat with the remaining beef. Add another tablespoon of oil, then add the noodles and stir-fry for 3–5 minutes, or until softened.
3 Add the garlic chives and stir-fry until just wilted. Stir in the extra oyster and soy sauces and sugar, return the beef to the wok and toss to heat through. Serve immediately.

NUTRITION PER SERVE (6)
Protein 33 g; Fat 13 g; Carbohydrate 40 g;
Dietary Fibre 1.5 g; Cholesterol 50 mg;
1295 kJ (310 cal)

Buy the fresh rice noodle as a block and cut it into thin strips.

Mix together the garlic, ginger, oyster and soy sauces to marinate the beef.

Stir-fry the noodles until they are softened, then add the garlic chives.

VERMICELLI, BEEF AND THAI BASIL SALAD

Preparation time: 20 minutes
Total cooking time: 10–15 minutes
Serves 4

125 g (4 oz) dried rice vermicelli
600 g (1¼ lb) rump steak
oil, for cooking
2–3 cloves garlic, thinly sliced
1 small red chilli, finely chopped
1 small red capsicum, thinly
    sliced
1 red onion, thinly sliced
1 cup (30 g/1 oz) coriander leaves
1 cup (30 g/1 oz) Thai basil leaves or
    green basil leaves

DRESSING
1–2 cloves garlic, crushed
1 red chilli, chopped
2 tablespoons soy sauce
2 tablespoons lime juice
1 tablespoon fish sauce
3 tablespoons grated palm sugar

1 Soak the noodles in hot water for 5 minutes, or until soft. Drain.
2 Combine the dressing ingredients; mix well and set aside.
3 Thinly slice the beef across the grain. Heat the wok until very hot, add 1 tablespoon of the oil and swirl it around to coat the side. Stir-fry the beef in 2–3 batches for 2 minutes, or until just brown, yet still pink in patches. (Ensure the wok is hot before

each addition.) Remove all the beef and set aside.
4 Heat another tablespoon of oil in the wok, then stir-fry the garlic, chilli, capsicum and onion for 2–3 minutes, or until soft but not browned.
5 Add the beef to the wok to just heat through quickly, then toss the mixture through the vermicelli. Pour on the dressing, and toss through the coriander and Thai basil leaves.

NUTRITION PER SERVE
Protein 40 g; Fat 15 g; Carbohydrate 35 g; Dietary Fibre 2 g; Cholesterol 100 mg; 1795 kJ (425 cal)

Slice the rump steak thinly across the grain, so it holds together well.

Stir-fry the beef in batches so that it is just beginning to turn brown.

Add the beef and toss through the vermicelli until it is just heated through.

BEEF WITH BOK CHOY

Preparation time: 20 minutes
Total cooking time: 10 minutes
Serves 4

1 bunch bok choy (see VARIATION)
oil, for cooking
2 cloves garlic, crushed
250 g (8 oz) rump steak, thinly sliced
2 tablespoons soy sauce
1 tablespoon sweet sherry
2 tablespoons chopped basil
2 teaspoons sesame oil

1 Wash the bok choy and drain. Cut the leaves into wide strips and the stems into thin strips. Heat the wok until very hot, add 1 tablespoon of the oil and swirl to coat the side. Add the garlic and stir-fry for 30 seconds.
2 Add another tablespoon of oil to the wok and add the meat in batches. Stir-fry for 3 minutes over high heat until the meat has browned but not cooked through. Remove from the wok.
3 Add the bok choy to the wok and stir-fry for 30 seconds or until just wilted. Add the meat, soy sauce and sherry. Stir-fry for 2–3 minutes or until

the meat is tender.
4 Add the basil and sesame oil and toss well. Serve immediately.

NUTRITION PER SERVE
Protein 60 g; Fat 40 g; Carbohydrate 0.5 g;
Dietary Fibre 1 g; Cholesterol 42 mg;
790 kJ (190 cal)

VARIATION: The Asian vegetable, choy sum, has a similar flavour to bok choy and could also be used for this recipe. It has a longer leaf and shorter stem. Baby bok choy could also be used for this recipe.

Cut the leaves of bok choy into wide strips and cut the stalks into thin strips.

Stir-fry the bok choy briefly until the leaves have just begun to wilt.

Return the meat to the wok with the soy sauce and sherry. Stir in the basil before serving.

FIVE-SPICE BEEF

Preparation time: 15 minutes
Total cooking time: 10 minutes
Serves 4

1 teaspoon five-spice powder
1/2 teaspoon black pepper
500 g (1 lb) rump steak
oil, for cooking
3 teaspoons finely grated ginger
4 spring onions, cut into short lengths

2 tablespoons soy sauce
2 tablespoons oyster sauce

1 Mix together the five-spice powder and black pepper and rub into both sides of the piece of meat. Cut the meat into thin strips.
2 Heat the wok until very hot, add 1 tablespoon of the oil and swirl it around to coat the base and side of the wok. Stir-fry the ginger and spring onion for 1 minute and then remove from the wok.

3 Stir-fry the meat in small batches until just browned. Return all the meat to the wok and add the soy and oyster sauces. Toss together to coat the meat in sauce and serve immediately.

NUTRITION PER SERVE
Protein 30 g; Fat 13 g; Carbohydrate 3 g;
Dietary Fibre 0 g; Cholesterol 84 mg;
1045 kJ (250 cal)

Rub the combined five-spice powder and pepper into both sides of the meat.

Stir-fry the ginger and spring onion for 1 minute and then remove from the wok.

Stir-fry the meat in small batches over high heat so that it browns rather than stews.

QUICK BEEF AND NOODLE SALAD

Preparation time: 15 minutes
Total cooking time: 10 minutes
Serves 4

500 g (1 lb) rump steak
1 tablespoon peanut oil
2 tablespoons oyster sauce
2 teaspoons mild curry powder
1 tablespoon soft brown sugar
1 small Lebanese cucumber, thinly
   sliced
1 red onion, sliced
1 red capsicum, cut into thin strips
1 small red chilli, seeded and chopped
1/4 cup (15 g/1/2 oz) chopped mint
1/3 cup (60 g/2 oz) chopped unsalted
   peanuts or cashews
500 g (1 lb) Hokkien noodles

DRESSING
1/2 cup (125 ml/4 fl oz) rice vinegar
   (see NOTE)
2 tablespoons fish sauce
1/4 cup (60 g/2 oz) caster sugar
2 teaspoons finely chopped fresh
   ginger
1 small red chilli, seeded and chopped
1 tablespoon chopped coriander
   leaves

1 Remove all visible fat from the meat. Combine the peanut oil, oyster sauce, curry powder and brown sugar in a small bowl.
2 Heat a wok over medium heat. Add the steak and cook for 6–8 minutes, turning and basting with half the sauce during cooking. Remove the steak from the wok.
3 To make the dressing, whisk together all the ingredients.
4 Place the cucumber, onion, capsicum and chilli in a large bowl. Add the mint and nuts. Thinly slice the meat, add to the bowl with the dressing and lightly toss to combine. If you have time, leave for a few minutes to marinate.
5 Place the noodles in the same wok and stir-fry over medium heat for 1–2 minutes. Stir in the remaining basting sauce and toss until heated through. Divide the noodles among serving bowls and top with the salad. Serve immediately.

NUTRITION PER SERVE
Protein 50 g; Fat 17 g; Carbohydrate 115 g;
Dietary Fibre 5.5 g; Cholesterol 105 mg;
3405 kJ (815 cal)

NOTE: Rice vinegar is available in Asian grocery stores.

While you cook the steak, turn it and baste often with the sauce.

Place the cucumber, onion, capsicum and chilli in a large bowl and add the mint and nuts.

Stir the remaining basting sauce into the noodles in the wok.

BEEF WITH NOODLES AND ASIAN GREENS

Preparation time: 15 minutes
Total cooking time: 10 minutes
Serves 4

SAUCE
2 teaspoons cornflour
1/2 cup (125 ml/4 fl oz) chicken stock
1/3 cup (80 ml/2³/4 fl ozl) light soy sauce
1/4 cup (60 ml/2 fl oz) oyster sauce
1/2 teaspoon sesame oil

450 g (14 oz) Hokkien noodles
oil, for cooking
500 g (1 lb) rump steak, thinly sliced
1 clove garlic, crushed

2 teaspoons grated fresh ginger
5 cm (2 inch) stem lemon grass, white part only, chopped
4 spring onions, cut into short lengths
200 g (6¹/2 oz) beans, cut into short lengths
2 bok choy, roughly chopped
1/2 bunch choy sum, roughly chopped

1 Blend the cornflour with a little of the stock until smooth. Add the remaining sauce ingredients.
2 Place the noodles in a large bowl. Cover with boiling water and leave for 2 minutes. Drain well.
3 Heat the wok until very hot, add 1 tablespoon of the oil and swirl it around to coat the side. Add half the beef strips and stir-fry over high heat for 2 minutes, or until just cooked.

Remove from the wok. Heat another tablespoon of oil, and cook the rest of the beef. Remove from the wok.
4 Heat another tablespoon of oil in the wok. Add the garlic, ginger, lemon grass, spring onion and beans and stir-fry for 2 minutes. Stir through the bok choy and choy sum and cook for 1 minute, or until just wilted.
5 Push the vegetables to one side. Add the cornflour mixture to the juices and stir for 2 minutes, or until thickened and heated through. Add the beef and noodles and stir-fry for a further 1 minute to coat in the sauce.

NUTRITION PER SERVE
Protein 40 g; Fat 30 g; Carbohydrate 87 g; Dietary Fibre 5 g; Cholesterol 100 mg; 3366 kJ (805 cal)

Use only the more tender white portion of the lemon grass, discarding the tough green part.

Soak the Hokkien noodles in water for a couple of minutes, then drain well.

Push the vegetables to one side of the wok and add the cornflour mixture.

Pork

PHAD THAI

Preparation time: 25 minutes
Total cooking time: 10–15 minutes
Serves 4

250 g (8 oz) thick rice stick noodles
2 tablespoons oil
3 cloves garlic, chopped
2 teaspoons chopped red chillies
150 g (5 oz) pork, thinly sliced
100 g (3¹/₂ oz) peeled raw prawns, chopped
¹/₂ bunch garlic chives, chopped
2 tablespoons fish sauce
2 tablespoons lime juice
2 teaspoons soft brown sugar
2 eggs, beaten
1 cup (90 g/3 oz) bean sprouts
sprigs of coriander
3 tablespoons chopped roasted peanuts
crisp-fried onion, soft brown sugar and chopped peanuts, to serve

1 Soak the rice stick noodles in warm water for 10 minutes or until they are soft. Drain and set aside. Heat the wok until very hot, then add the oil and swirl to coat the side. When the oil is very hot, add the garlic, chilli and pork and stir-fry for 2 minutes.

2 Add the prawns and stir-fry for 3 minutes. Add the garlic chives and drained noodles to the wok; cover and cook for another minute.

3 Add the fish sauce, lime juice, sugar and eggs to the wok. Toss well until heated through.

4 Serve immediately, sprinkled with the bean sprouts, sprigs of fresh coriander and chopped peanuts. Traditionally served with crisp-fried onion, soft brown sugar and more chopped peanuts on the side.

NUTRITION PER SERVE
Protein 20 g; Fat 17 g; Carbohydrate 20 g;
Dietary Fibre 2 g; Cholesterol 145 mg;
1334 kJ (320 cal)

After stir-frying the pork for 2 minutes, stir in the chopped prawns.

Use two wooden spoons or a pair of tongs to toss the stir-fry.

THAI CRISPY FRIED NOODLES

Preparation time: 30 minutes
Total cooking time: 20 minutes
Serves 4

100 g (3½ oz) rice vermicelli
2 cups (500 ml/16 fl oz) oil, for frying
100 g (3½ oz) deep-fried tofu puffs,
    cut into strips
2 cloves garlic, finely chopped
5 cm (2 inch) piece fresh ginger,
    grated
150 g (5 oz) pork mince
100 g (3½ oz) raw prawn meat, finely
    chopped
1 tablespoon white vinegar
2 tablespoons fish sauce
2 tablespoons soft brown sugar
2 tablespoons chilli sauce (page 248)
1 teaspoon chopped red chillies
2 small knobs pickled garlic, chopped
¼ bunch fresh garlic chives, chopped
1 cup (30 g/1 oz) coriander leaves

1 Place the vermicelli in a bowl of hot water for 1 minute; drain and allow to dry for 20 minutes. Heat the oil in a wok, add the tofu in two batches and cook for 1 minute or until golden and crisp. Remove from the wok and leave to drain.
2 Add the completely dry vermicelli to the oil in several batches, cooking for 10 seconds or until puffed and crisp. Remove immediately to prevent the vermicelli absorbing too much oil. Drain on paper towels and cool.
3 Drain all but 1 tablespoon of the oil from the wok. Reheat the wok over high heat and add the garlic, ginger, mince and prawn meat. Stir-fry for 2 minutes or until golden brown. Add the vinegar, fish sauce, brown sugar, chilli sauce and chillies and stir until the mixture comes to the boil.
4 Just before serving, add the noodles and tofu to the wok and toss thoroughly. Quickly toss through the pickled garlic, chives and coriander and serve immediately.

NUTRITION PER SERVE
Protein 8.5 g; Fat 13 g; Carbohydrate 17 g;
Dietary Fibre 2.5 g; Cholesterol 37 mg;
900 kJ (230 cal)

Cook the tofu for 1 minute until golden brown. Remove with a wire mesh strainer.

Add the vermicelli to the wok in batches and cook until puffed and crisp.

Add the chopped garlic, grated ginger, mince and prawn meat to the wok.

Just before serving, return the noodles and tofu to the wok and toss well.

CHIANG MAI NOODLES

Preparation time: 20 minutes
Total cooking time: 15 minutes
Serves 4

500 g (1 lb) fresh egg noodles
1 tablespoon oil
3 Asian or French shallots, chopped
6 cloves garlic, chopped
2 teaspoons finely chopped red
  chillies
1–2 tablespoons red curry paste
  (use the recipe on page 246 or
  ready-made paste)

350 g (12 oz) lean pork, finely sliced
1 carrot, cut into thin strips
2 tablespoons fish sauce
2 teaspoons soft brown sugar
3 spring onions, finely sliced
1/4 cup (7 g/1/4 oz) coriander leaves
nam prik dipping sauce (page 249), for
  serving

1 Cook the noodles in a wok or large pan of rapidly boiling water for 2–3 minutes, or until they are just tender. Drain and keep warm. Heat the oil in a wok until it is very hot. Add the shallots, garlic, chilli and curry paste and stir-fry for 2 minutes or until

fragrant. Add the pork in two batches and cook for 3 minutes or until the meat changes colour.

2 Return all the meat to the wok. Add the carrot, fish sauce and brown sugar and bring to the boil. Add the noodles and spring onion and toss well. Top with coriander leaves and serve immediately with nam prik.

NUTRITION PER SERVE
Protein 17 g; Fat 7.5 g; Carbohydrate 92 g;
Dietary Fibre 5 g; Cholesterol 23 mg;
2122 kJ (501 cal)

Use Asian shallots if you can find them. Otherwise French shallots will do.

Cook the noodles in a wok or pan of rapidly boiling water until just tender.

Return all the meat to the wok. Add the carrot, fish sauce and brown sugar.

SPICY SAUSAGE STIR-FRY

Preparation time: 40 minutes
Total cooking time: 15 minutes
Serves 4

2 tablespoons oil
500 g (1 lb) potato, cubed
500 g (1 lb) orange sweet potato,
    cubed
6 chorizo sausages, diagonally sliced
2 cloves garlic, thinly sliced
1 red onion, cut into wedges
200 g (6½ oz) broccoli, chopped

1 red capsicum, cut into short thick
    strips
½ cup (125 ml/4 fl oz) tomato purée
2 tablespoons chopped fresh parsley

1 Heat the wok until very hot, add the oil and swirl it around to coat the side. Stir-fry the potato and sweet potato over medium heat until tender and golden. Remove and drain on paper towels, then place on a serving plate and cover to keep warm.
2 Add the sausage to the wok and stir-fry in batches over high heat for 3–4 minutes, or until crisp. Remove

and drain on paper towels.
3 Add the garlic and onion to the wok and stir-fry for 2 minutes, or until the onion softens. Add the broccoli and capsicum, and stir-fry for 1 minute. Return the sausage to the wok, add the tomato purée and toss to combine. Add the parsley and season with salt and black pepper. Toss well and serve on top of the stir-fried potato.

NUTRITION PER SERVE
Protein 20 g; Fat 30 g; Carbohydrate 40 g;
Dietary Fibre 8 g; Cholesterol 55 mg;
2390 kJ (570 cal)

Peel the skin from the sweet potato and cut the flesh into cubes.

Chorizo is a spicy Spanish sausage. Cut the chorizo into thick diagonal slices.

Stir-fry the potato and sweet potato in the hot oil until tender and golden.

BARBECUED PORK AND BROCCOLI

Preparation time: 25 minutes
Total cooking time: 10 minutes
Serves 4–6

1 tablespoon oil
1 large onion, thinly sliced
2 carrots, cut into matchsticks
200 g (6¹/₂ oz) broccoli, chopped
6 spring onions, diagonally sliced
1 tablespoon finely chopped fresh
   ginger

3 cloves garlic, finely chopped
400 g (13 oz) Chinese barbecued
   pork, thinly sliced
2 tablespoons soy sauce
2 tablespoons mirin
2 cups (180 g/6 oz) bean sprouts

1 Heat the wok until very hot, add the oil and swirl it around to coat the side. Stir-fry the onion over medium heat for 3–4 minutes, or until slightly softened. Add the carrot, broccoli, spring onion, ginger and garlic and cook for 4–5 minutes, tossing the mixture constantly.

2 Increase the heat to high and add the barbecued pork. Toss constantly until the pork is well mixed with the vegetables and is heated through. Add the soy sauce and mirin, and toss until the ingredients are well coated. (The wok should be hot enough for the sauce to reduce into a glaze.) Add the bean sprouts and season well with salt and pepper. Serve immediately.

NUTRITION PER SERVE (6)
Protein 20 g; Fat 15 g; Carbohydrate 6.5 g;
Dietary Fibre 6 g; Cholesterol 40 mg;
920 kJ (220 cal)

Peel the carrots, if necessary, and cut them into even-sized matchsticks.

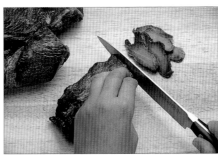

Cut the pieces of Chinese barbecued pork into thin slices.

Add the pork to the wok and toss until it is well mixed with the vegetables.

PORK WITH SNAKE BEANS

Preparation time: 15 minutes
Total cooking time: 20 minutes
Serves 4

oil, for cooking
400 g (13 oz) pork fillet, cut into
    thick slices
2 onions, thinly sliced
150 g (5 oz) snake beans, diagonally
    sliced (see NOTE)
3 cloves garlic, finely chopped
1 tablespoon finely chopped
    fresh ginger
1 red capsicum, thinly sliced
6 spring onions, diagonally sliced
2 tablespoons sweet chilli sauce

1 Heat the wok until very hot, add
2 teaspoons of the oil and swirl it
around to coat the side. Stir-fry the
pork in two batches over high heat
for 3–4 minutes, or until it is just
cooked, adding more oil when
necessary. Remove all the pork from
the wok.

2 Heat 1 tablespoon of the oil over
medium heat and add the sliced
onion. Cook for 3–4 minutes, or until
the onion has softened slightly. Add
the sliced snake beans and cook for
2–3 minutes. Add the garlic, ginger,
capsicum and spring onion, and toss
well. Increase the heat and cook for
3–4 minutes.

3 Return the pork to the wok, add the
sweet chilli sauce and toss well.
Remove from the heat and season with
salt and pepper. Serve immediately.

NUTRITION PER SERVE
Protein 25 g; Fat 12 g; Carbohydrate 8 g;
Dietary Fibre 4 g; Cholesterol 50 mg;
1005 kJ (240 cal)

NOTE: If you can't find snake beans
you can use ordinary green beans in
this recipe.

Top and tail the snake beans, then cut them into
diagonal slices.

SWEET AND SOUR PORK

Preparation time: 25 minutes
+ 30 minutes marinating
Total cooking time: 20 minutes
Serves 4

500 g (1 lb) pork fillet, cut into thick
    slices
2 tablespoons cornflour
1 tablespoon sherry
1 tablespoon soy sauce
1 tablespoon sugar
oil, for cooking
1 large onion, thinly sliced
1 green capsicum, cut into cubes
2 small carrots, thinly sliced
1 small Lebanese cucumber, seeded
    and chopped
5 spring onions, cut into short lengths
440 g (14 oz) can pineapple pieces in
    natural juice, drained, juice
    reserved
1/4 cup (60 ml/2 fl oz) white vinegar
1/2 teaspoon salt

1 Place the pork in a shallow glass or ceramic bowl. Combine the cornflour with the sherry, soy sauce and half the sugar and pour into the bowl. Cover and refrigerate for 30 minutes.
2 Drain the pork, reserving the marinade. Heat the wok until very hot, add 2 tablespoons of the oil and swirl to coat the side. Stir-fry half the pork over high heat for 4–5 minutes, or until the pork is golden brown and just cooked. Remove from the wok, add more oil if necessary and repeat with the remaining pork. Remove all the pork from the wok.
3 Reheat the wok, add 1 tablespoon of the oil and stir-fry the onion over high heat for 3–4 minutes, or until slightly softened. Add the capsicum

and carrot, and cook for 3–4 minutes, or until tender. Stir in the marinade, cucumber, spring onion, pineapple, vinegar, salt, remaining sugar and 4 tablespoons of the reserved pineapple juice.
4 Bring to the boil and simmer for 2–3 minutes, or until the sauce has

thickened slightly. Return the pork to the wok and toss until the pork is heated through. Serve immediately.

NUTRITION PER SERVE
Protein 25 g; Fat 12 g; Carbohydrate 25 g;
Dietary Fibre 4 g; Cholesterol 50 mg;
1325 kJ (315 cal)

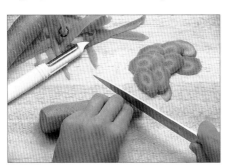
Peel the carrots, if necessary, and cut them into thin diagonal slices.

Halve the cucumber lengthways and scoop out the seeds with a teaspoon.

Stir-fry the pork until it is golden brown and just cooked through.

PEPPERED COCONUT PORK FILLET

Preparation time: 40 minutes
Total cooking time: 20 minutes
Serves 4

1 tablespoon cumin seeds
1 tablespoon coriander seeds
1 teaspoon black peppercorns
1²/₃ cups (100 g/3¹/₂ oz) shredded
    coconut
2 tablespoons cornflour
600 g (1¹/₄ lb) pork fillet
oil, for cooking
¹/₂ cup (125 ml/4 fl oz) thick coconut
    cream
¹/₄ cup (60 ml/2 fl oz) lime juice
2 tablespoons chopped coriander
¹/₄ teaspoon salt

1 Heat the wok, add the cumin and coriander seeds and dry-fry over low heat, shaking the wok regularly for 3 minutes, or until the seeds are fragrant. Place in a mortar and pestle with the peppercorns, and pound until finely ground. Alternatively, process in a spice mill or small food processor. Combine with the coconut and cornflour, mixing well.

2 Trim the pork of any fat and cut into slices about 1 cm (¹/₂ inch) thick, then cut across in half. Coat each slice in the spice mixture, using your fingertips to press the mixture on.

3 Reheat the wok until very hot, add 1 tablespoon of the oil and swirl it around to coat the side. Stir-fry the pork in three or four batches for about 2 minutes, or until it is golden brown and just cooked. Reheat the wok in between batches, adding more oil when necessary. Remove all the pork from the wok and keep warm.

4 Drain any oil from the wok and pour in the coconut cream and lime juice. Add the coriander and salt, to taste. Bring to a vigorous boil, stirring for 1 minute. Add the pork and toss to heat through and combine with the sauce. Serve immediately.

NUTRITION PER SERVE
Protein 35 g; Fat 35 g; Carbohydrate 8 g;
Dietary Fibre 4 g; Cholesterol 75 mg;
2030 kJ (485 cal)

Dry-fry the cumin and coriander seeds in the wok until they are fragrant.

Grind the seeds with the peppercorns in a mortar and pestle.

Press the spice mixture onto the pork slices to coat them.

Stir-fry the pork in batches until it is golden brown and just cooked.

PORK WITH SAGE AND APPLES

Preparation time: 25 minutes
Total cooking time: 20 minutes
Serves 4

500 g (1 lb) pork fillet, cut into strips
2 tablespoons oil
2 cloves garlic, finely chopped
40 g (1¼ oz) butter
1 large onion, thinly sliced
2 Granny Smith apples, cut into thin
   wedges

1 tablespoon soft brown sugar
2 tablespoons brandy
1 tablespoon chopped fresh sage
150 ml (5 fl oz) cream

1 Combine the pork, oil and garlic in a glass or ceramic bowl, and season well with salt and pepper.
2 Heat the wok and melt the butter over medium heat until foaming. Add the onion and apple and toss well. Sprinkle with the brown sugar and cook, stirring regularly, for 4 minutes, or until the apple is golden and softened. Remove from the wok.

3 Reheat the wok until very hot. Stir-fry the pork in batches over high heat for 2 minutes, tossing regularly until it turns white. Return all the pork to the wok with the apple. Add the brandy, sage and cream, and season well. Stir to combine. Serve immediately.

NUTRITION PER SERVE
Protein 30 g; Fat 35 g; Carbohydrate 15 g; Dietary Fibre 2.5 g; Cholesterol 140 mg; 2190 kJ (525 cal)

HINT: Never overcook the pork or it will be dry and tough.

Cut the Granny Smith apples into thin wedges, leaving the skin on.

Sprinkle the brown sugar over the apple and onion in the wok.

Cook the apple and onion, stirring regularly, until the apple is golden.

ITALIAN PORK WITH FENNEL

Preparation time: 15 minutes
Total cooking time: 15 minutes
Serves 4

140 g (4¹/₂ oz) fennel bulb, thinly
    sliced
oil, for cooking
30 g (1 oz) butter
600 g (1¹/₄ lb) pork fillet, cut into thin
    strips
1 tablespoon lemon juice
¹/₄ cup (60 ml/2 fl oz) chicken stock

2 tablespoons baby capers, rinsed
Parmesan shavings, to serve
1 tablespoon chopped fennel, to serve

1 Blanch the fennel in boiling water
for 1 minute. Drain and cool under
cold running water, then drain again.
2 Heat the wok until very hot, add
1 tablespoon of the oil and half the
butter and swirl it around to coat the
side. When the butter begins to sizzle,
add the sliced fennel. Stir-fry until
golden and tender. Remove from the
wok and keep warm.
3 Reheat the wok, add 2 teaspoons of
the oil and half the remaining butter.

Stir-fry the pork in two batches until
browned, adding more oil and butter
between batches. Return the pork and
fennel to the wok and add the lemon
juice and stock.
4 Add the capers and stir them
through the pork mixture, scraping
any bits from the bottom of the wok.
Season with salt and pepper, then
scatter with the Parmesan and extra
fennel. Serve immediately.

NUTRITION PER SERVE
Protein 40 g; Fat 20 g; Carbohydrate 2 g;
Dietary Fibre 1 g; Cholesterol 105 mg;
1525 kJ (365 cal)

Remove the top from the fennel and thinly slice
the bulb.

To make Parmesan shavings, draw a vegetable
peeler along the block.

Stir-fry the fennel in the oil and butter until it is
golden and tender.

CITRUS CHILLI PORK WITH CASHEW NUTS

Preparation time: 20 minutes
Total cooking time: 12 minutes
Serves 4

2 tablespoons oil
375 g (12 oz) pork fillet, thinly sliced
2 small red chillies, seeded and finely chopped
6 spring onions, chopped
1 tablespoon mild curry paste
2 tablespoons fish sauce
1–2 tablespoons lime juice
2 teaspoons crushed palm sugar
2 teaspoons cornflour
1/2–1 teaspoon seasoning sauce

1/3 cup (50 g/1 3/4 oz) roasted unsalted cashews
shredded lime rind, to garnish

1 Heat the wok until very hot, add the oil and swirl it around to coat the side. Stir-fry the pork slices, chilli and spring onion in batches over high heat for 2 minutes, or until the pork just changes colour. Stir in the curry paste and stir-fry for 1 minute. Remove from the wok and set aside.
2 Combine the fish sauce, lime juice, sugar and cornflour with 1/2 cup (125 ml/4 fl oz) water. Pour into the wok and stir for 1 minute, or until heated through and slightly thickened. Return the meat to the wok and toss until heated through.

3 Stir in the seasoning sauce, to taste, and cashews. Top with the lime rind.

NUTRITION PER SERVE
Protein 25 g; Fat 20 g; Carbohydrate 9 g; Dietary Fibre 1 g; Cholesterol 45 mg; 1215 kJ (290 cal)

Crush the palm sugar, using the flat blade of a large knife.

HOT ITALIAN SALAD

Preparation time: 15 minutes
Total cooking time: 15 minutes
Serves 4

olive oil, for cooking
4 slices prosciutto
2 onions, cut into wedges
1 clove garlic, crushed
250 g (8 oz) cherry tomatoes
1 yellow capsicum, cut into squares
1 green capsicum, cut into squares
180 g (6 oz) marinated artichoke
   hearts, halved

100 g (3¹/₂ oz) black olives
150 g (5 oz) rocket leaves
1 tablespoon balsamic vinegar
1 tablespoon extra virgin olive oil
Parmesan shavings, to serve

1 Heat the wok until very hot, add
2 teaspoons of the oil and swirl it
around to coat the side. Stir-fry the
prosciutto until crisp and golden.
Drain on paper towels and crumble.
2 Reheat the wok, add 2 teaspoons
of the oil and stir-fry the onion and
garlic over high heat for 3–4 minutes,
or until tender.
3 Stir in the tomatoes, capsicum and

artichokes, and cook for 4–5 minutes,
or until tender. Add the olives and
rocket and stir-fry until the rocket has
just wilted.
4 Combine the vinegar and olive oil,
and season. Pour into the wok and
toss thoroughly. Serve immediately,
sprinkled with the prosciutto and
Parmesan shavings.

NUTRITION PER SERVE
Protein 7.5 g; Fat 20 g; Carbohydrate 5 g;
Dietary Fibre 3.5 g; Cholesterol 10 mg;
870 kJ (210 cal)

Stir-fry the prosciutto slices until they are crisp
and golden.

Drain the prosciutto on paper towels, then
crumble into pieces with your fingers.

Stir the tomatoes, capsicum and artichokes into
the onion and garlic.

LARB (SPICY THAI PORK SALAD)

Preparation time: 20 minutes
Total cooking time: 8 minutes
Serves 4–6

1 tablespoon oil
2 stems lemon grass, white part only,
　　thinly sliced
2 fresh green chillies, finely chopped
500 g (1 lb) lean pork mince
1/4 cup (60 ml/2 fl oz) lime juice
2 teaspoons finely grated lime rind
2–6 teaspoons chilli sauce (page 248)
lettuce leaves, for serving
1/3 cup (10 g/1/4 oz) coriander leaves
1/4 cup (5 g/1/4 oz) small mint leaves
1 small onion, very finely sliced
1/3 cup (50 g/1 3/4 oz) roasted unsalted
　　peanuts, chopped
3 tablespoons crisp-fried garlic

1 Heat the oil in a wok. Add the lemon grass, chilli and pork mince. Stir-fry, breaking up any lumps with a fork or wooden spoon, over high heat for 6 minutes, or until cooked through. Transfer to a bowl and allow to cool.
2 Add the lime juice and rind and the chilli sauce to the cooled mince. Arrange the lettuce leaves on a serving plate. Stir most of the coriander and mint leaves, onion, peanuts and fried garlic through the mince. Spoon over the lettuce and sprinkle the rest of the leaves, onion, peanuts and garlic over the top to serve.

NUTRITION PER SERVE (6)
Protein 22 g; Fat 8.5 g; Carbohydrate 3.5 g;
Dietary Fibre 2 g; Cholesterol 40 mg;
760 kJ (180 cal)

Finely slice the white part of the lemon grass with a sharp knife.

Stir-fry the lemon grass, chilli and mince, breaking up the mince as it cooks.

Add the lime juice, lime rind and chilli sauce to the cooled mince.

SAN CHOY BAU

Preparation time: 25 minutes
+ 10 minutes soaking
Total cooking time: 8 minutes
Serves 4

4 dried Chinese mushrooms
oil, for cooking
1/4 cup (30 g/1 oz) slivered almonds,
    chopped
125 g (4 oz) water chestnuts, drained
    and finely chopped
1 carrot, finely chopped
4 spring onions, finely chopped
250 g (8 oz) lean pork mince
4 coriander roots, finely chopped
1 tablespoon grated fresh ginger
12 lettuce leaves
hoisin sauce, to serve

SAUCE
1 tablespoon light soy sauce
1 tablespoon lime juice
1 teaspoon sesame oil
1/4 cup (15 g/1/2 oz) chopped
    coriander
2 tablespoons chopped mint

1 Soak the mushrooms in a bowl of hot water for 10 minutes, or until softened. Discard the tough stems and chop the mushrooms finely. Set aside.
2 To make the sauce, combine the soy sauce, lime juice, oil, coriander and mint. Set aside.
3 Heat the wok until very hot, add 1 tablespoon of the oil and swirl it around to coat the side. Stir-fry the almonds, water chestnuts, carrot and spring onion for 1 minute, or until lightly cooked but not browned—they should still be crisp. Remove from the wok and set aside.
4 Reheat the wok and add

1 tablespoon of the oil. Stir-fry the pork mince, coriander root, ginger and mushrooms over medium-high heat for 2–3 minutes, or until the pork changes colour, but do not overcook the pork or it will be tough.
5 Add the sauce and stir to combine. Return the vegetable mixture to the wok and stir-fry for 1–2 minutes, or until heated through and the mixture is

well combined. Spoon the pork mixture into the lettuce leaves and sprinkle with the hoisin sauce, to taste. Serve more hoisin sauce for dipping.

NUTRITION PER SERVE
Protein 3.5 g; Fat 20 g; Carbohydrate 15 g;
Dietary Fibre 5 g; Cholesterol 0 mg;
1525 kJ (365 cal)

Water chestnuts are available canned. Drain them and then chop.

Soak the Chinese mushrooms, then discard the tough stems and finely chop them.

Stir-fry the pork mince with the coriander root, ginger and mushrooms.

BLACK BEAN PORK WITH BOK CHOY

Preparation time: 20 minutes
Total cooking time: 10 minutes
Serves 4

400 g (13 oz) lean pork leg steaks
1 tablespoon canned salted black
  beans, rinsed
500 g (1 lb) baby bok choy
2 teaspoons sesame oil
2 onions, finely sliced
2 cloves garlic, finely chopped
2–3 teaspoons chopped ginger

1 red capsicum, cut into strips
1/2 cup (90 g/3 oz) water chestnuts,
  finely sliced
2 tablespoons oyster sauce
1 tablespoon soy sauce
2 teaspoons fish sauce

1 Slice the pork steaks into strips, cutting across the grain. Roughly chop the beans. Separate the leaves of the bok choy, trim away the tough ends and shred the leaves.

2 Heat half the sesame oil in a large wok. Cook the onion, garlic and ginger over high heat for 3–4 minutes, add the capsicum and cook for 2–3 minutes. Remove from the wok. Heat the remaining sesame oil and stir-fry the pork in batches over high heat.

3 Return all the pork to the wok along with the onion mixture, black beans, shredded bok choy, water chestnuts and oyster, soy and fish sauces. Toss quickly to combine the ingredients, lower the heat, cover and steam for 3–4 minutes, or until the bok choy has just wilted. Serve immediately.

NUTRITION PER SERVE
Protein 30 g; Fat 3 g; Carbohydrate 20 g;
Dietary Fibre 3.5 g; Cholesterol 55 mg;
910 kJ (215 cal)

Separate the leaves of the bok choy and then trim the tough ends.

Stir-fry the pork strips in batches over high heat until brown.

Toss all the ingredients quickly until combined, then lower the heat.

STIR-FRIED PORK AND PEANUT DIP

Preparation time: 25 minutes
Total cooking time: 20 minutes
Serves 6–8

1 teaspoon green peppercorns
1 tablespoon oil
2 coriander roots, very finely chopped
2 cloves garlic, finely chopped
150 g (5 oz) pork mince
1/2 cup (125 ml/4 fl oz) coconut milk
3 tablespoons crunchy peanut butter
1 tablespoon fish sauce

2 teaspoons soft brown sugar
1/2 cup (15 g/1/2 oz) coriander leaves, chopped
roasted chopped unsalted peanuts
chilli sauce (see page 248)
vegetable crudités or savoury biscuits, to serve

1 Finely crush the peppercorns. Heat the oil in a wok.

2 Add the peppercorns, coriander roots and garlic to the wok and stir for 30 seconds over medium heat. Add the pork mince and stir-fry for 5 minutes, breaking up any lumps of meat with a fork or wooden spoon. Add the coconut milk, peanut butter and 1/2 cup (125 ml/4 fl oz) water. Bring to the boil, stirring. Reduce the heat and allow to simmer for 10 minutes.

3 Stir in the fish sauce and brown sugar. Pour into a serving bowl and sprinkle with the coriander and peanuts. Drizzle with chilli sauce. Serve warm or at room temperature, with crudités and savoury biscuits for dipping.

NUTRITION PER SERVE (8)
Protein 8 g; Fat 12 g; Carbohydrate 3 g;
Dietary Fibre 1.5 g; Cholesterol 9 mg;
625 kJ (150 cal)

Finely crush the green peppercorns, using the flat side of the blade of a knife.

Add the pork mince to the wok after cooking the peppercorns, coriander and garlic.

Add the fish sauce and brown sugar to the mixture in the wok and stir.

SPICY PORK AND PRAWN LETTUCE PARCELS

Preparation time: 20 minutes
 + 30 minutes for lettuce crisping
Total cooking time: 10 minutes
Serves 4–6

1–2 large lettuces
1 tablespoon oil
3 spring onions, chopped
2 teaspoons red curry paste (use the recipe on page 246 or ready-made paste)
100 g (3½ oz) pork mince
100 g (3½ oz) small raw prawns, peeled and deveined
3 tablespoons coconut milk
1–2 teaspoons chopped red chillies
2 teaspoons fish sauce
1 teaspoon soft brown sugar
2 teaspoons grated lime rind
3 tablespoons finely chopped roasted unsalted peanuts

1 Separate the lettuce leaves, wash them and pat dry, then wrap in a dry tea towel and refrigerate for about 30 minutes to crisp up.
2 Heat the oil in a wok. Add the spring onions and curry paste and stir-fry for 2 minutes over medium heat.
3 Add the pork mince and stir-fry until browned. Add the prawns, coconut milk and chillies and stir-fry for 3 minutes.
4 Add the fish sauce, brown sugar and lime rind and stir well. Stir in the peanuts, then leave to cool for 15 minutes. Place a spoonful of spicy pork on each lettuce leaf—the parcels can be rolled for easy eating.

NUTRITION PER SERVE (6)
Protein 10 g; Fat 8.5 g; Carbohydrate 3 g;
Dietary Fibre 2 g; Cholesterol 33 mg;
535 kJ (128 cal)

NOTE: The filling must be cooled so that all liquid will be absorbed, making it moist and succulent.

Separate the lettuce leaves, wash and pat dry, then wrap in a tea towel and refrigerate.

Use a wooden spoon to stir the spring onions and curry paste in the wok.

Add the prawns, coconut milk and chillies to the wok and stir for 3 minutes.

Finally, add the chopped peanuts and stir through the mixture.

THAI RED PORK CURRY WITH CORN AND PEAS

Preparation time: 15 minutes
Total cooking time: 25 minutes
Serves 4

1 tablespoon oil
1–2 tablespoons red curry paste (use the recipe on page 246 or ready-made paste)
500 g (1 lb) lean, diced pork
1 cup (250 ml/8 fl oz) coconut milk
1 cup (200 g/6$^{1/2}$ oz) fresh corn kernels or 150 g baby corn spears
$^{1/2}$ cup (90 g/3 oz) fresh peas
1 tablespoon fish sauce
2 teaspoons soft brown sugar
2 teaspoons finely grated lime rind
$^{1/2}$ cup (30 g/1 oz) shredded Thai basil

1 Heat the oil in a wok. Add the curry paste and stir-fry for 1 minute. Add the pork and stir-fry until lightly browned.
2 Add the coconut milk and 1 cup (250 ml/8 fl oz) water and bring to the boil. Simmer for 15 minutes.
3 Add the corn and peas to the wok and cook for 5 minutes. Add the fish sauce, brown sugar, lime rind and basil leaves and toss well.

NUTRITION PER SERVE
Protein 30 g; Fat 20 g; Carbohydrate 13 g; Dietary Fibre 3.5 g; Cholesterol 62 mg; 1535 kJ (367 cal)

HINT: Remove the kernels from two fresh corn cobs to make 1 cupful. Use a sharp knife to scrape down the length of the sides to remove kernels. Frozen corn can also be used.

Add the diced pork to the wok and toss the meat until it turns light brown.

Simmer the mixture in the wok for 15 minutes so that the sauce reduces and thickens.

Stir in the corn and peas and cook the curry for another 5 minutes.

THAI RED PORK AND PUMPKIN CURRY

Preparation time: 20 minutes
Total cooking time: 25 minutes
Serves 4

1 tablespoon oil
1–2 tablespoons red curry paste (use the recipe on page 246 or ready-made paste)
500 g (1 lb) lean pork, cubed
1 cup (250 ml/8 fl oz) coconut milk

350 g (11 oz) butternut or Japanese pumpkin, peeled and cubed
6 kaffir lime leaves
1/4 cup (60 ml/2 fl oz) coconut cream
1 tablespoon fish sauce
1 teaspoon soft brown sugar
2 red chillies, thinly sliced

1 Heat the oil in a wok, add the curry paste and stir for 1 minute.
2 Add the pork to the wok and stir-fry over medium-high heat until golden brown. Add the coconut milk, pumpkin, kaffir lime leaves and 125 ml

(4 fl oz) water, reduce the heat and simmer for 15 minutes, or until the pork is tender.
3 Add the coconut cream, fish sauce and brown sugar and stir to combine. Scatter chilli over the top to serve.

NUTRITION PER SERVE
Protein 30 g; Fat 11 g; Carbohydrate 9 g; Dietary Fibre 1.5 g; Cholesterol 62 mg; 1085 kJ (260 cal)

NOTE: Butternut and Japanese pumpkins are tender, sweet varieties.

Add the curry paste to the hot oil and stir with a wooden spoon for 1 minute.

Add the pork pieces to the wok and stir-fry over medium-high heat until golden brown.

Add the coconut cream, fish sauce and brown sugar to the wok and stir well.

CORIANDER PORK WITH FRESH PINEAPPLE

Preparation time: 25 minutes
Total cooking time: 10–12 minutes
Serves 4

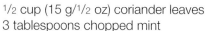

400 g (13 oz) pork loin or fillet
1/4 pineapple
1 tablespoon oil
4 cloves garlic, chopped
4 spring onions, chopped
1 tablespoon fish sauce
1 tablespoon lime juice

1/2 cup (15 g/1/2 oz) coriander leaves
3 tablespoons chopped mint

1 Cut the pork into thin slices, using a very sharp knife (see HINT).
2 Trim the skin from the pineapple and cut the flesh into small bite-sized pieces. Heat the oil in a wok, add the garlic and spring onion and cook for 1 minute. Remove from the wok.
3 Heat the wok to very hot; add the pork in 2 or 3 batches and stir-fry each batch for 3 minutes or until the meat is just cooked. Return the meat, garlic and spring onion to the wok and then add the pineapple pieces, fish sauce and lime juice. Toss well. Just before serving, sprinkle with the coriander leaves and chopped mint and then toss together lightly.

NUTRITION PER SERVE
Protein 24 g; Fat 7 g; Carbohydrate 7 g;
Dietary Fibre 2 g; Cholesterol 50 mg;
762 kJ (182 cal)

HINT: To make the meat easier to slice, freeze it until it is just firm and slice thinly while still frozen.

Buy pork loin or fillet and use a sharp knife to cut it into thin slices.

Slice the skin from the pineapple and cut the flesh into small, bite-sized pieces.

Stir-fry each batch of pork for 3 minutes, or until just cooked.

FRIED NOODLES WITH MUSHROOMS AND BARBECUED PORK

Preparation time: 30 minutes
Total cooking time: 6 minutes
Serves 4

8 dried Chinese mushrooms
2 tablespoons oil
4 cloves garlic, chopped
5 cm (2 inches) fresh ginger, grated
1–2 teaspoons chopped red
    chillies
100 g (3½ oz) barbecued pork, cut
    into small pieces
200 g (6½ oz) fresh egg noodles
2 teaspoons fish sauce
2 tablespoons lime juice
2 teaspoons soft brown sugar
2 tablespoons crisp-fried garlic
2 tablespoons crisp-fried onion
chilli flakes

1 Soak the mushrooms in hot water for 20 minutes. Drain and cut them into quarters.
2 Heat the oil in a large wok. Add the garlic, ginger and chilli and stir-fry for 1 minute over high heat. Add the pork to the wok and stir for 1 minute.
3 Add the egg noodles and mushrooms and toss well. Sprinkle the fish sauce, lime juice and soft brown sugar over the pork and then toss quickly, cover and steam for 30 seconds. Sprinkle the fried garlic and onion and chilli flakes over the top before serving.

NUTRITION PER SERVE
Protein 16 g; Fat 12 g; Carbohydrate 40 g;
Dietary Fibre 3 g; Cholesterol 32 mg;
1375 kJ (328 cal)

Drain the Chinese mushrooms and use a sharp knife to cut them into quarters.

Add the pork pieces to the wok and stir with a wooden spoon for a minute.

Cover the wok and allow the noodles to steam for 30 seconds.

FRIED RICE WITH CORIANDER AND BASIL

Preparation time: 20 minutes
Total cooking time: 20 minutes
Serves 4

2 tablespoons oil
2.5 cm (1 inch) piece pork fat, chopped
4 cloves garlic, chopped
5 cm (2 inch) piece fresh ginger, grated
2 teaspoons chopped red chillies
2 chicken thigh fillets, diced
100 g (3¹/₂ oz) pork loin, diced
2¹/₂ cups (500 g/1 lb) cold cooked jasmine rice
1 tablespoon fish sauce
2 teaspoons Golden Mountain sauce
2 spring onions, chopped
1 cup (30 g/1 oz) Thai basil leaves, chopped
¹/₂ cup (15 g/¹/₂ oz) coriander leaves, chopped, plus some to garnish

1 Heat the oil in a wok. When the oil is very hot, add the pork fat, garlic, ginger and chilli and stir-fry for 2 minutes.
2 Add the diced chicken and pork to the wok and stir-fry for 3 minutes, or until the meat changes colour. Add the rice to the wok and toss well using two wooden spoons, breaking up any lumps. When the rice has warmed, add the sauces and toss through with the spring onions, Thai basil and coriander. Serve immediately.

NUTRITION PER SERVE
Protein 25 g; Fat 40 g; Carbohydrate 45 g;
Dietary Fibre 5 g; Cholesterol 46 mg;
2752 kJ (657 cal)

Buy pork loin and then finely dice it with a sharp knife.

Add the pork fat, garlic, ginger and chillies to the wok and stir with a wooden spoon.

Add the cold cooked rice to the wok and toss well, breaking up any lumps.

PORK BALL CURRY WITH EGG NOODLES

Preparation time: 15 minutes
Total cooking time: 20 minutes
Serves 4

200 g (6¹/2 oz) pork mince
3 cloves garlic, chopped
2 stems lemon grass (white part only), finely chopped
2.5 cm (1 inch) piece ginger, grated
1 tablespoon oil
1–2 tablespoons green curry paste (use the recipe on page 246 or ready-made paste)
1¹/2 cups (375 ml/12 fl oz) coconut milk

2 tablespoons fish sauce
2 teaspoons soft brown sugar
¹/2 cup (15 g/¹/2 oz) chopped Thai basil leaves
200 g (6¹/2 oz) fresh egg noodles
sliced spring onions, coriander leaves and sliced chillies, to serve

1 Finely chop the pork mince with a cleaver or large knife. Combine the mince, garlic, lemon grass and ginger in a bowl and mix thoroughly. Form teaspoonfuls into small balls.
2 Heat the oil in a wok, add the curry paste and cook over low heat, stirring constantly, for 1 minute or until fragrant. Add the coconut milk and 1 cup (250 ml/8 fl oz) water to the wok. Stir until boiling, then reduce

the heat and simmer for 5 minutes. Add the pork balls and simmer for 5 minutes or until cooked. Add the fish sauce, brown sugar and Thai basil.
3 Cook the noodles in boiling water for 4 minutes or until tender, then drain. Toss with the pork balls and curry sauce and then serve immediately, as the noodles will soak up the sauce. Scatter spring onions, coriander and chillies over the top.

NUTRITION PER SERVE
Protein 20 g; Fat 25 g; Carbohydrate 42 g;
Dietary Fibre 3.5 g; Cholesterol 34 mg;
1980 kJ (475 cal)

Mix together the mince, garlic, lemon grass and ginger and form into meatballs.

Add the coconut milk and water to the wok and stir until boiling.

Add the noodles to rapidly boiling water and cook for 4 minutes.

PORK AND GREEN BEANS WITH GINGER SAUCE

Preparation time: 15 minutes
Total cooking time: 10 minutes
Serves 4

3/4 cup (185 ml/6 fl oz) soy sauce
4 tablespoons white or rice wine
    vinegar
1 teaspoon sugar
pinch of dried chilli flakes
3 teaspoons cornflour
600 g (11/4 lb) pork fillet, trimmed and
    cut into thin slices
2 tablespoons peanut oil

350 g (11 oz) green beans, cut into
    short lengths
2 cloves garlic, chopped
2 tablespoons grated fresh ginger

1 Place the soy sauce, vinegar, sugar, chilli flakes, cornflour and 1/3 cup (80 ml/2³/4 fl oz) water in a bowl and mix well. Add the pork and toss to coat well.
2 Heat a wok over high heat, add half the oil and swirl to coat the side. Drain the pork, reserving the liquid, and add to the wok. Stir-fry over high heat for 1–2 minutes, or until brown. Remove the pork from the wok.
3 Heat the remaining oil, add the

beans and stir-fry for 3–4 minutes. Add the garlic and ginger and stir-fry for 1 minute, or until fragrant. Return the pork and any juices to the pan and add the reserved marinade. Bring to the boil and cook, stirring, for 1–2 minutes, or until slightly thickened. Serve with steamed rice.

NUTRITION PER SERVE
Protein 51 g; Fat 23 g; Carbohydrate 11 g;
Dietary Fibre 3.5 g; Cholesterol 100 mg;
1917 kJ (458 cal)

NOTE: Rice wine vinegar is made by oxidising beer or wine made from fermented rice starch.

Add the pork to the wok and stir-fry until the meat is browned.

Heat the remaining oil in the wok and stir-fry the green beans.

Return the pork and reserved marinade to the wok and toss well.

SAVOURY RICE AND EGGS

Preparation time: 20 minutes
Total cooking time: 12 minutes
Serves 4

2 tablespoons ghee (see NOTE) or oil
1 onion, finely chopped
1/2 red capsicum, finely chopped
10 spring onions, thinly sliced
2–3 small red chillies, seeded and
    finely chopped
2–3 cloves garlic, finely chopped
1 tablespoon grated fresh ginger
125 g (4 oz) Chinese barbecued pork,
    finely chopped
6 eggs, lightly beaten

4 cups (740 g/1 1/2 lb) cold cooked
    jasmine rice
1–2 teaspoons seasoning sauce
1/3 cup (20 g/3/4 oz) chopped
    coriander
onion flakes, to garnish

1 Heat the wok until very hot, add the ghee and swirl it around to coat the side. Stir-fry the onion, capsicum, spring onion, chilli, garlic and ginger over medium-high heat for 2–3 minutes, or until the vegetables are cooked but not brown. Add the barbecued pork and toss to combine.
2 Reduce the heat, then pour in the beaten eggs. Season well with salt and pepper. Gently stir the egg mixture until it is creamy and almost set. Add the rice and gently stir-fry to incorporate all the ingredients and heat the mixture through.
3 Sprinkle with the seasoning sauce and stir in the coriander. Serve the savoury rice immediately, sprinkled with onion flakes.

NUTRITION PER SERVE
Protein 15 g; Fat 20 g; Carbohydrate 60 g;
Dietary Fibre 3.5 g; Cholesterol 295 mg;
2105 kJ (500 cal)

NOTE: Ghee is a form of clarified butter. It is the main type of fat used in Indian cooking and is available in most supermarkets.

Cut the Chinese barbecued pork into slices, then chop it finely.

Add the barbecued pork to the onion mixture and toss to combine.

Add the egg, season well and stir gently until the mixture is creamy.

FRIED RICE NOODLES

Preparation time: 30 minutes
Total cooking time: 15 minutes
Serves 4

2 Chinese dried pork sausages (see
    NOTE)
2 tablespoons oil
2 cloves garlic, finely chopped
1 onion, finely chopped
3 red chillies, seeded and chopped
250 g (8 oz) Chinese barbecued pork,
    finely chopped
200 g (6¹/₂ oz) peeled raw prawns
500 g (1 lb) fresh thick rice noodles,
    gently separated
150 g (5 oz) garlic chives, cut into
    3 cm (1¹/₄ inch) pieces

2 tablespoons kecap manis
3 eggs, lightly beaten
1 tablespoon rice vinegar
100 g (3¹/₂ oz) bean sprouts, straggly
    ends removed

1 Diagonally slice the dried pork sausages into paper-thin slices. Heat the oil in a large wok. Fry the sausage, tossing regularly, until golden and very crisp. Using a slotted spoon, remove from the wok and leave to drain on paper towels.
2 Reheat the oil in the wok, add the garlic, onion, chilli and pork and stir-fry for 2 minutes. Add the prawns and toss constantly, until the prawns change colour.
3 Add the noodles, chives and kecap manis and toss. Cook for 1 minute or

until the noodles begin to soften. Pour the combined eggs and vinegar over the top of the noodles and toss for 1 minute. Be careful not to overcook the noodles, or let the egg-coated noodles burn on the base of the wok. Toss in the bean sprouts.
4 Arrange on a large serving platter, scatter the sausage over the top and toss a little to mix a few slices among the noodles. Serve immediately.

NUTRITION PER SERVE
Protein 47 g; Fat 17 g; Carbohydrate 30 g;
Dietary Fibre 3 g; Cholesterol 285 mg;
1996 kJ (470 cal)

NOTE: Chinese pork sausages (*lup chiang*) must always be cooked before eating.

Chop the Chinese barbecued pork into very small pieces, using a sharp knife.

Remove the crisp Chinese sausage slices from the wok and drain on paper towels.

Pour the combined eggs and vinegar over the top of the noodles and toss.

SINGAPORE NOODLES

Preparation time: 20 minutes
Total cooking time: 10 minutes
Serves 4–6

150 g (5 oz) dried rice vermicelli
oil, for cooking
250 g (8 oz) Chinese barbecued pork, cut into small pieces
250 g (8 oz) peeled raw prawns, cut into small pieces
2 tablespoons Madras curry powder
2 cloves garlic, crushed
100 g (3¹/₂ oz) shiitake mushrooms, thinly sliced
1 onion, thinly sliced
100 g (3¹/₂ oz) green beans, thinly sliced on the diagonal
1 tablespoon soy sauce
4 spring onions, thinly sliced on the diagonal

1 Place the vermicelli in a large bowl, cover with boiling water and soak for 5 minutes. Drain well and spread out on a clean tea towel to dry.

2 Heat the wok until very hot, add 1 tablespoon of the oil and swirl it around to coat the side. Stir-fry the barbecued pork and the prawn pieces in batches over high heat. Remove from the wok and set aside.

3 Reheat the wok, add 2 tablespoons of the oil and stir-fry the curry powder and garlic for 1–2 minutes, or until fragrant. Add the mushrooms and onion and stir-fry over medium heat for 2–3 minutes, or until the onion and mushrooms are soft.

4 Return the pork and prawns to the wok, add the beans and 2 teaspoons water, and toss to combine. Add the drained noodles, soy sauce and spring onion. Toss well and serve.

NUTRITION PER SERVE (6)
Protein 10 g; Fat 7.5 g; Carbohydrate 25 g; Dietary Fibre 3 g; Cholesterol 60 mg; 905 kJ (215 cal)

Cut the barbecued pork into slices, then into small pieces.

Put the vermicelli in a heatproof bowl, cover with boiling water and leave to soak.

Stir-fry the curry powder and garlic in the oil until the mixture is fragrant.

NOODLES WITH BARBECUED PORK AND GREENS

Preparation time: 20 minutes
Total cooking time: 25 minutes
Serves 4

250 g (8 oz) fresh thick egg noodles
1 tablespoon oil
1 tablespoon sesame oil
250 g (8 oz) Chinese barbecued pork, cut into small cubes
1 large onion, very thinly sliced
2 cloves garlic, finely chopped
400 g (13 oz) green vegetables (beans, broccoli, celery), cut into bite-sized pieces
2 tablespoons hoisin sauce
1 tablespoon kecap manis
100 g (3¹/₂ oz) snow peas
3 baby bok choy, cut into quarters lengthways
230 g (7¹/₂ oz) can water chestnuts, sliced

1 Two-thirds fill a pan with water and bring to the boil. Add the noodles and cook for about 3 minutes, or until just tender. Drain well.
2 Heat the wok until very hot, add the oils and swirl them around to coat the side. Stir-fry the pork over medium heat for 2 minutes, or until crisp. Drain on paper towels.
3 Reheat the wok, add the onion and garlic, and stir-fry over very high heat for about 1 minute, or until just softened. Add the vegetables and cook, tossing regularly, for 2 minutes, or until just softened. Stir in the hoisin sauce, kecap manis, snow peas, bok choy, water chestnuts and 1 tablespoon of water. Cook for 2 minutes, covered. Add the noodles and stir-fried pork, and toss gently to combine. Serve immediately.

NUTRITION PER SERVE
Protein 10 g; Fat 20 g; Carbohydrate 60 g; Dietary Fibre 10 g; Cholesterol 40 mg; 3910 kJ (930 cal)

NOTE: Chinese barbecued pork is also known as *char siew*. You can buy it at Chinese barbecue shops.

Cut the barbecued pork into strips, then into small cubes.

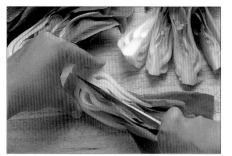
Trim the base of the baby bok choy, then cut them into quarters lengthways.

Drain the can of water chestnuts and then slice them thinly.

JAPANESE FRIED PORK AND NOODLES

Preparation time: 30 minutes
Total cooking time: 15 minutes
Serves 4

1 tablespoon oil
150 g (5 oz) pork loin, thinly sliced
5 spring onions, cut into short lengths
1 carrot, cut into thin strips
200 g (6½ oz) Chinese cabbage, shredded
500 g (1 lb) Hokkien noodles, gently pulled apart to separate
2 tablespoons shoshoyu
1 tablespoon Worcestershire sauce
1 tablespoon mirin
2 teaspoons caster sugar
1 cup (90 g/3 oz) bean sprouts, scraggly ends removed
1 sheet toasted nori, shredded

1 Heat the oil in a large wok over medium heat. Stir-fry the pork, spring onion and carrot for 1–2 minutes, or until the pork just changes colour.

2 Add the cabbage, noodles, shoshoyu, Worcestershire sauce, mirin, sugar and 2 tablespoons water. Cover and cook for 1 minute.

3 Add the bean sprouts and toss well to coat the vegetables and noodles in the sauce. Serve immediately, sprinkled with the shredded nori.

NUTRITION PER SERVE
Protein 25 g; Fat 8 g; Carbohydrate 93 g;
Dietary Fibre 5.5 g; Cholesterol 40 mg;
2300 kJ (550 cal)

Finely shred the Chinese cabbage with a large, sharp knife.

Use your fingers to remove the scraggly ends from the bean sprouts.

Stir-fry the pork, spring onion and carrot until the pork just changes colour.

MA POR TOFU

Preparation time: 15 minutes
  + 10 minutes marinating
Total cooking time: 15 minutes
Serves 4

3 teaspoons cornflour
2 teaspoons soy sauce
1 teaspoon oyster sauce
1 clove garlic, finely chopped
250 g (8 oz) pork mince
1 tablespoon oil

3 teaspoons red bean chilli paste
3 teaspoons preserved bean curd
750 g (1 1/2 lb) firm tofu, drained,
  cubed
2 spring onions, sliced
3 teaspoons oyster sauce, extra
2 teaspoons soy sauce, extra
1 1/2 teaspoons sugar

1 Put the cornflour, soy and oyster sauces and the garlic in a bowl and mix well. Add the mince, toss to coat and leave for 10 minutes.
2 Heat a wok until very hot, add the oil and swirl to coat the base and side of the wok with oil. Add the mince and stir-fry for 5 minutes, or until browned. Add the chilli paste and bean curd, and cook for 2 minutes, or until fragrant.
3 Add the remaining ingredients and stir for 3–5 minutes, or until the tofu is heated through.

NUTRITION PER SERVE
Protein 26 g; Fat 12 g; Carbohydrate 5 g;
Dietary Fibre 0 g; Cholesterol 30 mg;
1092 kJ (260 cal)

Drain the firm tofu from the liquid you buy it in, and cut it into cubes.

Add the minced pork to the cornflour, soy sauce, oyster sauce and garlic.

Stir-fry the pork mince until it is browned, then add the chilli paste and bean curd.

SESAME PORK

Preparation time: 10 minutes
Total cooking time: 20 minutes
Serves 4

2 tablespoons sesame seeds
3 tablespoons peanut oil
600 g (1 1/4 lb) pork fillets, thinly
  sliced
2 tablespoons hoisin sauce
2 tablespoons teriyaki sauce
2 teaspoons cornflour
2 teaspoons sesame oil
8 spring onions, sliced on the
  diagonal
2 cloves garlic, crushed

2 teaspoons finely grated fresh ginger
2 carrots, julienned
200 g (6 1/2 oz) snake beans, cut into
  short lengths

1 Preheat the oven to moderate 180°C (350°F/Gas 4). Place the sesame seeds on an oven tray and bake for 5 minutes, or until browned.
2 Heat a wok until very hot, add 1 tablespoon oil and swirl to coat. Add half the pork and stir-fry for 3 minutes, or until browned. Remove. Repeat with the remaining pork. Remove.
3 Combine the hoisin and teriyaki sauces, cornflour and 1 tablespoon water and mix until smooth.
4 Reheat the wok until very hot, add the remaining peanut oil and the sesame oil and swirl to coat. Add the spring onion, garlic and ginger, and stir-fry for 1 minute, or until fragrant.
5 Add the carrot and beans, and stir-fry for 3 minutes, or until almost cooked but still crunchy. Return the pork to the wok, add the cornflour mixture and stir until the sauce boils and thickens. Simmer until the meat is tender and the vegetables are just cooked. Toss through the sesame seeds and serve immediately.

NUTRITION PER SERVE
Protein 38 g; Fat 27 g; Carbohydra. .5 g;
Dietary Fibre 4.5 g; Cholesterol 75 mg;
1766 kJ (420 cal)

Cut the snake beans into shorter lengths for easy stir-frying.

Cook the pork in two batches, so that it fries rather than stews.

Mix together the hoisin and teriyaki sauces, cornflour and 1 tablespoon of water.

CHINESE PORK WITH BROCCOLI

Preparation time: 10 minutes
Total cooking time: 10 minutes
Serves 4

1.6 kg (3¼ lb) Chinese broccoli,
    cut into short lengths
1 tablespoon peanut oil
2.5 cm (1 inch) piece fresh ginger,
    julienned
2 cloves garlic, crushed

500 g (1 lb) Chinese barbecue pork,
    thinly sliced
¼ cup (60 ml/2 fl oz) chicken or
    vegetable stock
¼ cup (60 ml/2 fl oz) oyster sauce
1 tablespoon kecap manis

1 Place the broccoli in a steamer over a wok of simmering water and cook for 5 minutes, or until just tender but still crisp.
2 Drain the wok, dry thoroughly and heat until very hot. Add the oil and swirl to coat. Add the ginger and garlic and stir-fry for 30 seconds, or until fragrant. Add the broccoli and pork and toss to coat.
3 Mix together the stock, oyster sauce and kecap manis and add to the wok. Toss thoroughly until heated through and then serve immediately.

NUTRITION PER SERVE
Protein 30 g; Fat 7 g; Carbohydrate 4.5 g;
Dietary Fibre 2 g; Cholesterol 60 mg;
886 kJ (212 cal)

Peel the piece of fresh ginger and then cut it into julienne strips, like thin matchsticks.

Put the broccoli in a steamer over a wok of simmering water and cook until tender.

Stir-fry the ginger and garlic, then add the broccoli and pork to the wok.

SICHUAN PORK WITH CAPSICUM

Preparation time: 30 minutes
Total cooking time: 10 minutes
Serves 4–6

1¹/₂ tablespoons cornflour
1 tablespoon Sichuan peppercorns,
   ground
2 egg whites, beaten
500 g (1 lb) pork fillet, thinly sliced
2 tablespoons peanut oil, plus
   1 teaspoon, extra
1 red capsicum, thinly sliced
2 spring onions, sliced into short
   lengths
2 teaspoons chilli oil
4 star anise
2 cloves garlic, crushed

2 teaspoons finely chopped fresh
   ginger
2 tablespoons oyster sauce
2 tablespoons Chinese rice wine
2 tablespoons soy sauce
¹/₂ teaspoon sesame oil
2 teaspoons sugar

1 Place the cornflour, peppercorns, egg whites and ¹/₂ teaspoon salt in a bowl. Mix well, then add the pork and toss to coat.

2 Heat a wok until very hot, add 1 teaspoon peanut oil and swirl to coat the base and side of the wok with oil. Add the capsicum and spring onion and stir-fry for 1 minute. Remove from the wok.

3 Add 1 tablespoon peanut oil to the wok and swirl to coat the base and side of the wok. Add half the pork and stir-fry for 2 minutes, or until sealed. Remove. Repeat with the remaining oil and pork.

4 Add the chilli oil to the wok and swirl to coat. Add the star anise and stir-fry for 30 seconds, then add the garlic and ginger and stir-fry for another few seconds.

5 Combine the oyster sauce, rice wine, soy sauce, sesame oil and sugar, add to the wok and cook for 30 seconds. Return the pork to the wok and stir-fry for 1 minute, then stir in the vegetables and serve.

NUTRITION PER SERVE (6)
Protein 20 g; Fat 11 g; Carbohydrate 4 g;
Dietary Fibre 0.5 g; Cholesterol 40 mg;
865 kJ (207 cal)

Mix together the cornflour, peppercorns, egg whites and salt, then add the pork.

Stir-fry the capsicum and spring onion in the peanut oil for 1 minute.

Add half of the pork to the wok so that it doesn't overcrowd and stew in its juices.

PORK WITH PUMPKIN AND CASHEW NUTS

Preparation time: 20 minutes
Total cooking time: 20 minutes
Serves 4

2–3 tablespoons oil
1/2 cup (90 g/3 oz) cashew nuts
750 g (11/2 lb) pork neck, cut into
    long, thin strips
500 g (1 lb) pumpkin, cubed
1 tablespoon grated fresh ginger
1/3 cup (80 ml/23/4 fl oz) chicken stock
1/4 cup (60 ml/2 fl oz) dry sherry

11/2 tablespoons soy sauce
1/2 teaspoon cornflour
500 g (1 lb) baby bok choy, chopped
1–2 tablespoons coriander leaves

1 Heat a wok until very hot, add
1 tablespoon oil and swirl to coat the
side of the wok. Stir-fry the cashews
for 1–2 minutes, or until browned.
Drain on paper towels.
2 Reheat the wok, add a little extra oil
and swirl to coat. Stir-fry the pork in
batches for 5 minutes, or until lightly
browned. Remove from the wok. Add
1 tablespoon oil to the wok and stir-fry
the pumpkin and ginger for 3 minutes,

or until lightly browned. Add the
stock, sherry and soy sauce, and cook
for 3 minutes, or until the pumpkin
is tender.
3 Blend the cornflour with 1 teaspoon
water until smooth, add to the wok
and stir until the mixture boils and
thickens. Return the pork and cashews
to the wok and add the bok choy and
coriander. Stir until the bok choy has
just wilted. Serve immediately.

NUTRITION PER SERVE
Protein 46 g; Fat 28 g; Carbohydrate 15 g;
Dietary Fibre 8 g; Cholesterol 75 mg;
2112 kJ (505 cal)

Stir-fry the cashew nuts for 1–2 minutes, or until
they are just browned.

Reheat the wok and brown the pork in batches
so that it fries rather than stews.

Add the stock, sherry and soy sauce and cook
until the pumpkin is tender.

UDON NOODLES WITH GINGER PORK AND PICKLES

Preparation time: 30 minutes
+ 20 minutes marinating
Total cooking time: 25 minutes
Serves 4

10 cm (4 inch) piece fresh ginger, peeled
pinch of sugar
200 g (6½ oz) pork loin
500 g (1 lb) dried udon noodles
2 tablespoons cornflour
2 tablespoons oil
150 g (5 oz) broccoli, cut into long thin florets
100 g (3½ oz) Chinese pickled vegetables, finely sliced

4 spring onions, sliced
3 tablespoons soy sauce
3 tablespoons mirin or sherry
1 Lebanese cucumber, halved and finely sliced
2 tablespoons toasted sesame seeds

1 Slice one third of the ginger paper-thin and place in a bowl, then finely grate the rest. Squeeze the grated ginger over the ginger slices and discard the dry pulp. Season well with salt, pepper and the sugar.
2 Cut the pork into 5 cm (2 inch) strips. Add to the ginger. Mix well and leave to marinate for 20 minutes.
3 Cook the noodles in plenty of salted boiling water for 12 minutes, or until tender. Drain, rinse and set aside.
4 Remove the ginger from the pork. Scatter the cornflour over the pork and mix well. Heat half the oil in a wok over medium-high heat. Quickly stir-fry the pork until golden, adding the ginger at the end. Remove and set aside.
5 Heat the remaining oil and stir-fry the broccoli, pickles and spring onion for 30 seconds. Add 1 tablespoon of water, then cover and steam for 30 seconds.
6 Add the noodles, soy sauce and mirin to the wok and toss well until heated through. Add the pork and ginger and toss well. Divide between bowls, garnish with cucumber and sesame seeds and serve at once.

NUTRITION PER SERVE
Protein 30 g; Fat 15 g; Carbohydrate 105 g; Dietary Fibre 4 g; Cholesterol 25 mg; 2880 kJ (685 cal)

Buy the Chinese pickled vegetables from Asian food stores and slice them finely.

Slice a third of the ginger as thinly as you can, then grate the rest over it.

Add the noodles, soy sauce and mirin to the wok and toss well.

Lamb

LAMB WITH MIXED GREENS

Preparation time: 10 minutes
Total cooking time: 15 minutes
Serves 4

500 g (1 lb) lamb fillets, cut into strips
    about 2.5 cm (1 inch) wide
1 egg white, lightly beaten
1 tablespoon cornflour
2–3 tablespoons oil
2.5 cm (1 inch) piece fresh ginger,
    thinly sliced
2 cloves garlic, crushed
2 tablespoons soy sauce
2 leeks, finely sliced
250 g (8 oz) baby English spinach
    leaves, torn
1 small bunch bok choy, cut into short
    lengths
3/4 cup (115 g/4 oz) frozen peas
1 teaspoon sugar
3 tablespoons chicken stock
dash of chilli sauce

1 Season the strips of lamb with salt and pepper, dip in the egg white and dust with cornflour.
2 Heat half the oil in a wok and add the ginger, garlic and soy sauce. Stir-fry over high heat for 30 seconds. Add the lamb and stir-fry for 1 minute or until browned. Reduce the heat, cover and cook for 3 minutes. Remove the lamb from the wok.
3 Heat the remaining oil in the wok and add the leek. Stir-fry over high heat for 3 minutes, or until the leek has softened.
4 Add the spinach, bok choy and frozen peas to the wok and stir-fry for 1 minute. Reduce the heat and cover the wok to steam the vegetables for 2 minutes. Combine the sugar, stock and chilli sauce and add to the wok. Add the lamb and stir well. Stir-fry for 2 minutes or until the lamb and vegetables are just tender.

NUTRITION PER SERVE
Protein 35 g; Fat 30 g; Carbohydrate 7 g;
Dietary Fibre 5 g; Cholesterol 100 mg;
1775 kJ (425 cal)

Season the meat with salt and pepper, then dip in the egg white and cornflour.

Add the spinach, bok choy and frozen peas to the wok and stir-fry for 1 minute.

SPICY LAMB AND EGGPLANT

Preparation time: 15 minutes
Total cooking time: 20 minutes
Serves 4

oil, for cooking
1 onion, finely chopped
500 g (1 lb) eggplant,
    peeled and cut into batons
600 g (1¼ lb) lamb fillet, cut
    diagonally into thin slices
2 cloves garlic, finely chopped
1 small red chilli, seeded and finely
    chopped
1 tablespoon ground cumin

1 tablespoon ground coriander
2 teaspoons ground turmeric
1 teaspoon ground cinnamon
1 cup (250 ml/8 fl oz) thick coconut
    cream
1 tablespoon chopped mint
2 tablespoons chopped parsley
lemon wedges, to serve

1 Heat the wok until very hot, add 2 teaspoons of the oil and swirl it around to coat the side. Stir-fry the onion until soft and golden. Remove from the wok and set aside.
2 Add 1 tablespoon of the oil to the wok and cook the eggplant in two batches over high heat until golden brown and cooked through. Remove

and drain on paper towels.
3 Reheat the wok and add 2 teaspoons of the oil. Stir-fry the lamb in two batches over high heat until browned and just cooked.
4 Return all the lamb to the wok with the onion and eggplant. Add the garlic, chilli and spices, and cook for 1 minute. Pour in the coconut cream and bring to the boil.
5 Stir in the fresh herbs and season with salt and pepper. Serve with the lemon wedges.

NUTRITION PER SERVE
Protein 35 g; Fat 30 g; Carbohydrate 7 g;
Dietary Fibre 5 g; Cholesterol 100 mg;
1775 kJ (425 cal)

Peel the eggplant, remove the ends and cut the eggplant into batons.

Cook the eggplant in the oil until it has turned golden brown.

Return the lamb, onion and eggplant to the wok and add the garlic, chilli and spices.

INDIAN LAMB AND SPINACH

Preparation time: 20 minutes
+ 2 hours marinating
Total cooking time: 20 minutes
Serves 4

2 cloves garlic, finely chopped
1 tablespoon finely chopped fresh
   ginger
1/2 teaspoon salt
1 tablespoon ground cumin
1 tablespoon ground coriander
1 teaspoon ground cinnamon
1/2 teaspoon ground allspice
1/4 cup (60 ml/2 fl oz) oil

600 g (1 1/4 lb) lamb fillet, sliced
   diagonally
oil, for cooking
2 onions, thinly sliced
500 g (1 lb) English spinach, shredded
1 tablespoon lime juice
2 tablespoons toasted pine nuts

1 Combine the garlic, ginger, salt, spices and oil in a shallow glass or ceramic bowl. Add the sliced lamb and mix until well combined. Cover and refrigerate for at least 2 hours.
2 Heat the wok until very hot, and stir-fry the lamb in three batches over high heat for 2–3 minutes, or until the lamb is golden brown and just cooked. Remove the lamb from the wok and cover to keep warm.
3 Reheat the wok and add 1 tablespoon of the oil. Stir-fry the sliced onion over medium-high heat for 2–3 minutes, or until slightly softened. Add the spinach, cover and steam for 1–2 minutes, or until the spinach has just wilted. Return all the lamb and juices to the wok along with the lime juice and toasted pine nuts. Toss until thoroughly combined and season well with salt and pepper. Serve immediately.

NUTRITION PER SERVE
Protein 40 g; Fat 25 g; Carbohydrate 5 g; Dietary Fibre 5 g; Cholesterol 100 mg; 1735 kJ (415 cal)

Toast the pine nuts by dry-frying them in the wok before you start.

Stir-fry the marinated lamb in batches so that it fries rather than stews.

Cover the wok and steam the spinach until it has just wilted.

SATAY LAMB

Preparation time: 20 minutes
Total cooking time: 15 minutes
Serves 4–6

oil, for cooking
500 g (1 lb) lamb fillet, thinly sliced
1 onion, chopped
2 cloves garlic, crushed
2 teaspoons grated fresh ginger
1–2 red chillies, seeded and finely
  chopped
1 teaspoon ground cumin
1 teaspoon ground coriander
1/2 cup (125 g/4 oz) crunchy peanut
  butter
1 tablespoon soy sauce
2 tablespoons lemon juice
1/2 cup (125 ml/4 fl oz) coconut cream

1 Heat the wok until very hot, add 1 tablespoon oil and swirl it around to coat the side. Stir-fry the lamb in batches over high heat until it is well browned and cooked, adding more oil when necessary. Remove the lamb from the wok and set aside.

2 Reheat the wok, add 1 tablespoon of the oil and stir-fry the onion over medium heat for 2–3 minutes, or until soft and transparent. Stir in the garlic, ginger, chilli, cumin and coriander, and cook for 1 minute.

3 Stir in the peanut butter, soy sauce, lemon juice, coconut cream and 1/2 cup (125 ml/4 fl oz) water. Slowly bring to the boil. Return the lamb to the wok and stir until heated through.

NUTRITION PER SERVE (6)
Protein 25 g; Fat 25 g; Carbohydrate 5 g;
Dietary Fibre 3 g; Cholesterol 55 mg;
1390 kJ (330 cal)

Stir-fry the onion over medium heat until it is soft and transparent.

Add the garlic, ginger, chilli, cumin and coriander to the onion.

Add the peanut butter, soy sauce, lemon juice, coconut cream and water to the wok.

MINTED PESTO LAMB

Preparation time: 20 minutes
Total cooking time: 15 minutes
Serves 4

2 cups (40 g/1¼ oz) mint leaves
2 cloves garlic
¼ cup (40 g/1¼ oz) toasted pine nuts
½ cup (50 g/1¾ oz) grated Parmesan
¼ cup (60 ml/2 fl oz) olive oil
oil, for cooking
500 g (1 lb) lamb fillet, thinly sliced

1 onion, sliced
300 g (10 oz) mixed mushrooms, such as enoki, oyster, button, shimeji or Swiss brown

1 Place the mint, garlic, pine nuts and Parmesan in a food processor, and process for 10 seconds, or until finely chopped. With the motor running, gradually add the olive oil to form a paste. Season well.

2 Heat the wok until very hot, add 1 tablespoon of the oil and stir-fry the lamb in batches over medium-high heat until well browned. Remove all the lamb from the wok.

3 Reheat the wok, add 1 tablespoon of the oil and stir-fry the onion for 3–4 minutes, or until tender. Add the mushrooms and cook for 2 minutes.
4 Stir in the mint pesto. Return the lamb to the wok and toss over high heat for 5 minutes, or until the mushrooms are soft and the lamb is heated through. Season well.

NUTRITION PER SERVE
Protein 35 g; Fat 40 g; Carbohydrate 3 g; Dietary Fibre 3 g; Cholesterol 95 mg; 2145 kJ (510 cal)

Prepare the mushrooms, cutting any particularly large mushrooms in half.

Mix the mint, garlic, pine nuts and Parmesan in a food processor to make mint pesto.

Gradually pour the olive oil into the food processor while the motor is running.

MONGOLIAN LAMB

Preparation time: 15 minutes
Total cooking time: 12 minutes
Serves 4

oil, for cooking
500 g (1 lb) lamb backstrap
    (tender eye of the lamb loin),
    cut into thin strips
2 cloves garlic, crushed
4 spring onions, thickly sliced
2 tablespoons soy sauce
1/3 cup (80 ml/2³/4 fl oz) dry sherry
2 tablespoons sweet chilli sauce
2 teaspoons sesame seeds, toasted

1 Heat the wok until very hot, add
1 tablespoon of the oil and swirl it
around to coat the side of the wok.
Stir-fry the lamb strips in batches over
high heat, adding more oil whenever
necessary. Remove all the lamb from
the wok.
2 Reheat the wok, add 1 tablespoon
of oil and stir-fry the garlic and spring
onion for 2 minutes. Remove from the
wok and set aside. Add the soy sauce,
sherry and sweet chilli sauce to the
wok. Bring to the boil, reduce the heat
and simmer for 3–4 minutes, or until
the sauce thickens slightly.
3 Return the meat, with any juices,
and the spring onion to the wok,
and toss to coat with the sauce.
Serve sprinkled with the toasted
sesame seeds.

NUTRITION PER SERVE
Protein 30 g; Fat 20 g; Carbohydrate 7 g;
Dietary Fibre 1.5 g; Cholesterol 80 mg;
1445 kJ (345 cal)

Slice the lamb backstrap into thin strips with a
sharp knife.

Stir-fry the lamb strips in batches over high heat
so that they fry rather than stew.

Add the soy sauce, sherry and sweet chilli sauce
to the wok and bring to the boil.

LAMB WITH CANNELLINI BEANS AND ROSEMARY

Preparation time: 20 minutes
Total cooking time: 10 minutes
Serves 4

2 tomatoes
oil, for cooking
600 g (1¼ lb) lamb fillet,
    diagonally sliced
3 cloves garlic, finely chopped
1 teaspoon cumin seeds
2 teaspoons finely chopped
    rosemary
2 tablespoons red wine vinegar
1 tablespoon lemon juice
300 g (10 oz) can cannellini beans,
    rinsed
1 tablespoon flat-leaf parsley leaves

1 Score a cross in the base of each
tomato with a sharp knife. Put the
tomatoes in a heatproof bowl and
cover with boiling water for
30 seconds. Transfer to iced water and
then peel the skin away from the cross
and remove the stalks. Scoop out the
seeds with a teaspoon and finely chop
the flesh into cubes.
2 Heat the wok until very hot, add
2 teaspoons of the oil and swirl it
around to coat the side. Stir-fry the
lamb in two batches over very high
heat until it is browned.
3 Return all the lamb to the wok and
add the garlic, cumin seeds and
rosemary. Cook for 1 minute. Reduce
the heat and add the vinegar and
lemon juice. Stir to combine, scraping
any bits from the bottom of the wok.
4 Add the tomato and cannellini
beans and stir-fry until warmed
through. Season with salt and black
pepper, then scatter with the parsley.

NUTRITION PER SERVE
Protein 35 g; Fat 6 g; Carbohydrate 3 g;
Dietary Fibre 3 g; Cholesterol 100 mg;
890 kJ (210 cal)

Peel the skin in a downwards motion, away from
the cross. Remove the stalk.

Cut the tomatoes in half and scoop out the seeds
with a teaspoon.

Using a sharp knife, chop the tomatoes into very
fine cubes.

SWEET MUSTARD LAMB STIR-FRY

Preparation time: 15 minutes
Total cooking time: 15 minutes
Serves 4

oil, for cooking
500 g (1 lb) lamb fillet, cut into thin
    strips
2 cloves garlic, crushed
250 g (8 oz) snow peas
1 onion, cut into large wedges
20 g (³/₄ oz) butter
¹/₄ cup (60 g/2 oz) wholegrain mustard
1 tablespoon honey
¹/₂ cup (125 ml/4 fl oz) cream
2 tablespoons brandy, optional

1 Heat the wok until very hot, add
1 tablespoon of the oil and swirl it
around to coat the side. Stir-fry the
lamb strips in batches over high heat.
Remove from the wok and set aside.
2 Heat 1 tablespoon of the oil in the
wok and add the crushed garlic, snow
peas and onion wedges. Stir-fry over
medium heat for 3–4 minutes, or until
the onion softens slightly. Remove
from the wok and keep warm.
3 Reduce the heat and add the butter,
wholegrain mustard, honey, cream
and brandy to the wok. Simmer the
sauce gently for 3–4 minutes. Return
the meat and the snow pea mixture to
the wok and stir until the meat and
vegetables are heated through and
combined with the sauce.

NUTRITION PER SERVE
Protein 30 g; Fat 30 g; Carbohydrate 15 g;
Dietary Fibre 4 g; Cholesterol 140 mg;
2030 kJ (485 cal)

Remove any fat or sinew from the lamb fillet and
cut the lamb into thin strips.

Stir-fry the lamb slices in batches over high heat
so that the meat browns.

Heat the oil and add the garlic, snow peas and
onion wedges.

GARLIC LAMB WITH WILTED MUSHROOMS AND NOODLES

Preparation time: 30 minutes
Total cooking time: 20 minutes
Serves 4

350 g (12 oz) lamb fillet,
   cut into diagonal strips
8 Asian shallots, very thinly sliced
4 cloves garlic, finely chopped
1¹/₂ tablespoons oil
1 teaspoon soft brown sugar
1 teaspoon salt
1 teaspoon freshly ground black
   pepper

300 g (10 oz) fresh egg noodles
oil, extra, for cooking
200 g (6¹/₂ oz) button mushrooms,
   sliced
150 g (5 oz) small oyster mushrooms
2 tablespoons teriyaki sauce
75 g (2¹/₂ oz) fresh garlic chives,
   cut into short pieces

1 Combine the lamb, shallots, garlic, oil, brown sugar, salt and pepper in a bowl. Mix well.
2 Cook the noodles in boiling salted water for 3 minutes, or until just tender. Rinse with cold water.
3 Heat the wok until very hot, add 1 tablespoon of oil and swirl it around to coat the side. Stir-fry the lamb in three batches until browned, adding a little more oil when needed. Remove all the meat from the wok.
4 Add the button mushrooms to the wok with 2 teaspoons of water and stir-fry for 1 minute. Add the oyster mushrooms and teriyaki sauce and toss well. Cover and steam for about 10 seconds.
5 Return all the lamb and any juices to the wok with the noodles and chives. Toss well to heat through. Serve immediately.

NUTRITION PER SERVE
Protein 30 g; Fat 20 g; Carbohydrate 40 g;
Dietary Fibre 3 g; Cholesterol 60 mg;
1920 kJ (460 cal)

Trim any fat from the lamb fillet and cut the fillet into diagonal strips.

Asian shallots look rather like large cloves of garlic with a pink papery skin.

Stir-fry the marinated lamb in batches, tossing constantly until it is well browned.

PEPPERED LAMB AND ASPARAGUS

Preparation time: 35 minutes
 + 20 minutes marinating
Total cooking time: 20 minutes
Serves 4

400 g (13 oz) lamb fillets
2 teaspoons green peppercorns, finely chopped
3 cloves garlic, finely chopped
1 tablespoon vegetable oil
1 onion, cut into small wedges
1/3 cup (80 ml/2³/4 fl oz) dry sherry
1 green capsicum, cut into strips

1/2 teaspoon sugar
16 small asparagus spears, chopped, tough ends discarded
200 g (6¹/2 oz) broccoli florets
2 tablespoons oyster sauce
garlic chives, snipped, to garnish

1 Trim away any sinew from the lamb and cut the lamb into bite-sized pieces. Combine in a bowl with the green peppercorns, garlic and oil, then toss well and set aside for 20 minutes.
2 Heat a wok over high heat until slightly smoking. Add the lamb and stir-fry in batches until browned. Remove, cover and keep warm.
3 Reheat the wok and stir-fry the onion and 2 teaspoons of the sherry for 1 minute. Add the capsicum, sugar and a large pinch of salt. Cover and steam for 2 minutes. Add the asparagus, broccoli and the remaining sherry and stir-fry for 1 minute. Cover and steam for 3 minutes, or until the vegetables are just tender. Return the lamb to the wok, add the oyster sauce and stir well. Top with the chives.

NUTRITION PER SERVE
Protein 25 g; Fat 12 g; Carbohydrate 8 g; Dietary Fibre 4 g; Cholesterol 65 mg; 1100 kJ (265 cal)

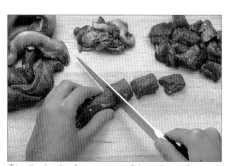

Trim the lamb of any excess fat or sinew, then cut into bite-sized pieces.

Stir-fry the lamb over high heat until brown and just cooked.

Add the asparagus and broccoli to the capsicum and onion.

WARM LAMB SALAD

Preparation time: 15 minutes
  + 3 hours refrigeration
Total cooking time: 15 minutes
Serves 4–6

2 tablespoons red curry paste
    (use the recipe on page 246 or
    ready-made paste)
1/4 cup (15 g/1/2 oz) chopped
    coriander leaves
1 tablespoon finely grated fresh ginger
3–4 tablespoons peanut oil
750 g (11/2 lb) lamb fillets, thinly sliced
200 g (61/2 oz) snow peas
600 g (11/4 lb) packet thick fresh rice
    noodles
1 red capsicum, thinly sliced

1 Lebanese cucumber, thinly sliced
6 spring onions, thinly sliced

MINT DRESSING
11/2 tablespoons peanut oil
1/4 cup (60 ml/2 fl oz) lime juice
2 tablespoons soft brown sugar
3 teaspoons fish sauce
3 teaspoons soy sauce
1/3 cup (20 g/3/4 oz) chopped mint
    leaves
1 clove garlic, crushed

1 Combine the curry paste, coriander,
ginger and 2 tablespoons oil in a bowl.
Add the lamb and coat well. Cover and
refrigerate for 2–3 hours.
2 Steam or boil the snow peas until
just tender, refresh under cold water
and drain.

3 Cover the noodles with boiling
water. Leave for 5 minutes, or until
tender, and drain.
4 To make the dressing, put all the
ingredients in a jar and shake well.
5 Heat a wok until very hot, add
1 tablespoon oil and swirl to coat.
Add half the lamb and stir-fry for
5 minutes, or until tender. Repeat with
the remaining lamb, using more oil
if needed.
6 Place the lamb, snow peas, noodles,
capsicum, cucumber and spring onion
in a large bowl, drizzle with the
dressing and toss before serving.

NUTRITION PER SERVE (6)
Protein 32 g; Fat 20 g; Carbohydrate 33 g;
Dietary Fibre 3 g; Cholesterol 83 mg;
1850 kJ (442 cal)

Mix together the curry paste, coriander, ginger
and 2 tablespoons oil.

Leave the thick fresh rice noodles in boiling water
until they are tender, then drain.

Put all the dressing ingredients in a screw-top jar
and shake well to mix them.

CHILLI LAMB AND CASHEWS

Preparation time: 10 minutes
Total cooking time: 10 minutes
Serves 4

750 g (1½ lb) lamb fillets
4 tablespoons peanut oil
1 cup (150 g/5 oz) cashew nuts
1 large onion, cut into wedges
200 g (6½ oz) snow peas
230 g (7½ oz) sliced bamboo shoots

2 tablespoons chilli sauce
1 tablespoon soy sauce

1 Trim the meat of any fat and sinew and then cut across the grain evenly into thin slices. Heat 2 tablespoons of the oil in a wok, swirling gently to coat the side. Stir-fry the lamb in small batches over high heat until browned but not cooked through. Remove from the wok and drain on paper towels.
2 Heat 1 tablespoon oil in the wok and fry the cashews until golden brown. Remove with a slotted spoon

and drain on paper towels.
3 Heat the remaining oil in the wok and stir-fry the onion and snow peas for 2 minutes. Add the bamboo shoots and stir-fry for 1 minute. Return the meat to the wok with the cashews, chilli and soy sauces. Stir-fry over high heat until the meat is cooked and the sauce is hot. Serve immediately.

NUTRITION PER SERVE
Protein 52 g; Fat 45 g; Carbohydrate 15 g;
Dietary Fibre 7 g; Cholesterol 124 mg;
2784 kJ (665 cal)

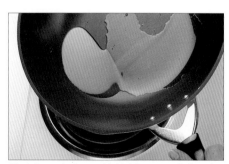

Heat the wok, then add 1 tablespoon of oil and heat it up, swirling to coat the side of the wok.

Stir-fry the cashews until they are golden brown, then remove with a slotted spoon.

Return the browned meat to the wok with the fried cashew nuts.

GREEK-STYLE LAMB

Preparation time: 20 minutes
Total cooking time: 8 minutes
Serves 4

400 g (13 oz) lamb fillets
2 tablespoons olive oil
1 large red onion, sliced
3 zucchini, thinly sliced
200 g (6¹/2 oz) cherry tomatoes, halved
3 cloves garlic, crushed
¹/3 cup (60 g/2 oz) pitted black olives, halved

2 tablespoons lemon juice
2 tablespoons oregano, finely chopped
100 g (3¹/2 oz) feta cheese, crumbled
¹/3 cup (60 g/2 oz) pine nuts, toasted

1 Cut the lamb fillets across the grain into thin strips. Heat a wok, then add the olive oil and heat for 30 seconds, swirling the wok to coat the base and side. Add the lamb in small batches and stir-fry each batch over high heat for 1–2 minutes or until browned. Remove all the lamb from the wok.
2 Add the onion and zucchini to the wok. Stir-fry over high heat for 2 minutes or until just tender. Add the cherry tomatoes and crushed garlic. Stir-fry for 1–2 minutes until the tomatoes have just softened. Return the meat to the wok and stir over high heat until heated through.
3 Remove the wok from the heat. Add the olives, lemon juice and oregano and toss until well combined. Sprinkle with crumbled feta cheese and pine nuts before serving.

NUTRITION PER SERVE
Protein 28 g; Fat 20 g; Carbohydrate 4 g;
Dietary Fibre 3 g; Cholesterol 83 mg;
1273 kJ (300 cal)

Before you start, toast the pine nuts for a couple of minutes under a hot grill or in the oven.

Cut the lamb fillets across the grain so that the strips hold together.

Stir-fry the lamb strips in small batches so they brown rather than stew.

Chicken & Duck

CHICKEN AND CASHEW NUTS

Preparation time: 30 minutes
Total cooking time: 20 minutes
Serves 4–6

oil, for cooking
750 g (1¹/₂ lb) chicken thigh fillets,
    cut into strips (see NOTE)
2 egg whites, lightly beaten
¹/₂ cup (60 g/2 oz) cornflour
2 onions, thinly sliced
1 red capsicum, thinly sliced
200 g (6¹/₂ oz) broccoli,
    cut into bite-sized pieces
2 tablespoons soy sauce
2 tablespoons sherry
1 tablespoon oyster sauce
¹/₃ cup (50 g/1³/₄ oz) roasted cashews
4 spring onions, diagonally sliced

1 Heat the wok until very hot, add
1 tablespoon of the oil and swirl it
around to coat the side. Dip about a
quarter of the chicken strips into
the egg white and then into the
cornflour. Add to the wok and stir-fry
for 3–5 minutes, or until the chicken is
golden brown and just cooked. Drain
on paper towels and repeat with the
remaining chicken, reheating the wok
and adding a little more oil each time.
2 Reheat the wok, add 1 tablespoon
of the oil and stir-fry the onion,
capsicum and broccoli over medium
heat for 4–5 minutes, or until the
vegetables have softened slightly.
Increase the heat to high and add the
soy sauce, sherry and oyster sauce.
Toss the vegetables well in the sauce
and bring to the boil.
3 Return the chicken to the wok and
toss over high heat for 1–2 minutes to
heat the chicken and make sure it is
entirely cooked through. Season well
with salt and freshly cracked pepper.
Toss the cashews and spring onion
through the chicken mixture, and
serve immediately.

NUTRITION PER SERVE (6)
Protein 35 g; Fat 15 g; Carbohydrate 15 g;
Dietary Fibre 3 g; Cholesterol 60 mg;
1375 kJ (330 cal)

NOTE: When choosing chicken, buy
free range if you can, as it has a better
flavour and texture. Yellowish flesh
indicates the chicken has been grain
fed but is not necessarily free range.

Dip the chicken strips into the egg white, then
into the cornflour.

Stir-fry the chicken in small batches until it is
golden brown.

HONEY CHICKEN

Preparation time: 15 minutes
Total cooking time: 25 minutes
Serves 4

oil, for cooking
500 g (1 lb) chicken thigh fillets, cubed
1 egg white, lightly beaten
1/3 cup (40 g/1 1/4 oz) cornflour
2 onions, thinly sliced
1 green capsicum, cubed
2 carrots, cut into batons
100 g (3 1/2 oz) snow peas, sliced
1/4 cup (90 g/3 oz) honey
2 tablespoons toasted almonds

1 Heat the wok until very hot, add 1 1/2 tablespoons of the oil and swirl it around to coat the side. Dip half of the chicken into the egg white, then lightly dust with the cornflour. Stir-fry over high heat for 4–5 minutes, or until the chicken is golden brown and just cooked. Remove from the wok and drain on paper towels. Repeat with the remaining chicken, then remove all the chicken from the wok.

2 Reheat the wok, add 1 tablespoon of the oil and stir-fry the sliced onion over high heat for 3–4 minutes, or until slightly softened. Add the capsicum and carrot, and cook, tossing constantly, for 3–4 minutes, or until tender. Stir in the snow peas and cook for 2 minutes.

3 Increase the heat, add the honey and toss the vegetables until well coated. Return the chicken to the wok and toss until it is heated through and is well coated in the honey. Remove from the heat and season well with salt and pepper. Serve immediately, sprinkled with the almonds.

NUTRITION PER SERVE
Protein 35 g; Fat 20 g; Carbohydrate 35 g; Dietary Fibre 4 g; Cholesterol 60 mg; 1815 kJ (435 cal)

Trim the excess fat from the chicken and cut the chicken into cubes.

Dip the chicken into the egg white, then lightly dust with the cornflour.

Stir-fry the chicken pieces until golden brown and just cooked.

CHICKEN IN TANGY LIME MARMALADE SAUCE

Preparation time: 25 minutes
Total cooking time: 20 minutes
Serves 4

500 g (1 lb) chicken thigh fillets,
    cut into strips
5 cm (2 inch) piece fresh ginger, cut
    into paper-thin slices (see HINT)
4 spring onions, thinly sliced
oil, for cooking
1 red capsicum, thinly sliced
1 tablespoon mirin
1 tablespoon lime marmalade
2 teaspoons grated lime rind
2 tablespoons lime juice

1 Put the chicken, ginger, spring onion and some ground black pepper in a dish. Toss well.
2 Heat the wok until very hot, add 1 tablespoon of the oil and swirl it around to coat the side of the wok. Stir-fry the chicken mixture in three batches over high heat for about 3 minutes each batch, or until it is golden brown and cooked through. Reheat the wok in between each batch, adding more oil when necessary. Remove all the chicken from the wok and set aside.

3 Reheat the wok, add the capsicum and stir-fry for 30 seconds. Add the mirin, marmalade, lime rind and juice, and season with salt and freshly ground black pepper. Cover and steam for 1 minute. Add the chicken and cook, uncovered, for 2 minutes, or until heated through.

NUTRITION PER SERVE
Protein 30 g; Fat 10 g; Carbohydrate 5.5 g; Dietary Fibre 2 g; Cholesterol 60 mg; 1050 kJ (250 cal)

HINT: Choose young ginger with thin skin and pink tips—it will be more tender and easy to slice.

Peel the piece of ginger, and then cut it into paper-thin slices.

Remove the seeds and membrane from the capsicum, and cut it into thin slices.

Combine the chicken, ginger, spring onion and some black pepper.

101

GOAN-STYLE CHICKEN WITH SULTANAS AND ALMONDS

Preparation time: 20 minutes
Total cooking time: 20 minutes
Serves 3–4

2 teaspoons ground cumin
2 teaspoons ground coriander
1 teaspoon ground cinnamon
1/2 teaspoon cayenne pepper
1/2 teaspoon ground cardamom
oil, for cooking
1 large onion, cut into thin wedges
2 cloves garlic, finely chopped
500 g (1 lb) chicken breast fillets,
     cubed
2 teaspoons finely grated orange rind
2 tablespoons orange juice
2 tablespoons sultanas
1 teaspoon soft brown sugar
1/4 cup (60 g/2 oz) thick natural
     yoghurt
1/3 cup (40 g/1 1/4 oz) slivered
     almonds, toasted

1 Dry-fry the spices in a wok over low heat for about 1 minute, or until fragrant, shaking the wok regularly.
2 Add 1 tablespoon oil and stir-fry the onion wedges and garlic over high heat for 3 minutes. Remove from the wok.
3 Reheat the wok, add 1 tablespoon of the oil and stir-fry the chicken in two batches until it is golden and just cooked. Return all the chicken to the wok with the onion mixture, orange rind, juice, sultanas and sugar. Cook for 1 minute, tossing until most of the juice evaporates.
4 Stir in the yoghurt and reheat gently, without boiling or the yoghurt will separate. Season well with salt and pepper. Serve garnished with the toasted almonds.

NUTRITION PER SERVE (4)
Protein 30 g; Fat 20 g; Carbohydrate 15 g;
Dietary Fibre 2.5 g; Cholesterol 65 mg;
1500 kJ (360 cal)

NOTE: Yoghurt separates easily when it is heated, due to its acid balance. Yoghurt also separates when shaken, whipped or stirred too much.

Toast the almonds by dry-frying them in the wok until golden brown.

Dry-fry the spices over low heat until they have become fragrant.

Stir-fry the onion and garlic until they are coated in the spices.

Add the onion mixture, orange rind, juice, sultanas and sugar to the chicken.

CHICKEN WITH OLIVES AND SUN-DRIED TOMATOES

Preparation time: 20 minutes
Total cooking time: 15 minutes
Serves 4

olive oil, for cooking
600 g (1¹/₄ lb) chicken breast fillets,
    cut diagonally into thin slices
1 red onion, thinly sliced
3 cloves garlic, finely chopped
2 tablespoons white wine vinegar
1 teaspoon sambal oelek
1 tablespoon lemon juice
12 Kalamata olives, pitted and
    quartered lengthways
¹/₄ cup (40 g/1¹/₄ oz) sun-dried
    tomatoes, cut into thin strips
¹/₄ cup (15 g/¹/₂ oz) chopped parsley
1 tablespoon shredded basil

1 Heat the wok until very hot, add
2 teaspoons of the oil and swirl it
around to coat the side. Stir-fry the
chicken slices in two batches until
browned and cooked through, adding
more oil between the batches. Remove
all the chicken from the wok and set
aside to keep warm.

2 Reheat the wok, add 1 tablespoon
of the oil and stir-fry the onion until it
is soft and golden. Add the garlic and
cook for 1 minute. Return the warm
chicken to the wok. Add the vinegar,
sambal oelek and lemon juice, and
toss well.

3 Stir in the olive pieces, sun-dried
tomato, parsley and basil, and season
with salt and black pepper. Heat
through thoroughly.

NUTRITION PER SERVE
Protein 35 g; Fat 15 g; Carbohydrate 2.5 g;
Dietary Fibre 1.5 g; Cholesterol 75 mg;
1420 kJ (335 cal)

Cut the chicken breast fillets diagonally into
thin slices.

Sambal oelek is a paste made from salt, vinegar
and chilli.

Drain the sun-dried tomatoes and then cut them
into thin strips.

SESAME CHICKEN AND LEEK

Preparation time: 15 minutes
Total cooking time: 16 minutes
Serves 4–6

2 tablespoons sesame seeds
1 tablespoon oil
2 teaspoons sesame oil
800 g (1 lb 10 oz) chicken tenderloins, cut diagonally into strips
1 leek, white part only, cut into julienne strips
2 cloves garlic, crushed

2 tablespoons soy sauce
1 tablespoon mirin
1 teaspoon sugar

1 Heat the wok until very hot, add the sesame seeds and dry-fry over high heat until they are golden. Remove the seeds from the wok.
2 Reheat the wok, add the oils and swirl them around to coat the side. Stir-fry the chicken strips in three batches over high heat, tossing constantly until just cooked. Reheat the wok before each addition. Return all the chicken to the wok.
3 Add the julienned leek and the garlic and cook for 1–2 minutes, or until the leek is soft and golden. Check that the chicken is cooked through: if it is not cooked, reduce the heat and cook, covered, for 2 minutes, or until it is completely cooked.
4 Add the soy sauce, mirin, sugar and toasted sesame seeds to the wok, and toss well to combine. Season with salt and black pepper, and serve immediately. Delicious with pasta.

NUTRITION PER SERVE (6)
Protein 2 g; Fat 8.5 g; Carbohydrate 2 g;
Dietary Fibre 1 g; Cholesterol 0 mg;
395 kJ (95 cal)

The tenderloins are the small strips from under chicken breasts. Slice them diagonally.

Cut the white part of the leek into julienne strips—very fine, thin lengths.

Fry the sesame seeds in the dry wok over high heat, stirring, until golden.

CHICKEN WITH LEMON AND CAPERS

Preparation time: 15 minutes
Total cooking time: 15 minutes
Serves 4

olive oil, for cooking
1 red onion, cut into thin wedges
25 g (3/4 oz) butter
800 g (1 lb 10 oz) chicken breast
    fillets, cut into bite-sized pieces
rind of 1 lemon, cut into thin strips
2 tablespoons baby capers, rinsed
    well and drained
1/3 cup (80 ml/2 3/4 fl oz) lemon juice
1/4 cup (15 g/1/2 oz) shredded basil

1 Heat the wok until very hot, add 2 teaspoons of the oil and swirl it around to coat the side. Add the red onion wedges and stir-fry until softened and golden. Remove from the wok and set aside.
2 Reheat the wok, add 2 teaspoons of the oil and half the butter, and stir-fry the chicken in two batches until it is browned, adding more oil and butter between batches. Return all the chicken to the wok with the onion.
3 Stir in the lemon rind, capers and lemon juice. Toss well and cook until warmed through. Add the shredded basil and season with salt and black pepper. Delicious served with creamy mashed potato.

NUTRITION PER SERVE
Protein 45 g; Fat 20 g; Carbohydrate 2.5 g;
Dietary Fibre 1 g; Cholesterol 115 mg;
1550 kJ (370 cal)

Peel the red onion, then cut it in half and cut it into thin wedges.

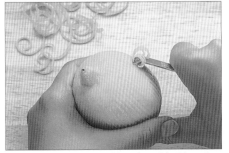

Use a zester to remove thin strips of rind from the lemon, without getting the pith from underneath.

Stir-fry the red onion wedges until they are soft and golden.

CHICKEN WITH BEANS AND ASPARAGUS

Preparation time: 25 minutes
+ 15 minutes marinating
Total cooking time: 15 minutes
Serves 4

1 stem lemon grass, white part only, chopped
5 cm (2 inch) piece fresh ginger, peeled and chopped
2–3 small red chillies, seeded and chopped
1 teaspoon grated kaffir lime or lime rind
2–3 cloves garlic, chopped
1/2 teaspoon ground black pepper
2 tablespoons oil
375 g (12 oz) chicken breast fillets, cut into thin strips
250 g (8 oz) green beans, cut into short pieces
1 celery stick, cut into short slices
185 g (6 oz) snow peas, halved
200 g (6 1/2 oz) asparagus, cut into short pieces
270 ml (9 fl oz) can coconut cream
2 tablespoons sweet chilli sauce
20 small basil leaves

1 Place the lemon grass, ginger, chilli, lime rind, garlic, black pepper and oil in a food processor or blender and process until the mixture forms a rough paste. Combine the paste and chicken strips in a glass or ceramic bowl, cover and refrigerate for at least 15 minutes.
2 Briefly blanch the beans, celery, snow peas and asparagus in a pan of boiling water. Drain and plunge into iced water. Drain again.
3 Heat the wok until very hot and stir-fry the chicken mixture in batches over high heat for 3–4 minutes, or until the chicken is cooked through. Stir constantly so the paste doesn't burn. Add the vegetables, coconut cream, sweet chilli sauce, to taste, and basil leaves. Stir-fry until heated through. Serve with rice or noodles.

NUTRITION PER SERVE
Protein 50 g; Fat 30 g; Carbohydrate 8 g; Dietary Fibre 6 g; Cholesterol 95 mg; 1990 kJ (475 cal)

Grating citrus rind is easier and less wasteful if you fit a piece of baking paper over the grater.

Process the lemon grass, ginger, chilli, lime rind, garlic, pepper and oil to a paste.

CHICKEN WITH WALNUTS AND STRAW MUSHROOMS

Preparation time: 20 minutes
Total cooking time: 15 minutes
Serves 4

375 g (12 oz) chicken breast fillets or
    tenderloins, cut into thin strips
1/2 teaspoon five-spice powder
2 teaspoons cornflour
2 tablespoons soy sauce
2 tablespoons oyster sauce
2 teaspoons soft brown sugar
1 teaspoon sesame oil
oil, for cooking
75 g (2 1/2 oz) walnuts
150 g (5 oz) snake beans or green
    beans, chopped

425 g (14 oz) can straw mushrooms,
    rinsed
6 spring onions, sliced
230 g (7 1/2 oz) can sliced bamboo
    shoots, rinsed

1 Dry the chicken with paper towels
and sprinkle with five-spice powder.
Mix the cornflour with the soy sauce in
a bowl until smooth. Add 1/2 cup
(125 ml/4 fl oz) water and the oyster
sauce, brown sugar and sesame oil.
2 Heat the wok until very hot, add
1 tablespoon of the oil and swirl it
around to coat the side. Stir-fry the
walnuts for 30 seconds, or until lightly
browned. Drain on paper towels.
3 Reheat the wok and add
1 tablespoon of the oil. Stir-fry the
chicken in batches over high heat for

2–3 minutes, or until just cooked
through. Remove all the chicken from
the wok and set aside.
4 Add the snake beans, straw
mushrooms, spring onions and
bamboo shoots to the wok and stir-fry
for 2 minutes. Remove from the wok.
Add the soy sauce mixture and heat
for 1 minute, or until slightly
thickened. Return the chicken and
vegetables to the wok, and toss to coat
with the sauce. Season well. Serve at
once, sprinkled with the fried walnuts.

NUTRITION PER SERVE
Protein 30 g; Fat 25 g; Carbohydrate 10 g;
Dietary Fibre 6.5 g; Cholesterol 45 mg;
1675 kJ (400 cal)

Wash the straw mushrooms in a sieve under cold
running water.

Top and tail the snake beans, and then cut them
into pieces.

Cook the walnuts in the oil until they are lightly
browned. Sprinkle them over the stir-fry.

CHICKEN WITH OYSTER SAUCE AND BASIL

Preparation time: 20 minutes
Total cooking time: 10 minutes
Serves 4

1/4 cup (60 ml/2 fl oz) oyster sauce
2 tablespoons fish sauce
1 tablespoon grated palm sugar
1 tablespoon oil
2–3 cloves garlic, crushed
1 tablespoon grated fresh ginger
1–2 red chillies, seeded and finely
 chopped
4 spring onions, finely chopped

375 g (12 oz) chicken breast fillets,
 cut into thin strips
250 g (8 oz) broccoli, cut into florets
230 g (7 1/2 oz) can water chestnuts,
 drained
230 g (7 1/2 oz) can sliced bamboo
 shoots, rinsed
20 basil leaves, shredded

1 Put 1/4 cup (60 ml/2 fl oz) water in a small jug with the oyster sauce, fish sauce and palm sugar. Mix well.
2 Heat the wok until very hot, add the oil and swirl it around to coat the side. Stir-fry the garlic, ginger, chilli and spring onion. Cook for 1 minute over medium heat. Increase the heat to medium-high, add the chicken and stir-fry for 2–3 minutes, or until it is just cooked. Remove from the wok.
3 Reheat the wok and add the broccoli, water chestnuts and bamboo shoots. Stir-fry for 2–3 minutes, tossing constantly. Add the sauce and bring to the boil, tossing constantly. Return the chicken to the wok and toss until it is heated through. Stir in the basil and serve at once.

NUTRITION PER SERVE
Protein 30 g; Fat 3.5 g; Carbohydrate 35 g;
Dietary Fibre 8 g; Cholesterol 45 mg;
1205 kJ (285 cal)

Palm sugar is bought in a block. Grate it or crush with the back of a large knife.

Remove the seeds from the chillies and chop the chillies finely.

Stir-fry the garlic, ginger, chilli and spring onion for 1 minute.

STIR-FRIED CHICKEN PASTA

Preparation time: 20 minutes
Total cooking time: 15 minutes
Serves 4–6

270 g (9 oz) jar sun-dried tomatoes
 in oil
500 g (1 lb) chicken breast fillets,
 cut into thin strips
2 cloves garlic, crushed
1/2 cup (125 ml/4 fl oz) cream
2 tablespoons shredded basil

400 g (13 oz) penne pasta, cooked
2 tablespoons pine nuts, toasted

1 Drain the sun-dried tomatoes, reserving the oil. Thinly slice the sun-dried tomatoes.
2 Heat the wok until very hot, add 1 tablespoon of the oil reserved from the sun-dried tomatoes and swirl it around to coat the side. Stir-fry the chicken strips in batches, adding more oil when necessary.
3 Return all the chicken strips to the wok and add the garlic, sun-dried tomatoes and cream. Simmer gently for 4–5 minutes.
4 Stir in the basil and pasta, and heat through. Season well. Serve topped with the toasted pine nuts.

NUTRITION PER SERVE (6)
Protein 30 g; Fat 30 g; Carbohydrate 5 g;
Dietary Fibre 4 g; Cholesterol 70 mg;
2696 kJ (640 cal)

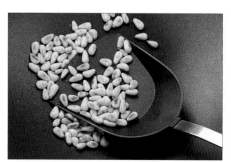
Toast the pine nuts by dry-frying them in the wok until they are lightly browned.

Drain the sun-dried tomatoes, reserving the oil, and thinly slice them.

Return the chicken to the wok with the garlic, sun-dried tomatoes and cream.

PEKING DUCK PANCAKES WITH PLUM SAUCE

Preparation time: 15 minutes
Total cooking time: 15 minutes
Serves 2–3

1/2 Chinese barbecued duck (about
    500 g/1 lb), boned
1 tablespoon oil
12 spring onions, cut into short
    lengths
1 large carrot, cut into batons
1 tablespoon cornflour
1 tablespoon honey
1 tablespoon sherry
1 tablespoon vinegar
1/4 cup (60 ml/2 fl oz) plum sauce
1 tablespoon soy sauce
12 Chinese barbecued duck
    pancakes, to serve

1 Remove and discard any excess fat and some of the skin from the duck. Cut the duck into bite-sized pieces. Heat the wok until very hot, add the duck pieces and cook over high heat for 3–4 minutes, or until the skin starts to become crispy. Remove the duck from the wok.
2 Reheat the wok, add the oil and swirl it around to coat the side. Stir-fry the spring onion and the carrot over medium heat for 3–4 minutes, or until the carrot has softened slightly. Combine the cornflour with the honey, sherry, vinegar, plum sauce and soy sauce. Increase the heat to high, return the duck to the wok and toss well. When the wok is very hot, add the sauce mixture and toss constantly for 2–3 minutes to coat the duck and vegetables. The sauce will begin to caramelize and reduce to form a glaze.
3 Remove the wok from the heat. Serve the stir-fried duck mixture with the pancakes, which have been steamed for 3–4 minutes or warmed in the microwave. Place a small portion of duck in the middle of each pancake, fold in the edges and roll up.

NUTRITION PER SERVE (3)
Protein 1 g; Fat 25 g; Carbohydrate 25 g;
Dietary Fibre 1 g; Cholesterol 0 mg;
1815 kJ (430 cal)

Ask to have the barbecued duck boned when you buy it.

Add the sauce and toss constantly until the sauce caramelizes and reduces.

DUCK AND ORANGE STIR-FRY

Preparation time: 25 minutes
Total cooking time: 15 minutes
Serves 4

1 Chinese barbecued duck
    (about 1 kg/2 lb), boned
1 tablespoon oil
1 onion, sliced
2 cloves garlic, crushed
2 teaspoons grated fresh ginger
1 tablespoon orange rind
2/3 cup (170 ml/5 1/2 fl oz) orange juice
1/4 cup (60 ml/2 fl oz) chicken stock

2 teaspoons soft brown sugar
2 teaspoons cornflour
1.5 kg (3 lb) baby bok choy,
    leaves separated
1 orange, segmented

1 Cut the duck meat into pieces. Reserve and thinly slice some crispy skin for garnish. Heat the wok until very hot, add the oil and swirl it around to coat the side. Stir-fry the onion for 3 minutes, or until tender. Stir in the garlic and ginger for 1–2 minutes. Pour in the combined orange rind, juice, stock and sugar. Bring to the boil.

2 Mix the cornflour with a little water to form a paste. Pour into the wok, stirring until the mixture boils and thickens. Place the duck pieces in the sauce and simmer for 1–2 minutes, or until heated through. Remove from the wok and keep warm.

3 Place the bok choy in the wok with 2 tablespoons water. Cover and steam until just wilted. Arrange on a serving plate, spoon the duck mixture over the top and garnish with the orange segments and the crispy duck skin.

NUTRITION PER SERVE
Protein 9 g; Fat 40 g; Carbohydrate 25 g;
Dietary Fibre 3.5 g; Cholesterol 0 mg;
2975 kJ (710 cal)

Cut downwards to remove the rind and pith from the orange.

Segment the orange by slicing between the membrane and the flesh.

Ask to have the barbecued duck boned when you buy it or remove the bones yourself.

GINGER CHICKEN WITH MUSHROOMS AND WHEAT NOODLES

Preparation time: 20 minutes + soaking
Total cooking time: 10 minutes
Serves 4

4 dried Chinese mushrooms
2 teaspoons cornflour
2 tablespoons soy sauce
2 tablespoons oyster sauce
1 tablespoon mirin or sweet sherry
200 g (6¹/2 oz) dried wheat noodles
1 teaspoon sesame oil
oil, for cooking
2–3 cloves garlic, crushed
8 cm (3 inch) piece fresh ginger,
    cut into matchsticks
375 g (12 oz) chicken breast fillets or
    tenderloins, cut into thin strips
1 red onion, cut into thin wedges
6 spring onions, cut into short lengths
185 g (6 oz) small field mushrooms,
    thickly sliced
1 cup (90 g/3 oz) bean sprouts
¹/3 cup (20 g/³/4 oz) chopped mint

1 Place the dried mushrooms in a small bowl and cover with hot water. Leave to soak for 10 minutes, or until softened. Drain and squeeze dry, then discard the hard centre stem and chop the mushrooms finely.
2 Combine the cornflour with ¹/4 cup (60 ml/2 fl oz) water and mix to a fine paste. Add the soy sauce, oyster sauce and mirin.
3 Cook the noodles in a large pan of boiling salted water for 1–2 minutes, or according to the manufacturer's instructions. Drain and set aside.
4 Heat the wok until very hot, add the sesame oil and 1 tablespoon of the oil, and swirl it around to coat the side. Stir-fry the garlic, ginger and chicken strips in batches over high heat for 2–3 minutes, or until the chicken has cooked through. Remove from the wok and set aside.
5 Reheat the wok, add 1 tablespoon of the oil and stir-fry the red onion and spring onion for 1–2 minutes, or until softened. Add the dried and field mushrooms, then stir-fry the mixture for 1–2 minutes, or until tender. Remove from the wok and set aside.

6 Add the soy sauce mixture to the wok and stir for 1–2 minutes, or until the sauce is well heated and slightly thickened. Return the chicken and vegetables to the wok with the bean sprouts, noodles and mint. Stir until well coated with sauce. Serve at once.

NUTRITION PER SERVE
Protein 30 g; Fat 9 g; Carbohydrate 45 g;
Dietary Fibre 6 g; Cholesterol 45 mg;
1650 kJ (395 cal)

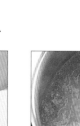

Cover the dried mushrooms with hot water and leave to soak.

Cook the noodles in a large pan of boiling salted water, then drain well.

SICHUAN PEPPER CHICKEN

Preparation time: 25 minutes
+ 2 hours marinating
Total cooking time: 20 minutes
Serves 4

3 teaspoons Sichuan pepper
500 g (1 lb) chicken thigh fillets,
    cut into strips
2 tablespoons soy sauce
1 clove garlic, crushed
1 teaspoon grated fresh ginger
3 teaspoons cornflour
100 g (3¹/₂ oz) dried thin egg noodles
oil, for cooking
1 onion, sliced
1 yellow capsicum, cut into thin strips
1 red capsicum, cut into thin strips
100 g (3¹/₂ oz) sugar snap peas
¹/₄ cup (60 ml/2 fl oz) chicken stock

1 Heat the wok until very hot and dry-fry the Sichuan pepper for 30 seconds. Remove from the wok and crush with a mortar and pestle or in a spice mill or small food processor.
2 Combine the chicken pieces with the soy sauce, garlic, ginger, cornflour and Sichuan pepper in a bowl. Cover and refrigerate for 2 hours.
3 Cook the egg noodles in boiling water for 5 minutes, or until tender. Drain, then drizzle with a little oil and toss it through the noodles to prevent them from sticking together. Set aside.
4 Heat the wok until very hot, add 1 tablespoon of the oil and swirl it around to coat the side. Stir-fry the chicken in batches over medium-high heat for 5 minutes, or until golden brown and cooked. Add more oil when necessary. Remove from the wok and set aside.

5 Reheat the wok, add 1 tablespoon of the oil and stir-fry the onion, capsicum and sugar snap peas over high heat for 2–3 minutes, or until the vegetables are tender. Add the chicken stock and bring to the boil.
6 Return the chicken and egg noodles to the wok and toss over high heat. Serve immediately.

NUTRITION PER SERVE
Protein 35 g; Fat 15 g; Carbohydrate 25 g;
Dietary Fibre 3 g; Cholesterol 65 mg;
1515 kJ (360 cal)

Heat the wok until very hot, then dry-fry the Sichuan pepper.

Crush the Sichuan pepper with a mortar and pestle or in a spice mill.

Toss the oil through the noodles to prevent them sticking together.

CHICKEN NASI GORENG

Preparation time: 25 minutes
Total cooking time: 15 minutes
Serves 4–6

5–8 long red chillies, seeded
   and chopped
2 teaspoons shrimp paste
8 cloves garlic, finely chopped
oil, for cooking
2 eggs, lightly beaten
350 g (12 oz) chicken thigh fillets, cut
   into thin strips
200 g (6^1/$_2$ oz) peeled raw prawns,
   deveined
8 cups (1.5 kg/3 lb) cooked rice
^{1}/$_3$ cup (80 ml/2^3/$_4$ fl oz) kecap manis
^{1}/$_3$ cup (80 ml/2^3/$_4$ fl oz) soy sauce
2 small Lebanese cucumbers,
   finely chopped
1 large tomato, finely chopped
lime wedges, to serve

1 Mix the chilli, shrimp paste and garlic in a food processor until the mixture resembles a paste.
2 Heat the wok until very hot, add 1 tablespoon of the oil and swirl it around to coat the side. Add the beaten eggs and, using a wok chan or metal egg flip, push the egg up the edges of the wok to form a large omelette. Cook for 1 minute over medium heat, or until the egg is set, then flip it over and cook the other side for 1 minute. Remove from the wok and cool before slicing into strips.
3 Reheat the wok, add 1 tablespoon of the oil and stir-fry the chicken and half the chilli paste over high heat until the chicken is just cooked. Remove the chicken from the wok.
4 Reheat the wok, add 1 tablespoon of the oil and stir-fry the prawns and the remaining chilli paste until the prawns are cooked. Remove from the wok and set aside.
5 Reheat the wok, add 1 tablespoon of the oil and the cooked rice, and toss constantly over medium heat for 4–5 minutes, or until the rice is heated through. Add the kecap manis and soy sauce, and toss constantly until all of the rice is coated in the sauces. Return the chicken and prawns to the wok, and toss until heated through. Season well with freshly cracked pepper and salt. Transfer to a large deep serving bowl and top with the omelette strips, cucumber and tomato. Serve with the lime wedges.

NUTRITION PER SERVE (6)
Protein 30 g; Fat 10 g; Carbohydrate 70 g; Dietary Fibre 3.5 g; Cholesterol 140 mg; 2105 kJ (505 cal)

Remove the seeds from the chillies and finely chop the flesh.

Slit the peeled prawns down the backs to remove the veins.

Process the chilli, shrimp paste and garlic until it forms a paste.

NOODLES WITH CHICKEN AND FRESH BLACK BEANS

Preparation time: 15 minutes
Total cooking time: 15 minutes
Serves 2–3

2 teaspoons salted black beans
oil, for cooking
2 teaspoons sesame oil
500 g (1 lb) chicken thigh fillets,
    cut into thin strips
3 cloves garlic, very thinly sliced
4 spring onions, chopped
1 teaspoon sugar

1 red capsicum, sliced
100 g (3½ oz) green beans,
    cut into short pieces
300 g (10 oz) Hokkien noodles
2 tablespoons oyster sauce
1 tablespoon soy sauce

1 Rinse the black beans in running water. Drain and roughly chop.
2 Heat the wok until very hot, add 1 tablespoon of oil and the sesame oil and swirl it around to coat the side. Stir-fry the chicken in three batches, until well browned, tossing regularly. Remove from the wok and set aside.
3 Reheat the wok, add 1 tablespoon of the oil and stir-fry the garlic and

spring onion for 1 minute. Add the black beans, sugar, capsicum and beans, and cook for 1 minute. Sprinkle with 2 tablespoons of water, cover and steam for 2 minutes.
4 Gently separate the noodles and add to the wok with the chicken, oyster sauce and soy sauce, and toss well. Cook, covered, for about 2 minutes, or until the noodles are just softened.

NUTRITION PER SERVE (3)
Protein 50 g; Fat 20 g; Carbohydrate 50 g;
Dietary Fibre 2 g; Cholesterol 85 mg;
2490 kJ (595 cal)

Cut the chicken thigh fillets into thin strips, removing any excess fat.

Rinse the salted black beans under running water, then roughly chop them.

Add the black beans, sugar and capsicum to the wok and cook for 1 minute.

CURRIED CHICKEN NOODLES

Preparation time: 20 minutes
Total cooking time: 10 minutes
Serves 4

100 g (3¹/₂ oz) dried rice vermicelli
oil, for cooking
500 g (1 lb) chicken breast fillets,
    cut into thin strips
2 cloves garlic, crushed
1 teaspoon grated fresh ginger
2 teaspoons Asian-style curry powder
1 red onion, sliced

1 red capsicum, cut into short thin
    strips
2 carrots, cut into matchsticks
2 zucchini, cut into matchsticks
1 tablespoon soy sauce

1 Cover the vermicelli with boiling water and soak for 5 minutes. Drain well and place on a tea towel to dry.
2 Heat the wok until very hot, add 1 tablespoon of the oil and swirl it around to coat the side. Stir-fry the chicken in batches over high heat until browned and tender. Remove all the chicken and drain on paper towels.
3 Reheat the wok, add 1 tablespoon

of oil and stir-fry the garlic, ginger, curry powder and onion for 1–2 minutes, or until fragrant. Add the capsicum, carrot and zucchini and stir-fry until well coated with the spices. Add 1 tablespoon water and stir-fry for 1 minute.
4 Add the drained noodles and chicken to the wok. Add the soy sauce and toss well. Season and serve.

NUTRITION PER SERVE
Protein 30 g; Fat 15 g; Carbohydrate 25 g;
Dietary Fibre 4 g; Cholesterol 60 mg;
1495 kJ (355 cal)

Trim any excess fat from the chicken and cut the chicken into thin strips.

Cut the carrot into strips that are the size and shape of matchsticks.

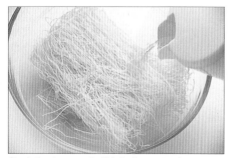

Soak the rice vermicelli in boiling water for 5 minutes.

RICE STICKS WITH CHICKEN AND GREENS

Preparation time: 25 minutes
Total cooking time: 10 minutes
Serves 4

6 baby bok choy
8 stems Chinese broccoli
150 g (5 oz) dried rice stick noodles
2 tablespoons oil
375 g (12 oz) chicken breast fillets or
    tenderloins, cut into thin strips
2–3 cloves garlic, crushed
5 cm (2 inch) piece fresh ginger,
    grated
6 spring onions, cut into short pieces
1 tablespoon sherry
1 cup (90 g/3 oz) bean sprouts

SAUCE
2 teaspoons cornflour
2 tablespoons soy sauce
2 tablespoons oyster sauce
2 teaspoons soft brown sugar
1 teaspoon sesame oil

1 Remove any tough outer leaves from the bok choy and Chinese broccoli. Cut the leaves and stems into bite-sized pieces. Wash well, then drain and dry thoroughly.
2 Place the rice stick noodles in a large heatproof bowl and cover with boiling water. Soak for 5–8 minutes, or until softened. Rinse, then drain. Cut into short lengths.
3 Meanwhile, to make the sauce, mix the cornflour and soy sauce to a smooth paste, then stir in the oyster sauce, brown sugar, sesame oil and 1/2 cup (125 ml/4 fl oz) water.
4 Heat the wok until very hot, add the oil and swirl it around to coat the side. Stir-fry the chicken, garlic, ginger and spring onion in batches over high heat for 3–4 minutes, or until the chicken is cooked. Remove from the wok.
5 Add the chopped bok choy, Chinese broccoli and sherry to the wok, cover and steam for 2 minutes, or until wilted. Remove from the wok. Add the sauce to the wok and stir until glossy and slightly thickened. Return the chicken, vegetables, noodles and bean sprouts to the wok, and stir until heated through. Serve at once.

NUTRITION PER SERVE
Protein 30 g; Fat 15 g; Carbohydrate 50 g;
Dietary Fibre 4 g; Cholesterol 45 mg;
1855 kJ (445 cal)

NOTE: Instead of the Chinese broccoli and bok choy, you can use broccoli and English spinach as the greens.

Cut the leaves and stems of the bok choy and Chinese broccoli into pieces.

Using a pair of scissors, cut the soaked noodles into short lengths.

CHICKEN CHOW MEIN

Preparation time: 25 minutes
  + 1 hour marinating
Total cooking time: 20 minutes
Serves 4–6

500 g (1 lb) chicken thigh fillets,
  cut into small cubes
1 tablespoon cornflour
2 tablespoons soy sauce
1 tablespoon oyster sauce
2 teaspoons sugar
oil, for cooking
2 onions, thinly sliced
2 cloves garlic, finely chopped
1 tablespoon finely chopped
  fresh ginger
1 green capsicum, cubed
2 celery sticks, diagonally sliced
8 spring onions, cut into short pieces
100 g (3½ oz) mushrooms, thinly
  sliced
½ cup (80 g/2¾ oz) water chestnuts,
  thinly sliced
2 teaspoons cornflour, extra
1 tablespoon sherry

½ cup (125 ml/4 fl oz) chicken stock
1 tablespoon soy sauce, extra
90 g (3 oz) Chinese cabbage, finely
  shredded
200 g (6½ oz) ready-made fried
  noodles

1 In a glass or ceramic bowl, combine the chicken with the cornflour, soy sauce, oyster sauce and sugar. Cover and refrigerate for 1 hour.

2 Heat the wok until very hot, add 1 tablespoon of the oil and swirl it around to coat the side. Stir-fry the chicken in two batches over high heat for 4–5 minutes, or until cooked. Add oil between batches. Remove all the chicken from the wok and set it aside.

3 Reheat the wok, add 1 tablespoon of the oil and stir-fry the onion over medium-high heat for 3–4 minutes, or until the onion is slightly softened. Add the garlic, ginger, capsicum, celery, spring onion, mushrooms and water chestnuts to the wok. Stir-fry over high heat for 3–4 minutes.

4 Combine the extra cornflour with the sherry, chicken stock and soy sauce. Add to the wok and bring to the boil. Simmer for 1–2 minutes, or until the sauce thickens slightly. Stir in the cabbage and cook, covered, for 1–2 minutes, or until the cabbage is just wilted. Return the chicken to the wok and toss until heated through. Season with salt and pepper. Arrange the noodles around the edge of a large platter and spoon the chicken mixture into the centre. Serve immediately.

NUTRITION PER SERVE (6)
Protein 25 g; Fat 8.5 g; Carbohydrate 20 g;
Dietary Fibre 4 g; Cholesterol 55 mg;
1110 kJ (265 cal)

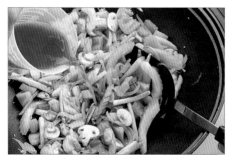

Combine the cornflour, sherry, stock and soy sauce and pour into the wok.

ORANGE CHILLI CHICKEN IN LETTUCE CUPS

Preparation time: 35–40 minutes
Total cooking time: 10–15 minutes
Serves 4

500 g (1 lb) chicken mince
1 tablespoon soy sauce
1 tablespoon rice wine vinegar
1 tablespoon sesame oil
peanut oil, for deep-frying
60 g (2 oz) dried rice vermicelli
   noodles, broken in sections
1 red capsicum, finely chopped
120 g (4 oz) can water chestnuts,
   drained and roughly chopped
2 spring onions, finely sliced
1 teaspoon grated fresh ginger
1 iceberg or romaine lettuce

SAUCE
2 tablespoons soy sauce
1 tablespoon teriyaki sauce
1 tablespoon mild-hot chilli sauce
2 tablespoons hoisin sauce
1 teaspoon sesame oil
2 teaspoons finely grated orange rind
1 teaspoon cornflour

1 Mix together the chicken mince, soy sauce, vinegar and sesame oil, cover and refrigerate.
2 Half-fill a deep-fryer or large pan with oil and heat to moderately hot. Add the rice noodles in small batches (they increase in size rapidly, causing the oil to rise) and fry for 1–2 seconds, or until puffed. Remove and drain on paper towels.
3 To make the sauce, combine all the ingredients and stir until the cornflour has dissolved. Set aside.
4 Heat a little peanut oil in a wok. Add the chicken mixture and fry for 3–4 minutes, breaking up any lumps with a fork or wooden spoon. Add the capsicum, water chestnuts, spring onion and ginger to the wok and toss for 1–2 minutes. Add the sauce to the wok and stir for about 1 minute, or until slightly thickened. Remove from the heat and mix in the noodles, reserving a few for garnish. Form the lettuce leaves into 6–8 cups and divide the chicken mixture among them. Sprinkle the reserved noodles on top.

NUTRITION PER SERVE
Protein 30 g; Fat 10 g; Carbohydrate 12 g;
Dietary Fibre 3 g; Cholesterol 65 mg;
1095 kJ (260 cal)

Finely chop the capsicum and slice 2 spring onions, including the green tops.

Use a slotted spoon to remove the cooked noodles from the pan.

Use a wooden spoon or fork to break up any lumps of mince as it cooks.

LEMON CHICKEN

Preparation time: 15 minutes
  + 30 minutes marinating
Total cooking time: 10 minutes
Serves 4

1 egg white, lightly beaten
2 teaspoons cornflour
1/2 teaspoon salt
1/4 teaspoon grated fresh ginger
500 g (1 lb) chicken breast fillets, cut
  into strips
3 tablespoons oil

LEMON SAUCE
2 teaspoons cornflour
1 1/2 tablespoons caster sugar
2 tablespoons lemon juice
3/4 cup (185 ml/6 fl oz) chicken stock
2 teaspoons soy sauce
1 teaspoon dry sherry

1 Combine the egg white, cornflour, salt and ginger in a bowl. Add the chicken and mix well to coat in the marinade. Leave in the fridge to marinate for 30 minutes.
2 Heat the oil in a wok, swirling gently to coat the side. Drain the chicken, discarding the marinade, and stir-fry until just cooked but not browned. Remove from the wok.
3 To make the lemon sauce, mix the cornflour with 2 tablespoons water to make a smooth paste. Add to the wok with the remaining sauce ingredients. Stir and boil for 1 minute. Return the chicken to the wok and stir to coat with the sauce. Serve immediately.

NUTRITION PER SERVE
Protein 30 g; Fat 15 g; Carbohydrate 10 g;
Dietary Fibre 0 g; Cholesterol 65 mg;
1315 kJ (315 cal)

Cut the chicken breast fillets into strips on the diagonal—they will hold together better.

Drain the chicken from the marinade and stir-fry until just cooked but not browned.

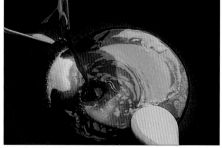

Mix the cornflour and water to a paste and add to the wok with the other sauce ingredients.

GINGER CHICKEN WITH BLACK FUNGUS

Preparation time: 25 minutes
Total cooking time: 15 minutes
Serves 4

3 tablespoons black fungus (see NOTE)
1 tablespoon oil
3 cloves garlic, chopped
5 cm (2 inches) ginger, shredded
500 g (1 lb) chicken breast fillets, sliced
4 spring onions, chopped
1 tablespoon Golden Mountain sauce
1 tablespoon fish sauce
2 teaspoons brown sugar
1/2 red capsicum, finely sliced
1/2 cup (15 g/1/2 oz) coriander leaves
1/2 cup (30 g/1 oz) shredded Thai basil leaves

1 Place the fungus in a bowl of hot water for 15 minutes until it is soft and swollen; drain and chop roughly.
2 Heat the oil in a large wok and stir-fry the garlic and ginger for 1 minute. Add the chicken in batches, stir-frying over high heat until it is cooked. Return all the chicken to the wok. Add the onions and Golden Mountain sauce and cook for 1 minute.
3 Add the fish sauce, brown sugar and fungus to the wok. Toss well, cover and steam for 2 minutes. Serve immediately, scattered with red capsicum, coriander and basil.

NUTRITION PER SERVE
Protein 6 g; Fat 5 g; Carbohydrate 4.5 g; Dietary Fibre 1 g; Cholesterol 8.5 mg; 359 kJ (86 cal)

NOTE: Black fungus is a dried mushroom that swells to many times its size when soaked in hot water. It is available from Asian food speciality stores and is also known as 'wood ear' or 'cloud ear' mushroom.

When the fungus is soft and swollen, drain it well and chop it with a sharp knife.

Add the spring onions and Golden Mountain sauce and stir-fry for a minute.

Cover the wok and allow the stir-fry to steam for 2 minutes.

121

THAI RED CURRY NOODLES AND CHICKEN

Preparation time: 25 minutes
Total cooking time: 10–15 minutes
Serves 4–6

200 g (6½ oz) thick rice stick noodles
1½ tablespoons oil
1 tablespoon red curry paste (use the recipe on page 246, or ready-made paste)
3 chicken thigh fillets, cut into strips
1–2 teaspoons chopped red chillies
2 tablespoons fish sauce
2 tablespoons lime juice

100 g (3½ oz) bean sprouts
½ cup (90 g/3 oz) roasted chopped peanuts
3 tablespoons crisp-fried onion
3 tablespoons crisp-fried garlic
1 cup (30 g/1 oz) coriander leaves

1 Cook the noodles in boiling water for 2 minutes. Drain and then toss with 2 teaspoons of the oil to prevent them sticking together.
2 Heat the remaining oil in a wok, add the curry paste and stir for 1 minute or until fragrant. Add the chicken in batches and stir-fry for 2 minutes or until golden brown. Return all the chicken to the wok.

3 Add the chilli, fish sauce and lime juice; bring to the boil and simmer for 1 minute. Add the bean sprouts and noodles and toss well. Arrange the noodles on a serving plate and sprinkle with peanuts, crisp-fried onion and garlic and coriander leaves. Serve immediately.

NUTRITION PER SERVE (6)
Protein 15 g; Fat 11 g; Carbohydrate 9 g;
Dietary Fibre 2 g; Cholesterol 25 mg;
812 kJ (194 cal)

NOTE: Rice stick noodles are flat and are available from Asian food stores and some supermarkets.

Toss 2 teaspoons of oil through the noodles to prevent them sticking together.

Cook each batch of chicken for 2 minutes and return all the chicken to the wok.

Add the bean sprouts and noodles to the wok and toss well to distribute evenly.

VIETNAMESE CHICKEN WITH PINEAPPLE AND CASHEWS

Preparation time: 35 minutes
Total cooking time: 25 minutes
Serves 4

1/2 cup (90 g/3 oz) raw cashew nuts
2 tablespoons oil
4 cloves garlic, finely chopped
1 large onion, cut in large chunks
2 teaspoons chopped red chillies
350 g (11 oz) chicken thigh fillets, chopped
1/2 red capsicum, chopped
1/2 green capsicum, chopped
2 tablespoons oyster sauce
1 tablespoon fish sauce
1 teaspoon sugar
2 cups (320 g/11 oz) chopped fresh pineapple
3 spring onions, chopped
2 tablespoons shredded coconut, toasted

1 Roast the cashews on an oven tray for about 15 minutes in a moderate 180°C (350°F/Gas 4) oven, until deep golden. Allow to cool.
2 Heat the oil in a wok and stir-fry the garlic, onion and chilli over medium heat for 2 minutes; remove from the wok. Increase the heat to high and stir-fry the chicken and capsicum, in 2 batches, tossing until the chicken is light brown.
3 Return the onion and chilli to the wok, add the oyster sauce, fish sauce, sugar and pineapple and toss for 2 minutes to heat through. Toss the cashews through. Arrange on a serving plate and scatter the spring onion and coconut over the top. Serve immediately.

NUTRITION PER SERVE
Protein 25 g; Fat 24 g; Carbohydrate 18 g;
Dietary Fibre 5 g; Cholesterol 44 mg;
1629 kJ (390 cal)

Roast the cashews on an oven tray for 15 minutes or until golden.

Stir-fry the chicken and capsicum until the chicken is light brown.

Return the onion and chilli to the wok and stir through with a wooden spoon.

COUNTRY CHICKEN KAPITAN

Preparation time: 35 minutes
Total cooking time: 35 minutes
Serves 4–6

30 g (1 oz) small dried prawns
4 tablespoons oil
4–8 red chillies, seeded and finely
　　chopped
4 cloves garlic, finely chopped
3 stems lemon grass (white part only),
　　finely chopped
2 teaspoons turmeric
10 candlenuts
2 large onions, chopped
1/4 teaspoon salt
1 cup (250 ml/8 fl oz) coconut milk
500 g (1 lb) chicken thigh fillets,
　　cut into bite-sized pieces
1/2 cup (125 ml/4 fl oz) coconut cream
2 tablespoons lime juice

1 Dry-fry the prawns over low heat for 3 minutes, shaking the wok regularly, until they are dark orange and have a strong aroma. Pound in a mortar and pestle until finely ground, or process in a small food processor.
2 Mix half the oil with the chilli, garlic, lemon grass, turmeric and candlenuts in a food processor, in short bursts, regularly scraping the bowl, until very finely chopped.
3 Add the remaining oil to a large wok and cook the onion and salt over low heat, stirring regularly, for 8 minutes, or until golden. Add the spice mixture and nearly all the ground prawns, setting a little aside to use as garnish. Stir for 5 minutes. If the mixture begins to stick to the bottom of the wok, add 2 tablespoons of the coconut milk. It is important for the

flavour to cook this thoroughly.
4 Add the chicken and stir well. Cook for 5 minutes or until the chicken begins to brown. Stir in the coconut milk and 1 cup (250 ml/8 fl oz) water and bring to the boil. Reduce the heat and simmer for 7 minutes or until the chicken is cooked and the sauce is thick. Add the coconut cream and

bring back to the boil, stirring constantly. Add the lime juice and serve immediately, sprinkled with the reserved ground prawns.

NUTRITION PER SERVE (6)
Protein 22 g; Fat 15 g; Carbohydrate 5.5 g;
Dietary Fibre 2.5 g; Cholesterol 50 mg;
1020 kJ (245 cal)

Pound the dry-fried prawns in a mortar and pestle until finely ground.

Process the chilli mixture in shorts bursts, regularly scraping the side of the bowl.

Stir-fry the onion and spice mixture for 5 minutes, taking care not to let it stick.

STIR-FRIED CHICKEN WITH SNOW PEAS

Preparation time: 10 minutes
Total cooking time: 10 minutes
Serves 4

1 tablespoon oil
2 teaspoons sesame oil
400 g (13 oz) chicken breast fillets,
    cut into strips
1 leek, white part only, julienned
2 cloves garlic, crushed
185 g (6 oz) snow peas, cut in half on
    the diagonal
2 tablespoons soy sauce
1 tablespoon mirin
1 teaspoon soft brown sugar
coriander leaves, to garnish

1 Heat a wok over high heat, add the oils and swirl to coat the side. Add the sliced chicken breast and stir-fry for 3–4 minutes, or until just cooked.
2 Add the leek and garlic and stir-fry for 1–2 minutes, or until the leek is soft and golden. Add the snow peas and stir-fry for 1 minute. Add the soy sauce, mirin and sugar to the wok, and toss well. Season well. Garnish with the coriander and serve immediately.

NUTRITION PER SERVE
Protein 50 g; Fat 17 g; Carbohydrate 10 g;
Dietary Fibre 4 g; Cholesterol 100 mg;
1664 kJ (398 cal)

Stir-fry the chicken in the combined oils until it is just cooked.

Add the soy sauce, mirin and sugar to the wok and toss well.

125

THAI CHICKEN AND HOLY BASIL

Preparation time: 15 minutes
Total cooking time: 7 minutes
Serves 4

3 tablespoons fish sauce
3 tablespoons lime juice
1 tomato, diced
1 cup (30 g/1 oz) loosely packed Thai
   basil leaves
2 tablespoons peanut or vegetable oil
3 cloves garlic, thinly sliced
4 spring onions, finely sliced
2 small red chillies, seeded and thinly
   sliced
4 chicken breast fillets, thinly sliced
250 g (8 oz) snow peas, trimmed

1 Place the fish sauce, lime juice, tomato, basil and 1 tablespoon water in a small bowl and mix well.
2 Heat a wok over high heat, add the oil and swirl to coat the side. Add the garlic, spring onion and chilli and stir-fry for 1 minute, or until fragrant. Add the chicken and cook for 3 minutes, or until lightly browned.
3 Add the snow peas and the fish sauce mixture and scrape any bits from the bottom of the wok. Reduce the heat and simmer for 2 minutes, or until the tomato is soft and the chicken cooked through. Serve immediately.

NUTRITION PER SERVE
Protein 57 g; Fat 20 g; Carbohydrate 10 g;
Dietary Fibre 6.5 g; Cholesterol 110 mg;
1887 kJ (450 cal)

Mix together the fish sauce, lime juice, tomato, basil and water.

Add the chicken to the wok and stir-fry until it is lightly browned.

Simmer until the tomato is soft and the chicken is cooked through.

CHICKEN WITH SOY AND HOKKIEN NOODLES

Preparation time: 10 minutes
  + 10 minutes standing
Total cooking time: 10 minutes
Serves 4

450 g (14 oz) Hokkien noodles
1 tablespoon oil
500 g (1 lb) chicken thigh fillets,
    trimmed and sliced
2 cloves garlic, chopped
5 cm (2 inch) piece fresh ginger,
    julienned

4 spring onions, sliced on the diagonal
2 carrots, finely sliced on the diagonal
250 g (8 oz) broccoli, cut into small
    florets
2 tablespoons mirin
4 tablespoons soy sauce
1 teaspoon soft brown sugar
2 tablespoons toasted sesame seeds

1 Cover the noodles with boiling water and leave for 10 minutes, or until tender.
2 Heat a wok over high heat, add the oil and swirl to coat the side. Add the chicken in batches and stir-fry for 5 minutes. Return all the chicken to the wok, add the garlic and ginger and cook for 1 minute, or until fragrant. Add the spring onion, carrot and broccoli and cook for 4–5 minutes, or until tender.
3 Mix together the mirin, soy sauce and sugar and stir into the chicken mixture. Drain the noodles, add to the wok and cook until heated through. Serve sprinkled with the sesame seeds.

NUTRITION PER SERVE
Protein 64 g; Fat 25 g; Carbohydrate 114 g;
Dietary Fibre 12 g; Cholesterol 100 mg;
3930 kJ (939 cal)

Add the garlic and ginger to the chicken and stir-fry for a further minute.

Add the spring onion, carrot and broccoli to the wok and cook until tender.

Drain the noodles, add to the wok and cook until heated through.

CHICKEN WITH SNOW PEA SPROUTS

Preparation time: 15 minutes
Total cooking time: 15 minutes
Serves 4

2 tablespoons oil
1 onion, finely sliced
3 kaffir lime leaves, shredded (see HINT)
3 chicken breast fillets, cubed
1 red capsicum, sliced
1/4 cup (60 ml/2 fl oz) lime juice
100 ml (3 1/2 fl oz) soy sauce
100 g (3 1/2 oz) snow pea sprouts
2 tablespoons chopped coriander leaves

1 Heat a wok over medium heat, add the oil and swirl to coat the base and side of the wok. Add the onion and kaffir lime leaves and stir-fry for 3–5 minutes, or until the onion begins to soften. Add the chicken and cook for a further 4 minutes. Add the capsicum and continue to cook for 2–3 minutes.
2 Stir in the lime juice and soy sauce and cook for 1–2 minutes, or until the sauce reduces slightly. Add the sprouts and coriander and cook until the sprouts have wilted slightly. Serve immediately.

NUTRITION PER SERVE
Protein 45 g; Fat 15 g; Carbohydrate 5.5 g; Dietary Fibre 2 g; Cholesterol 90 mg; 1375 kJ (330 cal)

HINT: Kaffir lime leaves are quite tough leaves with a wonderful aroma and flavour. Because of their toughness, however, it is necessary to shred them as finely as possible. Fold the leaves in half down their spines and then shred finely with a very sharp knife.

VARIATION: Use fresh asparagus instead of capsicum, and mint or basil instead of coriander.

Add the chicken and cook for 4 minutes, then add the capsicum.

Add the snow pea sprouts and coriander and cook until they have wilted a little.

CHICKEN AND ASPARAGUS STIR-FRY

Preparation time: 15 minutes
Total cooking time: 10 minutes
Serves 4

2 tablespoons oil
1 clove garlic, crushed
10 cm (4 inch) piece fresh ginger,
    peeled and thinly sliced
3 chicken breast fillets, sliced

4 spring onions, sliced
200 g (6^1/$_2$ oz) fresh asparagus
    spears, cut into short lengths
2 tablespoons soy sauce
^{1}/$_3$ cup (30 g/1 oz) slivered almonds,
    roasted

1 Heat a wok over high heat, add the oil and swirl to coat the side. Add the garlic, ginger and chicken and stir-fry for 1–2 minutes, or until the chicken changes colour.
2 Add the spring onion and asparagus and stir-fry for a further 2 minutes, or until the spring onion is soft.
3 Stir in the soy sauce and ^{1}/$_4$ cup (60 ml/2 fl oz) water, cover and simmer for 2 minutes, or until the chicken is tender and the vegetables are slightly crisp. Sprinkle with the almonds and serve immediately.

NUTRITION PER SERVE
Protein 30 g; Fat 12 g; Carbohydrate 2 g;
Dietary Fibre 1 g; Cholesterol 60 mg;
1010 kJ (240 cal)

Stir-fry the garlic, ginger and chicken until the chicken changes colour.

Add the spring onion and asparagus and stir-fry until the spring onion is soft.

Stir in the soy sauce and a little water and cover the wok to steam the vegetables.

CREAMY CHICKEN WITH TARRAGON

Preparation time: 5 minutes
Total cooking time: 20 minutes
Serves 4

5 chicken breast fillets, cut into slices
2 tablespoons oil
1 tablespoon chopped French
  tarragon
1 cup (250 ml/8 fl oz) cream
1 tablespoon lemon juice

1 Lightly season the slices of chicken with white pepper. Heat a wok over high heat, add the oil and swirl the wok to coat the base and side with oil. When the oil is hot, add the chicken, in batches, and cook over medium heat for 3–4 minutes, or until it is browned. Return all the chicken to the wok and stir through the tarragon.
2 Add the cream, bring to the boil and boil for 3 minutes, or until the sauce has thickened slightly. Add the lemon juice and season with salt and ground black pepper before serving.

NUTRITION PER SERVE
Protein 70 g; Fat 45 g; Carbohydrate 2 g;
Dietary Fibre 0 g; Cholesterol 315 mg;
2800 kJ (670 cal)

NOTE: If you are preparing this dish in advance, add the lemon juice after reheating to serve or the sauce will curdle. Avoid using Russian tarragon, which has a less subtle, slightly aniseed flavour. Tarragon vinegar is a good substitute for lemon juice.

Brown the chicken in batches so that the wok doesn't overcrowd and lower the temperature.

Add the cream and bring to the boil. Boil until the sauce has reduced and thickened.

SMOKED CHICKEN AND SPINACH

Preparation time: 10 minutes
Total cooking time: 10 minutes
Serves 4

300 g (10 oz) smoked chicken breast
(see NOTE)
1 tablespoon olive oil
100 g (3¹/₂ oz) marinated chargrilled
capsicum, cut into thin strips
¹/₃ cup (50 g/1³/₄ oz) pine nuts
1 bunch (500 g/1 lb) English spinach,
trimmed
1 tablespoon light sour cream
2 teaspoons wholegrain mustard
¹/₄ cup (7 g/¹/₄ oz) basil leaves, finely
shredded

1 Cut the chicken into thin strips.
2 Heat a wok over high heat, add the oil and swirl to coat the base and side of the wok with oil. Add the chicken, capsicum and pine nuts and stir-fry for 3–4 minutes, or until the nuts are golden. Add the spinach and stir-fry for 2–3 minutes, or until wilted.
3 Add the sour cream, mustard and basil to the wok and toss well to thoroughly combine. Season with salt and pepper before serving.

NUTRITION PER SERVE
Protein 22 g; Fat 13 g; Carbohydrate 2.5 g;
Dietary Fibre 4.5 g; Cholesterol 45 mg;
900 kJ (215 cal)

NOTE: Smoked chicken breast and marinated chargrilled capsicum are available at speciality delicatessens.

Cut the smoked chicken breast into thin strips for quick and even stir-frying.

Stir-fry the chicken, capsicum and pine nuts until the nuts are golden.

Add the sour cream, mustard and basil to the stir-fry and toss through.

PEPPERED CHICKEN

Preparation time: 10 minutes
Total cooking time: 10 minutes
Serves 4

1 tablespoon oil
2 chicken breast fillets, cut into strips
2¹/₂ teaspoons seasoned
    peppercorns (see NOTE)
1 onion, cut into wedges
1 red capsicum, cut into strips

2 tablespoons oyster sauce
1 teaspoon soy sauce
1 teaspoon sugar

1 Heat a wok over high heat, add the oil and swirl to coat the base and side of the wok. Add the chicken strips and stir-fry for 2–3 minutes, or until they are browned.
2 Add the peppercorns and stir-fry until they are fragrant. Add the onion and capsicum and stir-fry for 2 minutes, or until the vegetables have

softened slightly.
3 Reduce the heat and stir in the oyster sauce, soy and sugar. Toss well to thoroughly combine before serving.

NUTRITION PER SERVE
Protein 18 g; Fat 6.5 g; Carbohydrate 6 g;
Dietary Fibre 1 g; Cholesterol 40 mg;
665 kJ (160 cal)

NOTE: Seasoned peppercorns are available in the herb and spice section of large supermarkets.

Add the onion and capsicum and stir-fry until they have softened slightly.

Add the oyster sauce, soy sauce and sugar to the stir-fry and toss through.

Add the strips of chicken breast to the wok and stir-fry until browned.

CHICKEN SAN CHOY BAU

Preparation time: 10 minutes
Total cooking time: 5 minutes
Serves 4 as a starter

1 tablespoon oil
700 g (1 lb 6 oz) chicken mince
2 cloves garlic, finely chopped
100 g (3½ oz) can water chestnuts,
    drained, chopped
1½ tablespoons oyster sauce
3 teaspoons soy sauce
1 teaspoon sugar
5 spring onions, finely sliced
4 lettuce leaves

1 Heat a wok over high heat, add the oil and swirl to coat the base and side of the wok. Add the chicken mince and garlic and stir-fry for 3–4 minutes, or until browned and cooked through, breaking up any lumps with the back of a spoon. Pour off any excess liquid.
2 Reduce the heat and add the water chestnuts, oyster sauce, soy sauce, sugar and spring onion.
3 Trim the lettuce leaves around the edges to neaten them and to form each one into a cup shape. Divide the chicken mixture among the lettuce cups and serve hot, with extra oyster sauce if you like.

NUTRITION PER SERVE
Protein 40 g; Fat 9 g; Carbohydrate 6 g;
Dietary Fibre 2 g; Cholesterol 88 mg;
1142 kJ (273 cal)

Stir-fry the chicken mince, breaking up any lumps with the back of a spoon.

Add the water chestnuts, oyster sauce, soy sauce, sugar and spring onion.

Trim the edges of the lettuce leaves and form them into cup shapes to hold the mince.

SWEET CHILLI CHICKEN

Preparation time: 10 minutes
Total cooking time: 10 minutes
Serves 4–6

375 g (12 oz) Hokkien noodles
4 chicken thigh fillets, cut into small
   pieces (see NOTE)
1–2 tablespoons sweet chilli sauce
2 teaspoons fish sauce
1 tablespoon oil
100 g (3¹/₂ oz) baby sweet corn,
   halved lengthways
150 g (5 oz) sugar snap peas
1 tablespoon lime juice

1 Place the noodles in a large bowl,
cover with boiling water and gently
pull apart with a fork. Leave for
5 minutes, then drain.
2 Combine the chicken, sweet chilli
sauce and fish sauce in a bowl.
3 Heat a wok over high heat, add the
oil and swirl to coat. Add the chicken
pieces and stir-fry for 3–5 minutes, or
until cooked through. Add the corn
and sugar snap peas and stir-fry for
2 minutes. Add the noodles and lime
juice and serve.

NUTRITION PER SERVE (6)
Protein 30 g; Fat 6.5 g; Carbohydrate 50 g;
Dietary Fibre 4 g; Cholesterol 53 mg;
1593 kJ (380 cal)

NOTE: If thigh fillets are unavailable,
use 3 breast fillets.

Soak the noodles in boiling water and separate
them with a fork.

Mix together the chicken pieces, sweet chilli
sauce and fish sauce.

Add the noodles and lime juice to the wok just
before serving.

TANGY ORANGE AND GINGER CHICKEN

Preparation time: 15 minutes
Total cooking time: 15–20 minutes
Serves 4

2 tablespoons sesame seeds
3 tablespoons light olive oil
10 chicken thigh fillets,
    cut into small pieces
3 teaspoons grated fresh
    ginger
1 teaspoon grated orange rind
1/2 cup (125 ml/4 fl oz) chicken
    stock
2 teaspoons honey
1 bunch (500 g/1 lb) bok choy,
    trimmed and halved

1 Toast the sesame seeds by dry-frying them in the wok, placing under a hot grill, or roasting them in a 200°C (400°F/Gas 6) oven for 5 minutes on a baking tray.
2 Heat a wok over high heat, add the oil and swirl to coat the base and side of the wok with oil. Add the chicken, in batches, and stir-fry for 3–4 minutes, or until golden.
3 Return all the chicken to the wok, add the ginger and orange rind, and cook for 20 seconds, or until fragrant. Add the stock and the honey and stir to combine. Increase the heat and cook for 3–4 minutes, or until the sauce has thickened slightly.
4 Add the bok choy to the wok and cook until it has slightly wilted. Season with salt and black pepper. Sprinkle with the toasted sesame seeds and serve immediately.

NUTRITION PER SERVE
Protein 70 g; Fat 20 g; Carbohydrate 3.5 g; Dietary Fibre 0.5 g; Cholesterol 150 mg; 2005 kJ (480 cal)

HINT: Toasting the sesame seeds before use brings out their flavour.

Stir-fry the chicken in batches so that the wok doesn't overcrowd.

Add the stock and honey and cook until the sauce has thickened slightly.

CHICKEN SAUSAGE STIR-FRY

Preparation time: 15 minutes
Total cooking time: 25 minutes
Serves 4–6

6 thick chicken sausages
2 tablespoons chicken stock
1 tablespoon oyster sauce
1 teaspoon soy sauce
1 tablespoon oil
1 red onion, halved, thinly sliced
1 red capsicum, julienned
100 g (3 1/2 oz) snow peas, larger ones
  halved on the diagonal

1 Place the sausages on a grill tray and cook under high heat, turning, for 10–15 minutes, or until cooked through. Allow to cool and thinly slice on the diagonal.
2 Combine the chicken stock, oyster sauce and soy sauce in a bowl.
3 Heat a wok over high heat, add the oil and swirl to coat. Add the onion and stir-fry for 2 minutes. Add the capsicum, snow peas and sausage and stir-fry for 1–2 minutes. Add the chicken stock mixture and stir-fry for a further 3–5 minutes, or until the vegetables are cooked and the sauce has reduced slightly. Season with salt and pepper and serve immediately.

NUTRITION PER SERVE (6)
Protein 15 g; Fat 26 g; Carbohydrate 6 g;
Dietary Fibre 4 g; Cholesterol 57 mg;
1305 kJ (312 cal)

Grill the sausages under high heat, then thinly slice on the diagonal.

Mix together the chicken stock, oyster sauce and soy sauce.

Stir-fry until the vegetables are cooked and the sauce has reduced and thickened a little.

MIDDLE-EASTERN CHICKEN

Preparation time: 10 minutes
Total cooking time: 20 minutes
Serves 4

2 tablespoons oil
2 chicken breast fillets, thinly sliced
1 red onion, thinly sliced
310 g (10 oz) can chickpeas, drained
1/2 cup (75 g/2 1/2 oz) unsalted
　pistachio kernels

1 tomato, chopped
juice of 1 orange
1/4 cup (7 g/1/4 oz) finely chopped
　flat-leaf parsley

1 Heat a wok over high heat, add half the oil and swirl to coat the base and side of the wok. Add the chicken and stir-fry, in batches, for 3–5 minutes, or until cooked. Remove from the wok and keep warm.
2 Add the remaining oil to the wok and stir-fry the onion for 2 minutes, then add the chickpeas, pistachio

kernels and tomato. Stir-fry for 3–5 minutes, or until the chickpeas are warmed through.
3 Pour in the orange juice, return the chicken and its juices to the wok and stir-fry until half the juice has evaporated. Stir through the parsley. Season well and serve (couscous is the ideal accompaniment).

NUTRITION PER SERVE
Protein 37 g; Fat 25 g; Carbohydrate 17 g;
Dietary Fibre 6.5 g; Cholesterol 60 mg;
1785 kJ (425 cal)

Stir-fry the chicken in batches so that the wok isn't overcrowded.

Stir-fry the onion for 2 minutes, then add the chickpeas, pistachio nuts and tomato.

Stir-fry until half the juice has evaporated, then add the parsley and seasoning.

WOK-FRIED CHICKEN AND LEMON GRASS

Preparation time: 15 minutes
Total cooking time: 12 minutes
Serves 4

1 tablespoon fish sauce
3 teaspoons grated palm sugar
1 tablespoon peanut oil
2 teaspoons sesame oil
800 g (1 lb 10 oz) chicken breast
    fillets, cut into strips
1½ tablespoons grated fresh ginger

2 tablespoons finely chopped lemon
    grass, white part only
2 cloves garlic, finely chopped
2 tablespoons coriander leaves
2 limes, cut into wedges

1 Place the fish sauce and palm sugar in a small bowl and stir until all the sugar has dissolved.
2 Heat a large wok until very hot, add half the combined oils and swirl to coat. Add half the chicken and stir-fry for 4 minutes, then remove. Repeat with the remaining oil and the second batch of chicken and then remove

from the wok.
3 Add the ginger, lemon grass and garlic to the wok, and stir-fry for 1–2 minutes, then return all the chicken to the wok and stir-fry for 2 minutes more.
4 Stir in the combined fish sauce and palm sugar. Scatter with the coriander leaves and serve immediately with lime wedges.

NUTRITION PER SERVE
Protein 45 g; Fat 15 g; Carbohydrate 2 g;
Dietary Fibre 0 g; Cholesterol 100 mg;
1330 kJ (318 cal)

Palm sugar is bought in blocks. Grate the sugar, using an ordinary cheese grater.

Cut the chicken breast fillets into strips and then stir-fry in two batches.

Stir-fry the ginger, lemon grass and garlic and then return all the chicken to the wok.

BUTTER CHICKEN

Preparation time: 10 minutes
Total cooking time: 35 minutes
Serves 4–6

2 tablespoons peanut oil
1 kg (2 lb) chicken thigh fillets, cubed
60 g (2 oz) butter
2 teaspoons garam masala
2 teaspoons sweet paprika
2 teaspoons ground coriander
1 tablespoon finely chopped fresh
   ginger

1/4 teaspoon chilli powder
1 cinnamon stick
6 cardamom pods, bruised
350 g (12 oz) puréed tomatoes
1 tablespoon sugar
1/4 cup (60 g/2 oz) plain yoghurt
1/2 cup (125 ml/4 fl oz) cream
1 tablespoon lemon juice

1 Heat a wok until very hot, add
1 tablespoon oil and swirl to coat.
Stir-fry the chicken in two batches, for
4 minutes each batch, or until
browned. Remove from the wok.
2 Reduce the heat and add the butter

to the wok. Add the spices and stir-fry
for 1 minute, or until fragrant. Add the
chicken and coat in the spices.
3 Add the tomato and sugar and
simmer, stirring, for 15 minutes, or
until the chicken is tender and the
sauce is thick. Add the yoghurt, cream
and juice, and warm through for
5 minutes. Remove the cinnamon and
cardamom pods before serving.

NUTRITION PER SERVE (6)
Protein 32 g; Fat 27 g; Carbohydrate 7.5 g;
Dietary Fibre 1 g; Cholesterol 122 mg;
1669 kJ (397 cal)

Bruise the cardamom pods by crushing them
with the back of a knife to release the flavour.

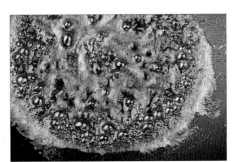

Melt the butter in the wok, then stir-fry the spices
for 1 minute, or until fragrant.

Add the tomato and sugar to the wok and then
simmer, stirring, for 15 minutes.

WARM CURRIED CHICKEN SALAD

Preparation time: 15 minutes
  + overnight marinating
Total cooking time: 10 minutes
Serves 4–6

3 tablespoons mild Indian curry paste
1/4 cup (60 ml/2 fl oz) coconut milk
750 g (11/2 lb) chicken breast fillets,
    sliced
150 g (5 oz) green beans, halved
2 tablespoons peanut oil
1/3 cup (30 g/1 oz) flaked almonds,
    toasted

1 red capsicum, sliced
250 g (8 oz) rocket
100 g (31/2 oz) fried egg noodles

LEMON DRESSING
1/3 cup (80 ml/23/4 fl oz) olive oil
2 tablespoons lemon juice
2 cloves garlic, crushed
1 teaspoon soft brown sugar

1 Mix together the curry paste and coconut milk, add the chicken, toss to coat, cover and refrigerate overnight.
2 Cook the beans in boiling water for 30 seconds, or until just tender. Refresh under cold water. Drain.
3 Heat a wok until very hot, add half the oil and swirl to coat. Cook the chicken in two batches, for 5 minutes each batch, until browned, using the remaining oil for the second batch. Remove from the wok.
4 To make the dressing, place the ingredients in a jar and shake well.
5 Place the chicken, beans, almonds, capsicum, rocket and dressing in a large bowl and mix well. Stir in the noodles and serve.

NUTRITION PER SERVE (6)
Protein 32 g; Fat 29 g; Carbohydrate 6.5 g;
Dietary Fibre 2.5 g; Cholesterol 72 mg;
1730 kJ (412 cal)

Toast the flaked almonds on a baking tray in the oven or under a grill before you start.

Cook the beans in boiling water for 30 seconds and then refresh in cold water.

Brown the chicken in two batches, using half the oil for each batch.

CARAMEL CORIANDER CHICKEN

Preparation time: 20 minutes
  + overnight refrigeration
Total cooking time: 20 minutes
Serves 4–6

2 teaspoons ground turmeric
6 cloves garlic, crushed
2 tablespoons grated fresh ginger
2 tablespoons soy sauce
1/4 cup (60 ml/2 fl oz) Chinese rice
    wine or sherry
2 egg yolks, beaten
1 kg (2 lb) chicken thigh fillets,
    cut into cubes
1/2 cup (60 g/2 oz) plain flour
1/2 cup (125 ml/4 fl oz) oil

1/2 cup (90 g/3 oz) soft brown sugar
1/2 cup (30 g/1 oz) chopped coriander
1/4 cup (60 ml/2 fl oz) rice vinegar

1 Place the turmeric, 2 crushed garlic cloves, the ginger, soy, rice wine, egg yolks, 1 teaspoon salt and 1 teaspoon white pepper in a large bowl and mix together well. Add the chicken and toss to coat. Cover with plastic wrap and refrigerate overnight.
2 Pour away any excess liquid from the chicken, add the flour and toss to mix well.
3 Heat a wok until very hot, add 1 tablespoon oil and swirl to coat. Add a third of the chicken and stir-fry for 4 minutes, or until golden brown. Remove from the wok. Cook the other two batches of chicken, adding more

oil as necessary. Remove all the chicken from the wok and keep warm.
4 Reduce the heat to medium, add the remaining oil, brown sugar and remaining garlic. Mix together and then leave for 1–2 minutes, or until the sugar caramelizes and liquefies.
5 Return the chicken to the wok, and add the coriander and vinegar. Stir gently for 4 minutes, or until the chicken is cooked through and well coated with the sauce.

NUTRITION PER SERVE (6)
Protein 35 g; Fat 25 g; Carbohydrate 30 g;
Dietary Fibre 2 g; Cholesterol 130 mg;
2070 kJ (495 cal)

Cut the chicken thigh fillets into bite-sized cubes for even stir-frying.

Mix together the turmeric, garlic, ginger, soy, rice wine, egg yolks, salt and pepper.

Leave the sauce to cook until the sugar caramelizes and liquifies.

VIETNAMESE CHICKEN SALAD

Preparation time: 25 minutes
Total cooking time: 10 minutes
Serves 6

1 small Chinese cabbage, finely
    shredded
2 tablespoons oil
2 onions, halved and sliced thinly
500 g (1 lb) chicken thigh fillets,
    trimmed and cut into strips
1/4 cup (60 g/2 oz) sugar

1/4 cup (60 ml/2 fl oz) fish sauce
1/3 cup (80 ml/2³/4 fl oz) lime juice
1 tablespoon white vinegar
2/3 cup (30 g/1 oz) chopped
    Vietnamese mint or common mint
2/3 cup (30 g) chopped coriander
Vietnamese mint leaves, extra, to
    garnish

1 Place the cabbage in a large bowl,
cover with plastic wrap and chill.
2 Heat a wok until very hot, add
1 tablespoon oil and swirl to coat. Add
half the onion and half the chicken,
and stir-fry for 4–5 minutes, or until

the chicken is cooked through.
Remove and repeat with the remaining
oil, onion and chicken. Cool.
3 To make the dressing, mix together
the sugar, fish sauce, lime juice,
vinegar and 1/2 teaspoon salt with a
fork. To serve, toss together the
cabbage, chicken and onion, dressing,
mint and coriander and garnish with
the mint leaves.

NUTRITION PER SERVE
Protein 17 g; Fat 8 g; Carbohydrate 13 g;
Dietary Fibre 1.5 g; Cholesterol 35 mg;
805 kJ (190 cal)

Finely shred the small Chinese cabbage and then
leave to chill.

Stir-fry half the onion and half the chicken strips
for 4–5 minutes.

Mix together the dressing ingredients with a fork,
then toss with the salad.

DUCK AND PINEAPPLE CURRY

Preparation time: 10 minutes
Total cooking time: 15 minutes
Serves 4–6

1 tablespoon peanut oil
8 spring onions, cut into short lengths
2 cloves garlic, crushed
1 tablespoon red curry paste (use the recipe on page 246 or ready-made paste)

750 g (1½ lb) Chinese barbecued duck, chopped (see NOTE)
400 ml (13 fl oz) coconut milk
450 g (14 oz) can pineapple pieces in syrup, drained
3 kaffir lime leaves
¼ cup (15 g/½ oz) chopped coriander
2 tablespoons chopped mint

1 Heat a wok until very hot, add the oil and swirl to coat. Add the spring onion, garlic and curry paste to the wok, and stir-fry for 1 minute, or until the paste is fragrant.

2 Add the remaining ingredients. Bring to the boil, then reduce the heat and simmer for 10 minutes, or until the duck is heated through.

NUTRITION PER SERVE (6)
Protein 4 g; Fat 32 g; Carbohydrate 25 g; Dietary Fibre 4.5 g; Cholesterol 10 mg; 1705 kJ (405 cal)

NOTE: You can chop the duck yourself if you have a cleaver, or ask for it to be done when you buy it.

Chop the barbecued duck into smaller pieces, or ask for this to be done when you buy it.

Cook the spring onion, garlic and curry paste for 1 minute, or until the paste is fragrant.

Add the remaining ingredients to the wok and simmer for 10 minutes.

NONYA LIME CHICKEN

Preparation time: 20 minutes
Total cooking time: 25 minutes
Serves 4–6

²/₃ cup (90 g/3 oz) Asian shallots
4 cloves garlic
2 stems lemon grass, white part only, chopped
2 teaspoons finely chopped fresh galangal
1 teaspoon ground turmeric
2 tablespoons sambal oelek
1 tablespoon shrimp paste
¹/₄ cup (60 ml/2 fl oz) oil

1 kg (2 lb) chicken thigh fillets, cut into cubes
410 ml (13 fl oz) coconut milk
1 teaspoon finely grated lime rind
¹/₂ cup (125 ml/4 fl oz) lime juice
6 kaffir lime leaves, finely shredded
2 tablespoons tamarind concentrate
lime wedges and kaffir lime leaves, to garnish

1 Place the shallots, garlic, lemon grass, galangal, turmeric, sambal oelek and shrimp paste in a blender and blend until smooth.
2 Heat a wok until very hot, add the oil and swirl to coat. Add the spice paste and stir-fry for 1–2 minutes, or until fragrant. Add the chicken and stir-fry for 5 minutes, or until browned.
3 Add the coconut milk, lime rind and juice, lime leaves and tamarind concentrate. Reduce the heat and simmer for 15 minutes, or until the chicken is cooked and the sauce has reduced and thickened slightly. Season well with salt. Garnish with lime wedges and lime leaves to serve.

NUTRITION PER SERVE (6)
Protein 32 g; Fat 25 g; Carbohydrate 4 g; Dietary Fibre 1.5 g; Cholesterol 65 mg; 1590 kJ (380 cal)

Fresh galangal is similar to fresh ginger. Peel it and then finely chop or grate.

Blend the shallots, garlic, lemon grass, galangal, turmeric, sambal oelek and shrimp paste.

Stir-fry the chicken in the spice paste for 5 minutes or until it is browned.

CHILLI-CRUSTED CHICKEN NOODLES

Preparation time: 25 minutes
Total cooking time: 20 minutes
Serves 4–6

1½ teaspoons chilli powder
3 tablespoons cornflour
1½ teaspoons salt
2 tablespoons oil
350 g (12 oz) chicken thigh fillets, sliced
4 spring onions, sliced
1 carrot, sliced
1 celery stick, sliced
2 tablespoons mirin or sherry
500 g (1 lb) Hokkien noodles, gently pulled apart
2 tablespoons oyster sauce
250 g (8 oz) baby bok choy, washed, trimmed, leaves separated

1 Combine the chilli powder, cornflour and salt and mix well. Heat the oil in a wok over high heat. Coat the chicken strips in the cornflour mix and stir-fry in batches for 3 minutes each batch, or until golden. Drain on paper towels and remove all the chicken from the wok.

2 Reheat the wok over medium heat. Add the spring onion, carrot and celery and stir-fry for 1 minute. Add the mirin and the noodles, tossing well until the vegetables have softened.

3 Add the oyster sauce and 2 tablespoons water; cover and steam for 2–4 minutes, or until the noodles are tender.

4 Add the chicken and bok choy and toss well. Cover and steam for 30 seconds only. Serve immediately.

NUTRITION PER SERVE (6)
Protein 15 g; Fat 9 g; Carbohydrate 30 g;
Dietary Fibre 3 g; Cholesterol 40 mg;
1165 kJ (275 cal)

Gently pull apart the Hokkien noodles before you cook them.

Coat the chicken in the mixture of cornflour, chilli powder and salt.

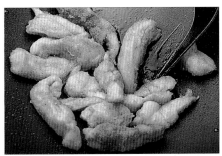

Stir-fry the chicken in small batches so that the wok doesn't overcrowd and cool down.

SOY CHICKEN AND CRISPY NOODLES

Preparation time: 30 minutes
Total cooking time: 35 minutes
Serves 4–6

750 g (1¹/₂ lb) chicken thigh fillets
3 teaspoons cornflour
¹/₃ cup (80 ml/2³/₄ fl oz) soy sauce
oil, for deep-frying
100 g (3¹/₂ oz) dried rice vermicelli
1 clove garlic, crushed
2 teaspoons grated fresh ginger
1 carrot, sliced
2 sticks celery, sliced
1 red capsicum, sliced

1 green capsicum, sliced
100 g (3¹/₂ oz) snow peas, trimmed
6 spring onions, sliced
¹/₄ cup (60 ml/2 fl oz) chicken stock

1 Cut the chicken into 2 cm (³/₄ inch) cubes. Mix the cornflour with half the soy sauce; add the chicken, then cover and refrigerate until ready to use.
2 Heat the oil in a large pan. Break the vermicelli into small pieces. Drop a noodle into the oil: if it fizzes and puffs, the oil is hot enough. Add the noodles in small amounts and cook until puffed and white. Drain on paper towels and set aside.
3 Heat 1 tablespoon of oil in a wok, add the chicken and stir-fry in batches

over high heat for about 4 minutes, or until cooked. Remove the chicken from the wok and set aside.
4 Heat 1 tablespoon of oil in the wok and cook the garlic and ginger for 30 seconds. Add the vegetables and cook, tossing well, for 2–3 minutes.
5 Add the chicken, stock and remaining soy sauce and stir until boiled and thickened. Transfer to serving plates and arrange the noodles around the outside of the plates.

NUTRITION PER SERVE (6)
Protein 30 g; Fat 9 g; Carbohydrate 20 g;
Dietary Fibre 2 g; Cholesterol 85 mg;
1150 kJ (275 cal)

Mix the cornflour with half the soy sauce and then add the chicken and leave to marinate.

To test if the oil is hot, add one noodle. If the noodle fizzes and puffs, the oil is hot enough.

Cook the noodles in the hot oil until they are puffed and white.

QUICK THAI CHICKEN

Preparation time: 15 minutes
Total cooking time: 15 minutes
Serves 4

1 tablespoon red curry paste (use the recipe on page 246 or ready-made paste)
2 tablespoons oil
2 tablespoons fish sauce
2 tablespoons lime juice
1/4 cup (15 g/1/2 oz) chopped coriander leaves
1 tablespoon grated fresh ginger
1 teaspoon caster sugar
1 teaspoon sesame oil
750 g (11/2 lb) chicken thigh fillets, cut into strips
1 tablespoon oil, extra
10 spring onions, cut into short lengths
100 g (31/2 oz) snow peas, trimmed

1 Whisk together the curry paste, oil, fish sauce, lime juice, coriander, ginger, sugar and sesame oil in a large non-metallic bowl. Add the chicken strips and toss to coat thoroughly.

2 Heat the extra oil in a wok. Add the chicken in batches and stir-fry for 3–5 minutes, or until browned all over, then remove from the wok and set aside. Add the spring onion and snow peas and stir-fry for 2 minutes. Return the chicken and any juices to the wok and stir-fry for 2–3 minutes, or until the chicken is heated through. Season with salt and pepper and serve.

NUTRITION PER SERVE
Protein 45 g; Fat 10 g; Carbohydrate 6 g; Dietary Fibre 2.5 g; Cholesterol 95 mg; 1275 kJ (305 cal)

Cut the chicken thigh fillets into strips, then marinate in the Thai sauce.

Brown the chicken in batches so that the wok doesn't overcrowd and cool down.

Stir-fry the spring onion and snow peas for a couple of minutes before adding the chicken.

Seafood

LIME AND GARLIC PRAWNS WITH SUGAR SNAP PEAS

Preparation time: 10 minutes
Total cooking time: 3 minutes
Serves 4

1/2 cup (125 ml/4 fl oz) freshly
squeezed lime juice
3 tablespoons soy sauce
1 1/2 tablespoons honey
1 tablespoon peanut oil
2 cloves garlic, crushed
4 kaffir lime leaves, shredded
16 ears of baby corn, halved
lengthways
150 g (5 oz) sugar snap peas
24 raw prawns, peeled and deveined,
tails intact
4 tablespoons fresh coriander leaves,
chopped

1 Place the lime juice, soy sauce and honey in a small bowl and stir until the honey dissolves.
2 Heat a wok over high heat, add the oil and swirl to coat the side. Add the garlic, lime leaves and baby corn and stir-fry for 1–2 minutes.
3 Add the sugar snap peas, prawns and lime juice mixture and stir-fry for a further minute, or until the prawns are cooked through. Stir in the coriander leaves and serve immediately.

NUTRITION PER SERVE
Protein 27 g; Fat 5.5 g; Carbohydrate 23 g;
Dietary Fibre 5 g; Cholesterol 150 mg;
930 kJ (222 cal)

NOTE: To keep kaffir lime leaves fresh, keep them in an airtight container or plastic bag in the freezer. They will defrost within 1 minute.

Stir the lime juice, soy sauce and honey until the honey dissolves.

Add the sugar snap peas, prawns and lime juice mixture to the wok and stir-fry.

MARINATED CHILLI SQUID

Preparation time: 10 minutes
  + 2–3 hours marinating
Total cooking time: 15 minutes
Serves 4

500 g (1 lb) squid tubes
1 tablespoon finely chopped
    fresh ginger
2–3 teaspoons finely chopped
    red chilli
3 cloves garlic, finely chopped
¼ cup (60 ml/2 fl oz) oil
2 onions, thinly sliced
500 g (1 lb) baby bok choy,
    roughly chopped

1 Wash the squid well and dry with paper towels. Cut into 1 cm (½ inch) rings and place in a bowl with the ginger, chilli, garlic and oil. Toss well. Cover and refrigerate for 2–3 hours.
2 Heat the wok until very hot and stir-fry the squid rings over high heat in three batches for 1–2 minutes, reserving the marinade. Remove from the wok as soon as the squid turns white. Keep the wok very hot and don't cook the squid for too long or it will toughen. Remove all the squid from the wok.
3 Pour the reserved marinade into the wok and bring to the boil. Add the onion and cook over medium heat for 3–4 minutes, or until slightly softened. Add the bok choy, cover and steam for 2 minutes, or until wilted. Add the squid and toss. Serve immediately.

NUTRITION PER SERVE
Protein 25 g; Fat 15 g; Carbohydrate 7 g;
Dietary Fibre 2 g; Cholesterol 250 mg;
1105 kJ (265 cal)

Wash the squid tubes well and pat them dry with paper towels.

Using a sharp knife, slice the washed squid tubes into rings.

Remove the squid from the wok as soon as it turns white, or it will be rubbery.

SMOKED SALMON WITH CANNELLINI BEANS

Preparation time: 20 minutes
Total cooking time: 15 minutes
Serves 4

olive oil, for cooking
6 slices white bread, cubed
3 cloves garlic, crushed
6 spring onions, sliced
300 g (10 oz) smoked salmon, cut into
    thin strips
300 g (10 oz) can cannellini beans,
    rinsed
4 Roma tomatoes, chopped
175 g (6 oz) iceberg lettuce, shredded
2 tablespoons chopped fresh dill
2 tablespoons lemon juice

1 Heat the wok until very hot, add
$1/3$ cup (80 ml/$2^3/_4$ fl oz) oil and swirl
it around to coat the side. Stir-fry the
bread over high heat until crisp and
golden. Remove from the wok and
drain the croutons on paper towels.
2 Reheat the wok, add 1 tablespoon
of the oil and stir-fry the garlic and half
the spring onion for 2 minutes.
Remove from the wok.
3 Reheat the wok and stir-fry the
salmon until it is slightly crisp. Add the
cannellini beans and tomato and cook
for 2–3 minutes, or until heated
through. Remove the wok from the
heat and quickly stir in the lettuce,
dill, and the spring onion and
garlic mixture.
4 Whisk the lemon juice with
2 tablespoons olive oil to make a

dressing and pour over the salad. Add
the croutons and toss. Garnish with
the remaining spring onion.

NUTRITION PER SERVE
Protein 25 g; Fat 25 g; Carbohydrate 25 g;
Dietary Fibre 5 g; Cholesterol 35 mg;
1700 kJ (405 cal)

Make the croutons by stir-frying the bread cubes
until crisp and golden.

SALMON WITH LEEK AND CAMEMBERT IN HONEY MUSTARD SAUCE

Preparation time: 10 minutes
Total cooking time: 15 minutes
Serves 4

500 g (1 lb) salmon fillet, cut into thick strips
1/4 cup (60 g/2 oz) wholegrain mustard
1 tablespoon lime juice
2 tablespoons oil
1 leek, white part only, julienned
2 tablespoons tamari
2 teaspoons fish sauce
1 tablespoon honey
75 g (2¹/₂ oz) snow pea sprouts
¹/₂ cup (15 g/¹/₂ oz) coriander leaves, plus extra to garnish
100 g (3¹/₂ oz) Camembert, sliced
lime wedges, to serve

1 Place the salmon strips in a glass or ceramic bowl. Add the mustard and lime juice and toss to coat the salmon.
2 Heat the wok until very hot, add the oil and swirl it around to coat the side. Stir-fry the salmon in batches over high heat until it is slightly browned. Remove from the wok.
3 Add 1 tablespoon water to the wok, then add the leek and stir-fry until it is golden brown. Return the salmon to the wok, with the tamari, fish sauce and honey. Cook until the salmon is heated through.
4 Remove the wok from the heat and toss the snow pea sprouts and coriander leaves through the salmon. Serve topped with the Camembert and extra coriander, and the lime wedges on the side.

NUTRITION PER SERVE
Protein 30 g; Fat 30 g; Carbohydrate 7 g; Dietary Fibre 2 g; Cholesterol 110 mg; 1770 kJ (420 cal)

Remove the skin from the salmon, pull out any bones, then cut into thick strips.

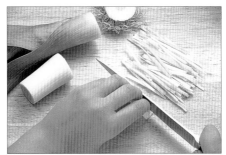

Cut the leek into julienne strips, using only the white part.

Stir-fry the salmon until it turns a soft pink colour and is slightly browned.

SWORDFISH WITH BOK CHOY

Preparation time: 20 minutes
Total cooking time: 10 minutes
Serves 4

500 g (1 lb) swordfish steak, cubed
2 tablespoons cracked black pepper
oil, for cooking
3 cloves garlic, thinly sliced
1 onion, sliced
1 kg (2 lb) baby bok choy, leaves
   separated
100 g (3¹/₂ oz) shiitake mushrooms,
   sliced

2 tablespoons hoisin sauce
2 tablespoons rice wine
1 tablespoon oyster sauce
1 tablespoon soy sauce
1 tablespoon toasted sesame seeds
1 teaspoon sesame oil

1 Dip the swordfish in cracked black pepper until coated, then shake off any excess.
2 Heat the wok until very hot, add 2 tablespoons of the oil and swirl it around to coat the side. Stir-fry the swordfish in batches over high heat until tender. Do not overcook or the fish will break up. Remove from the wok and keep warm.

3 Reheat the wok, add 1 tablespoon of the oil and stir-fry the garlic until crisp and golden. Add the onion and stir-fry until golden. Add the bok choy and mushrooms and cook until the leaves wilt. Combine the hoisin sauce, rice wine, oyster sauce and soy sauce, pour into the wok and heat.
4 Return the swordfish to the wok and toss. Serve sprinkled with sesame seeds and drizzled with the oil.

NUTRITION PER SERVE
Protein 35 g; Fat 15 g; Carbohydrate 15 g;
Dietary Fibre 3 g; Cholesterol 90 mg;
1490 kJ (355 cal)

Use a sharp knife to cut the swordfish steak into bite-sized cubes.

Wipe the mushrooms with a damp paper towel, then cut into slices.

Dip the pieces of swordfish in the cracked black pepper and shake off any excess.

153

SALT-AND-PEPPER SQUID

Preparation time: 40 minutes
  + 20 minutes marinating
Total cooking time: 10 minutes
Serves 4

500 g (1 lb) squid tubes
1/3 cup (80 ml/2¾ fl oz) oil
4 cloves garlic, finely chopped
1/2 teaspoon sugar
2 teaspoons sea salt
1 teaspoon ground black pepper
150 g (5 oz) baby English spinach
  leaves
100 g (3½ oz) cherry tomatoes,
  quartered
2 tablespoons lime juice
lime quarters, to garnish

1 Cut the squid tubes in half
lengthways and open them out. Rinse
and pat dry with paper towels. Lay on
a chopping board with the inside
facing upwards. Honeycomb the squid
by scoring along the length of each
piece very finely, then diagonally
across the width to create a fine
diamond pattern. Cut the squid into
pieces 5 x 3 cm (2 x 1¼ inches).
Combine the squid, oil, garlic, sugar
and half the salt and pepper, cover and
refrigerate for 20 minutes.
2 Arrange the spinach leaves and
tomatoes on a large serving platter.
3 Heat the wok until it is very hot and
stir-fry the squid over high heat in
several batches, tossing constantly, for
1–2 minutes, or until the squid just
turns white and curls. Keep the wok
very hot and don't cook the squid for
too long or it will toughen.
4 Return all the squid pieces to the
wok with the lime juice and the
remaining salt and pepper. Stir briefly
until heated through. Arrange on top
of the spinach and garnish with the
lime wedges. Serve immediately.

NUTRITION PER SERVE
Protein 20 g; Fat 15 g; Carbohydrate 3 g;
Dietary Fibre 2 g; Cholesterol 250 mg;
1020 kJ (250 cal)

HINT: Tenderize squid by marinating
in puréed papaya or pawpaw mixed
with a little milk. Rinse and drain.

Cut the squid tubes in half lengthways, and open them out.

Score very finely along the length, then diagonally to create a diamond pattern.

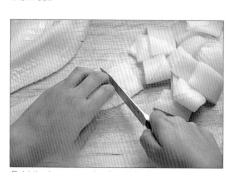

Fold the honeycombed squid tubes over and cut them into pieces.

Stir-fry the squid in batches until it turns white and curls up. Take care not to overcook.

SICHUAN PRAWNS WITH SNOW PEAS

Preparation time: 30 minutes
  + 20 minutes marinating
Total cooking time: 20 minutes
Serves 4

2 teaspoons Sichuan pepper
750 g (1½ lb) raw prawns, peeled and
    deveined, tails intact
2 tablespoons grated fresh ginger
3 cloves garlic, finely chopped
2 tablespoons Chinese rice wine or
    dry sherry
oil, for cooking
2 eggs, lightly beaten
½ red capsicum, cut into strips
½ green capsicum, cut into strips
4 spring onions, cut into pieces
100 g (3½ oz) snow peas
½ teaspoon salt
75 g (2½ oz) roasted unsalted
    peanuts, roughly chopped
50 g (1¾ oz) snow pea sprouts

1 Heat the wok until very hot and dry-fry the Sichuan pepper until it is fragrant. Remove from the wok and crush with a mortar and pestle or in a spice grinder.
2 Combine the prawns with the Sichuan pepper, ginger, garlic and wine in a glass or ceramic dish. Cover and refrigerate for 20 minutes.
3 Heat the wok until very hot, add 1½ tablespoons of the oil and swirl it around to coat the side. Dip three or four prawns in the beaten eggs, then stir-fry for about 1 minute, or until the prawns just change colour and are cooked. Remove from the wok. Repeat with the remaining prawns, reheating the wok to very hot for each batch and adding a little oil when needed.

Remove the prawns from the wok.
4 Add the capsicum, spring onion, snow peas and salt to the wok. Stir-fry for 2 minutes, or until the vegetables are just crisp and tender.
5 Return the prawns to the wok with the peanuts and toss gently to combine. Serve immediately on a bed of snow pea sprouts.

NUTRITION PER SERVE
Protein 50 g; Fat 20 g; Carbohydrate 8 g;
Dietary Fibre 4.5 g; Cholesterol 370 mg;
1710 kJ (410 cal)

Peel the prawns, leaving the tails intact, and pull out the dark veins from their backs.

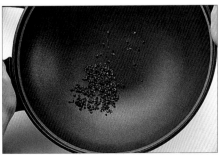

Dry-fry the Sichuan pepper in a hot wok until it becomes fragrant.

Crush the fried Sichuan pepper with a mortar and pestle or in a spice grinder.

155

BABY OCTOPUS WITH GINGER AND LIME

Preparation time: 30 minutes
+ overnight marinating
Total cooking time: 10 minutes
Serves 4

500 g (1 lb) baby octopus
1/4 cup (15 g/1/2 oz) chopped
    coriander
2 cloves garlic, finely chopped
2 red chillies, seeded and chopped
2 teaspoons grated fresh ginger
2 stems lemon grass, white part only,
    chopped
1 tablespoon oil
2 tablespoons lime juice
oil, for cooking
550 g (1 lb 2 oz) bok choy, leaves
    separated
400 g (13 oz) choy sum, leaves
    separated
2 cloves garlic, crushed, extra
1 teaspoon grated fresh ginger, extra

1 To prepare the baby octopus, remove the head, cut off the eyes, and remove the gut by slitting the head open. Grasp the body firmly and push the beak out with your index finger. Clean the octopus thoroughly under cold running water and pat dry with paper towels. Cut the head into two or three pieces.
2 Place the octopus, coriander, garlic, chilli, ginger, lemon grass, oil and lime juice in a glass bowl. Cover and refrigerate overnight, or for 2 hours.
3 Heat the wok until very hot, add 1 tablespoon of the oil and swirl it around to coat the side. Stir-fry the vegetables with 1 tablespoon water. Cover and steam until just wilted. Spread on a serving plate.
4 Reheat the wok, add 1 tablespoon of the oil and stir-fry the extra garlic and ginger for 30 seconds, or until fragrant. Add the octopus and stir-fry over high heat for 7–8 minutes, or until cooked through. Serve on top of the wilted greens.

NUTRITION PER SERVE
Protein 25 g; Fat 6 g; Carbohydrate 8 g;
Dietary Fibre 2 g; Cholesterol 0 mg;
735 kJ (175 cal)

Remove the eyes from the octopus by cutting them off the base of the head.

Remove and discard the beak by pushing it out of the octopus.

SEAFOOD WITH MIRIN

Preparation time: 20 minutes
Total cooking time: 15 minutes
Serves 4–6

200 g (6¹/₂ oz) squid tubes
olive oil, for cooking
350 g (12 oz) raw prawns, peeled and
    deveined, tails intact
250 g (8 oz) firm white fish fillets, cut
    into strips
250 g (8 oz) scallops, cleaned
2 onions, thinly sliced
3 cloves garlic, finely chopped
2 tablespoons finely grated fresh
    ginger
1 green capsicum, thinly sliced
5 spring onions, diagonally sliced
2 tablespoons mirin
¹/₂ teaspoon salt

1 Rinse and dry the squid tubes and slice into rings. Heat the wok until very hot, add 2 teaspoons of oil and swirl it around to coat the side. Stir-fry the prawns and squid rings in batches over high heat until they change colour. Remove from the wok.
2 Reheat the wok, add 2 teaspoons of the oil and stir-fry the fish strips and scallops until just cooked. Do not overcook the seafood or it will break up. Remove from the wok.
3 Reheat the wok, add 1 tablespoon of the oil and stir-fry the sliced onion over medium-high heat for about 3–4 minutes, or until it has just softened. Add the garlic, ginger, capsicum and spring onion. Increase the heat to high and toss constantly for 3–4 minutes.
4 Add the mirin and salt to the wok with some cracked pepper, and toss well. Return all of the seafood to the wok and toss until well combined and heated through.

NUTRITION PER SERVE (6)
Protein 30 g; Fat 8.5 g; Carbohydrate 2 g;
Dietary Fibre 1 g; Cholesterol 195 mg;
880 kJ (210 cal)

Peel the prawns, leaving the tails intact, and pull out the dark veins from the backs.

Wash and dry the squid tubes and then slice them into rings.

Stir-fry the prawns and squid rings until they have just changed colour—don't overcook them.

CHILLI SQUID WITH SUGAR SNAP PEAS

Preparation time: 30 minutes
Total cooking time: 10 minutes
Serves 4

500 g (1 lb) squid tubes
3 teaspoons grated fresh ginger
2 small red chillies, seeded and finely chopped
1 green chilli, seeded and finely sliced
1 tablespoon green peppercorns in brine, drained
oil, for cooking
1 large red capsicum, cut into strips
1 large green capsicum, cut into strips

1 tablespoon honey
1 tablespoon sweet chilli sauce
200 g (6½ oz) sugar snap peas
2 teaspoons grated lime rind

1 Cut the squid tubes in half lengthways and open them out. Rinse and pat dry with paper towels. Place on a chopping board with the inside facing upwards. Cut into thin strips about 5 cm (2 inches) long and 5 mm (¼ inch) wide. Mix with the ginger, chilli, peppercorns and some salt.
2 Heat the wok until very hot, add 1 tablespoon of the oil and swirl it around to coat the side. Stir-fry the squid in three batches for about 2 minutes, or until it turns white. Keep

the wok hot and add a little more oil if necessary. Do not overcook the squid or it will toughen. Remove the squid from the wok and set aside.
3 Add the capsicum and toss for 1 minute. Drizzle with the honey and chilli sauce and toss well. Cover and steam for 2 minutes. Add the sugar snap peas, tossing well, cover and steam for 1 minute. Add the squid and any juices to the wok with the lime rind and toss well. Serve immediately.

NUTRITION PER SERVE
Protein 25 g; Fat 10 g; Carbohydrate 15 g; Dietary Fibre 4 g; Cholesterol 250 mg; 1075 kJ (255 cal)

Cut the squid tubes in half lengthways and open them out.

Lay the squid on a chopping board with the inside facing upwards and cut into thin strips.

Stir-fry the squid in batches until it turns white, but do not overcook it.

GINGER GARLIC PRAWN SALAD

Preparation time: 35 minutes
Total cooking time: 15 minutes
Serves 4

oil, for cooking
5 cloves garlic, finely chopped
1 tablespoon grated fresh ginger
1 onion, sliced
500 g (1 lb) raw prawns, peeled and
    deveined, tails intact
1 carrot, cut into matchsticks
2 celery sticks, cut into matchsticks
100 g (3¹/₂ oz) snow peas, sliced
100 g (3¹/₂ oz) green beans,
    cut into short lengths
2 teaspoons cornflour
¹/₄ cup (60 ml/2 fl oz) vegetable stock
2 tablespoons soy sauce
2 teaspoons soft brown sugar
500 g (1 lb) watercress
¹/₄ cup (40 g/1¹/₄ oz) roasted unsalted
    peanuts, roughly chopped

1 Heat the wok until very hot, add 1 tablespoon of the oil and swirl it around to coat the side. Stir-fry the garlic, ginger, onion and prawns over high heat for 5 minutes, or until the prawns have turned pink and are cooked. Remove from the wok.
2 Reheat the wok, add 1 tablespoon of the oil and stir-fry the carrot, celery, snow peas and beans over high heat for 3–4 minutes. Mix the cornflour with a little of the stock to form a paste. Mix in the remaining stock, soy sauce and sugar. Pour into the wok and stir until the sauce boils and thickens.
3 Return the prawns to the wok, stirring for 1–2 minutes, or until heated through. Serve on a bed of watercress, and sprinkle the chopped peanuts over the top.

NUTRITION PER SERVE
Protein 35 g; Fat 15 g; Carbohydrate 15 g;
Dietary Fibre 10 g; Cholesterol 185 mg;
1450 kJ (350 cal)

Peel the heads and shells from the prawns, leaving the tails intact.

Remove the dark veins from the prawns by pulling them out with your fingers.

Cut the celery sticks into pieces and then into short matchsticks for quick and even cooking.

Stir-fry the garlic, ginger, onion and prawns until the prawns turn pink.

CHILLI CRAB

Preparation time: 25 minutes
Total cooking time: 25 minutes
Serves 4

2 x 1 kg (2 lb) mud crabs
2 tablespoons oil
1 onion, chopped
4 cloves garlic, crushed
3 teaspoons grated fresh ginger
2–3 red chillies, finely chopped
440 ml (14 fl oz) tomato purée
1 tablespoon soy sauce
1 tablespoon soft brown sugar
2 teaspoons rice vinegar

1 Wash the crabs well with a scourer. Pull the apron back from underneath the crab and snap it off. Remove the feathery gills and internal organs. Twist off the legs and claws and pull the body apart. Using a cleaver or a heavy-bladed knife, cut the body in half or quarters. Crack the claws by giving them a good hit with the back of a cleaver.
2 Heat the wok until very hot, add the oil and swirl it around to coat the side of the wok. Stir-fry the crab in batches for 2–3 minutes, or until it turns bright red. Remove all the crab from the wok and set aside.
3 Add the onion to the wok and cook for 3 minutes. Add the garlic, ginger and chilli, and cook for 1–2 minutes. Stir in the tomato purée, soy sauce, sugar, vinegar and 1/2 cup (125 ml/ 4 fl oz) water. Bring to the boil, then reduce the heat and simmer for 5 minutes.
4 Return the crab to the wok and toss to coat with the tomato sauce mixture. Simmer for 8 minutes, turning the crab pieces frequently.

NUTRITION PER SERVE
Protein 65 g; Fat 15 g; Carbohydrate 20 g; Dietary Fibre 3 g; Cholesterol 420 mg; 1185 kJ (450 cal)

Snap the apron off the crab by pulling it back from underneath the crab.

Pull the feathery gills and the internal organs out of the crab.

Using a cleaver, cut the body of the crab in half or into quarters.

FRESH TUNA AND GREEN BEANS

Preparation time: 25 minutes
Total cooking time: 10 minutes
Serves 4

300 g (10 oz) small green beans, topped and tailed
2 tablespoons oil
600 g (11/4 lb) fresh tuna, cut into small cubes
250 g (8 oz) small cherry tomatoes
16 small black olives
2–3 tablespoons lemon juice
2 cloves garlic, finely chopped
8 anchovy fillets, rinsed, dried and finely chopped
1/4 cup (15 g/1/2 oz) small basil leaves (or larger leaves, torn)

1 Bring a small pan of water to the boil. Add the beans and cook for 2 minutes. Drain and refresh under very cold water so they keep their colour. Set aside.
2 Heat the wok until very hot, add the oil and swirl it around to coat the side. Stir-fry the tuna for about 5 minutes, or until it is cooked on the outside, but still pink on the inside.
3 Add the cherry tomatoes, olives and beans and gently toss until heated through. Stir in the lemon juice, garlic and anchovies. Season with salt and black pepper and serve scattered with the basil leaves.

NUTRITION PER SERVE
Protein 40 g; Fat 15 g; Carbohydrate 4 g; Dietary Fibre 4 g; Cholesterol 75 mg; 1390 kJ (330 cal)

Cut the tuna into long strips and then into small cubes.

Rinse and dry the anchovy fillets to reduce their saltiness, then chop them finely.

Tuna is best cooked until it is browned on the outside, but still pink inside.

GARLIC AND GINGER PRAWNS

Preparation time: 25 minutes
Total cooking time: 10 minutes
Serves 4

2 tablespoons oil
1 kg (2 lb) raw king prawns,
    peeled, deveined and butterflied,
    tails left intact
3–4 cloves garlic, finely chopped
5 cm (2 inch) piece fresh ginger,
    cut into matchsticks
2–3 small red chillies, seeded and
    finely chopped
6 coriander roots, finely chopped, plus
    a few leaves to garnish
8 spring onions, cut into short lengths
1/2 red capsicum, thinly sliced
2 tablespoons lemon juice
1/2 cup (125 ml/4 fl oz) white wine
2 teaspoons crushed palm sugar
2 teaspoons fish sauce

1 Heat the wok until very hot, add the oil and swirl to coat. Stir-fry the prawns, garlic, ginger, chilli and coriander root in two batches for 1–2 minutes over high heat, or until the prawns turn pink. Remove all the prawns from the wok and set aside.
2 Add the spring onion and capsicum to the wok. Cook over high heat for 2–3 minutes. Add the lemon juice, wine and palm sugar. Cook until the liquid has reduced by two thirds.
3 Add the prawns and sprinkle with fish sauce. Toss to heat through. Garnish with coriander to serve.

NUTRITION PER SERVE
Protein 1 g; Fat 10 g; Carbohydrate 4.5 g;
Dietary Fibre 1.5 g; Cholesterol 0 mg;
550 kJ (130 cal)

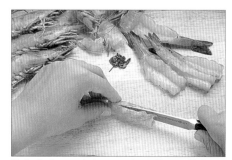

Butterfly the peeled prawns by cutting a slit down the backs and opening them out.

Using a large, sharp knife, finely chop the coriander roots.

Stir-fry the prawns in two batches with the garlic, ginger, chilli and coriander root.

SPICY CHILLI PRAWNS

Preparation time: 20 minutes
  + overnight marinating
Total cooking time: 5 minutes
Serves 4

20–24 raw prawns, unpeeled
crusty bread and lemon wedges, to
  serve

MARINADE
1 small red onion, finely chopped
1/2 cup (125 ml/4 fl oz) olive oil
1 tablespoon grated lime or lemon rind
2–3 cloves garlic, crushed
1/2 cup (125 ml/4 fl oz) lime or lemon
  juice
2–3 small red chillies, seeded and
  finely chopped
1 tablespoon grated fresh ginger
1 stem lemon grass, white part only,
  finely chopped
1 teaspoon ground turmeric

1 Place the prawns in a large glass or
ceramic bowl. Add the marinade
ingredients and toss well. Cover and
refrigerate overnight. Turn the prawns
once or twice while marinating.
2 Drain the prawns, reserving the
marinade. Heat the wok until very hot
and stir-fry the prawns in three batches
over high heat until they are pink and
very crispy. Remove from the wok.
3 Pour the reserved marinade into the
wok. Bring to the boil, then return the
prawns to the wok and toss well.
Season and serve immediately.

NUTRITION PER SERVE
Protein 25 g; Fat 30 g; Carbohydrate 30 g;
Dietary Fibre 3 g; Cholesterol 150 mg;
2150 kJ (515 cal)

NOTE: The whole prawn, including
the cripsy shell, can be eaten. If you
prefer, you can discard the prawn
heads before marinating.

Toss the whole prawns in the marinade before
refrigerating overnight.

Drain the prawns in a sieve, so that you can keep
the marinade.

Stir-fry the prawns until they are pink and the
shells are very crispy.

BLACK FUNGUS WITH PRAWNS

Preparation time: 25 minutes
Total cooking time: 8 minutes
Serves 4

20 g (³/₄ oz) dried black fungus
2 teaspoons cornflour
¹/₄ cup (60 ml/2 fl oz) mirin
1 tablespoon rice wine vinegar
1 tablespoon soy sauce
1–2 small red chillies, seeded and
    finely chopped
1–2 cloves garlic, crushed
2 teaspoons grated fresh ginger
1 tablespoon oil

500 g (1 lb) raw prawns, peeled,
    deveined and halved
¹/₂ red capsicum, cut into matchsticks
1 celery stick, cut into matchsticks
1 carrot, cut into matchsticks
4 spring onions, cut into short pieces
    and sliced lengthways
230 g (7¹/₂ oz) can water chestnuts,
    drained

1 Place the black fungus in a bowl and cover with boiling water. Leave until doubled in volume and softened. Drain, squeeze dry and chop roughly.
2 Mix the cornflour with ¹/₄ cup (60 ml/2 fl oz) water in a bowl until smooth. Add the mirin, vinegar, soy sauce, chilli, garlic and ginger.

3 Heat the wok until very hot, add the oil and swirl it around to coat the side. Stir-fry the prawns briefly until they are just starting to change colour. Add the capsicum, celery, carrot, spring onion, water chestnuts and black fungus and stir-fry over medium-high heat for 2–3 minutes, or until tender. Remove from the wok.
4 Add the sauce to the wok and stir until the mixture boils and thickens. Stir in the prawns and vegetables. Serve at once.

NUTRITION PER SERVE
Protein 30 g; Fat 6.5 g; Carbohydrate 30 g;
Dietary Fibre 5 g; Cholesterol 185 mg;
1205 kJ (290 cal)

Peel the prawns, removing the large veins from their backs, then cut them in half.

Put the black fungus in a bowl and cover it with boiling water.

When the fungus has doubled in volume, squeeze it dry and chop roughly.

SEAFOOD WITH CHILLI PLUM SAUCE

Preparation time: 30 minutes
Total cooking time: 15 minutes
Serves 4

150 g (5 oz) squid tubes
1 kg (2 lb) English spinach
oil, for cooking
500 g (1 lb) raw prawns, peeled and deveined
400 g (13 oz) scallops, cleaned
2 cloves garlic, crushed
1–2 red chillies, seeded and finely chopped
1/2 cup (125 ml/4 fl oz) plum sauce
1 teaspoon soft brown sugar
2 tablespoons lime juice
3 spring onions, sliced

1 Rinse the squid tubes, pat dry with paper towels and slice into rings.
2 Rinse the spinach and leave wet (so it won't stick to the wok). Heat the wok until very hot, add the spinach and toss over high heat until wilted. Transfer to a serving plate.
3 Heat the wok until very hot, add 1 tablespoon of the oil and swirl it around to coat the side. Stir-fry the squid rings, prawns and scallops in batches over high heat until they turn opaque and are cooked through. Remove all of the seafood from the wok and set aside. Heat 1 tablespoon of the oil and cook the garlic and chilli for 1–2 minutes, or until softened.
4 Add the plum sauce, brown sugar and lime juice to the wok. Bring to the boil, then reduce the heat and simmer for 4–5 minutes, or until the sauce thickens. Return the squid rings, prawns and scallops to the wok, add the sliced spring onion and toss to coat in the sauce. Serve the seafood on top of the stir-fried spinach.

NUTRITION PER SERVE
Protein 65 g; Fat 4 g; Carbohydrate 20 g;
Dietary Fibre 7.5 g; Cholesterol 470 mg;
1605 kJ (385 cal)

Peel the prawns and remove the dark veins from their backs.

Cut the hard white muscle and any dark veins from the scallops.

Wash and dry the squid tubes, then cut them into thin rings.

THAI NOODLES WITH PRAWNS

Preparation time: 25 minutes
Total cooking time: 10 minutes
Serves 4

200 g (6¹/₂ oz) dried thick rice stick
    noodles
1 tablespoon oil
2 cloves garlic, crushed
2 red chillies, seeded and chopped
1 chicken breast fillet, thinly sliced
150 g (5 oz) raw prawns, peeled,
    deveined and chopped
¹/₄ cup (30 g/1 oz) chopped garlic
    chives
2 tablespoons fish sauce
1 tablespoon soft brown sugar
2 tablespoons lemon juice
1 egg, lightly beaten
50 g (1³/₄ oz) deep-fried tofu puffs,
    cut into strips
¹/₄ cup (7 g/¹/₄ oz) coriander leaves
¹/₄ cup (25 g/³/₄ oz) bean sprouts
¹/₄ cup (40 g/1¹/₄ oz) roasted unsalted
    peanuts, chopped

1 Put the noodles in a heatproof bowl. Cover with boiling water and leave for 5–8 minutes, or until soft and tender. Drain and set aside.
2 Heat the wok until very hot, add the oil and swirl it around to coat the side. Stir-fry the garlic, chilli and sliced chicken over high heat for 2–3 minutes, or until the chicken is browned.
3 Add the prawn meat and cook for 2 minutes, or until the prawn meat turns opaque. Add the drained noodles and garlic chives and toss until thoroughly combined.
4 Add the fish sauce, brown sugar,

lemon juice, egg and tofu and toss gently to combine. Serve sprinkled with the coriander leaves, bean sprouts and peanuts. Serve with lemon wedges on the side.

NUTRITION PER SERVE
Protein 30 g; Fat 15 g; Carbohydrate 50 g;
Dietary Fibre 2 g; Cholesterol 130 mg;
1885 kJ (450 cal)

NOTE: Deep-fried tofu puffs are available from Asian grocery stores and some supermarkets.

Use a large sharp knife to cut the chicken breast fillet into thin slices.

Cover the noodles with boiling water in a heatproof bowl.

CRAB WITH ASPARAGUS AND BROCCOLI

Preparation time: 30 minutes
Total cooking time: 15 minutes
Serves 4

250 g (8 oz) thick dried rice stick
    noodles
oil, for cooking
3 stems lemon grass, white part only,
    very thinly sliced
1 tablespoon grated fresh ginger
4 spring onions, chopped
1/4 teaspoon green peppercorns in
    brine, crushed
750 g (1 1/2 lb) broccoli, cut into small
    florets
150 g (5 oz) asparagus, cut into short
    lengths
3 teaspoons sesame oil
1 teaspoon sugar
250 g (8 oz) cooked fresh crab meat
    (see HINT)
75 g (2 1/2 oz) garlic chives, chopped
2 tablespoons lemon juice

1 Soak the noodles in boiling water
for 8 minutes, or until soft and tender.
Drain, cool a little, then drizzle with
1/2 tablespoon of oil and mix in lightly
with your fingertips to prevent them
sticking together. Cover to keep warm.
2 Heat the wok until very hot, add
1 tablespoon of the oil and swirl it
around to coat the side. Stir-fry the
lemon grass, ginger and spring onion
for 15 seconds. Add the peppercorns,
broccoli and asparagus and stir-fry for
1 minute. Add the sesame oil
and sugar, and cook, covered, for
1–2 minutes, or until the asparagus
and broccoli are just tender. Add the
crab meat and cook for 1–2 minutes,
or until heated through.

3 Add the noodles, chives and lemon
juice, and toss well. Season well with
salt and pepper. Serve immediately.

NUTRITION PER SERVE
Protein 15 g; Fat 15 g; Carbohydrate 55 g;
Dietary Fibre 2.5 g; Cholesterol 50 mg;
1705 kJ (405 cal)

HINT: Good fishmongers sell fresh
crab meat in vacuum packets.
Alternatively, you can use the meat
from 2 very fresh cooked blue
swimmer crabs. Canned crab can
also be used.

Slice the lemon grass very thinly, using only the
white part of the stem.

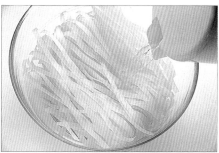

Cover the noodles with boiling water and leave for
8 minutes until they have softened.

Stir-fry the lemon grass, ginger and spring onion
quickly, before adding the vegetables.

SQUID WITH OLIVE OIL AND OREGANO DRESSING

Preparation time: 10 minutes
Total cooking time: 5 minutes
Serves 4

olive oil, for cooking
500 g (1 lb) squid tubes
2 teaspoons sea salt
2 teaspoons ground black pepper
mixed salad leaves, to serve

DRESSING
1 teaspoon grated lemon rind (see HINT)
2 tablespoons lemon juice
4 spring onions, finely sliced
2 teaspoons chopped oregano

1 To make the dressing, mix together 3 tablespoons olive oil with the lemon rind, lemon juice, spring onion and oregano.
2 Rinse the squid tubes in cold water and then pat dry with paper towels. Cut them in half and then into thin strips lengthways.
3 Place the salt and pepper in a bowl, mix well and add the squid strips. Toss to evenly coat.
4 Heat a wok over high heat, add 1 tablespoon of the oil and swirl to coat the side of the wok with oil. Cook the squid strips, in two batches, stir-frying for 1–2 minutes, or until they just change colour. Keep the wok hot and don't cook the squid for too long or it will toughen. Arrange the salad leaves on a serving platter, top with the stir-fried squid and drizzle with the dressing.

NUTRITION PER SERVE
Protein 40 g; Fat 45 g; Carbohydrate 1 g;
Dietary Fibre 1 g; Cholesterol 498 mg;
2449 kJ (585 cal)

HINT: When grating citrus rind, place a piece of baking paper over the grater. It will allow you to grate while making it easier to remove the rind from the grater.

Mix together the olive oil, lemon rind, lemon juice, spring onion and oregano.

Cut the squid hoods in half and then slice into thin strips lengthways.

Add the squid strips to the salt and pepper mixture and toss to coat.

Cook the squid strips in two batches over high heat, taking care not to overcook.

BLACK BEAN AND CHILLI MUSSELS

Preparation time: 10 minutes
Total cooking time: 8 minutes
Serves 4

3 teaspoons salted black beans,
   rinsed
1 tablespoon shredded fresh ginger
2 cloves garlic, chopped
1 tablespoon sugar
2 tablespoons oyster sauce
1 teaspoon soy sauce
2 teaspoons oil
1 small red chilli, seeded and thinly
   sliced
1.2 kg (2 lb 6 oz) black mussels,
   scrubbed, debearded (see NOTE)
2 teaspoons cornflour
4 spring onions, sliced on the diagonal
coriander leaves, to serve

1 Place the black beans, ginger, garlic, sugar, oyster sauce and soy sauce in a small bowl and mash with a fork.
2 Heat a wok over high heat, add the oil and swirl to coat the side. Add the chilli and stir-fry for 30 seconds, then add the black bean mixture and stir-fry for 1 minute, or until fragrant. Add the mussels and stir-fry for 3–5 minutes, or until they open. Discard any that do not open. Reduce the heat to low.
3 Place the cornflour and 1/2 cup (125 ml/4 fl oz) water in a bowl and stir until smooth. Add to the wok and bring to the boil, stirring until the sauce boils and thickens. Stir through the spring onion and coriander leaves.

NUTRITION PER SERVE
Protein 38 g; Fat 7.5 g; Carbohydrate 19 g; Dietary Fibre 1.5 g; Cholesterol 243 mg; 1240 kJ (295 cal)

NOTE: When buying live mussels make sure they are fresh. Live mussels will have tightly closed shells—some may be slightly opened. Give the shells a tap and if they close this will indicate that they are still alive. Discard any with broken or cracked shells. Always buy extra to allow for the ones that are cracked or do not open during cooking.

Mash together the black beans, ginger, garlic, sugar, oyster and soy sauce.

Stir-fry the mussels for 3–5 minutes, or until they open. Discard any that don't open.

Add the cornflour mixture to the wok and bring to the boil until the sauce thickens.

WARM PRAWN AND SCALLOP SALAD

Preparation time: 30 minutes
Total cooking time: 15 minutes
Serves 4

2 teaspoons five-spice powder
1–2 small red chillies, chopped
2–3 cloves garlic, crushed
2 teaspoons sesame oil
oil, for cooking
24 raw prawns, peeled and deveined,
    tails intact
20 scallops, cleaned
200 g (6¹/₂ oz) asparagus, cut into
    short lengths
150 g (5 oz) snow peas
125 g (4 oz) rocket leaves
2 tablespoons light soy sauce
2 tablespoons lemon juice
1 tablespoon mirin
1 tablespoon honey
6 spring onions, chopped
¹/₃ cup (20 g/³/₄ oz) chopped
    coriander leaves
1 tablespoon sesame seeds, toasted

1 Mix the five-spice powder, chilli, garlic, sesame oil and 2 tablespoons cooking oil in a large glass bowl. Add the prawns and scallops and toss to coat. Cover and refrigerate for at least 10 minutes.

2 Blanch the asparagus and snow peas briefly in a pan of boiling water. Drain and plunge into a bowl of iced water, then drain again. Tear the rocket leaves if they are too big. Arrange the asparagus, snow peas and rocket on four serving plates.

3 Put the soy sauce, lemon juice, mirin, honey and 1 tablespoon oil in a small bowl. Stir to combine.

4 Heat the wok until very hot and stir-fry the prawns, scallops and spring onion over high heat in three or four batches for 3–4 minutes, or until cooked through. Remove from the wok and set aside.

5 Add the sauce and coriander to the wok and bring to the boil. Cook over high heat for 1–2 minutes. Return the seafood to the wok and toss well. Sprinkle with sesame seeds to serve.

NUTRITION PER SERVE
Protein 35 g; Fat 20 g; Carbohydrate 10 g; Dietary Fibre 5 g; Cholesterol 170 mg; 1515 kJ (360 cal)

Peel the prawns, leaving the tails intact, and pull out the dark veins.

Slice or pull off any vein, membrane or hard white muscle from the scallops.

BALINESE CHILLI SQUID

Preparation time: 30 minutes
Total cooking time: 15 minutes
Serves 4

750 g (1¹/₂ lb) squid tubes
¹/₄ cup (60 ml/2 fl oz) lime juice
3 tablespoons vegetable oil
1 large red chilli, seeded and sliced
3 spring onions, sliced
1 tablespoon tamarind concentrate
1 stem lemon grass, white part only,
    finely sliced
1 cup (250 ml/8 fl oz) chicken stock
5 Thai basil leaves, shredded

SPICE PASTE
2 large red chillies, seeded and
    chopped
2 cloves garlic, chopped
2 cm (³/₄ inch) piece fresh ginger,
    chopped
2 cm (³/₄ inch) piece fresh turmeric,
    chopped
3 spring onions, chopped
1 tomato, peeled, seeded and
    chopped
2 teaspoons coriander seeds
1 teaspoon dried shrimp paste

1 Cut the squid into large pieces and score the tender flesh. Place in a bowl with the lime juice and season well.
2 To make the spice paste, grind the chilli, garlic, ginger, turmeric, spring onion, tomato, coriander and shrimp paste in a food processor.
3 Heat 2 tablespoons of the oil in a wok. Cook the squid, chilli and spring onion in batches for 2 minutes over high heat—don't overcook the squid. Remove from the wok.
4 Heat the remaining oil and add the spice paste, tamarind concentrate and lemon grass. Cook, stirring, over medium heat for 5 minutes.
5 Return the squid to the wok and add the stock. Season with pepper and add the basil. Bring to the boil, then reduce the heat and simmer for 2 minutes. Serve immediately.

NUTRITION PER SERVE
Protein 35 g; Fat 15 g; Carbohydrate 3 g;
Dietary Fibre 2 g; Cholesterol 375 mg;
1245 kJ (295 cal)

Remove the hot seeds from the fresh red chillies, before slicing with a sharp knife.

Cut the squid into large pieces and score the tender flesh.

After adding the lime juice, season the squid pieces well with salt and pepper.

Cook the squid in batches for 2 minutes over high heat—don't overcook or it will toughen.

FRIED CLAMS IN ROASTED CHILLI PASTE

Preparation time: 15 minutes
Total cooking time: 15 minutes
Serves 4

ROASTED CHILLI PASTE
2 tablespoons vegetable oil
2 spring onions, sliced
2 cloves garlic, sliced
1/4 cup (85 g/2³/4 oz) small dried
    shrimps
6 small red chillies, seeded
2 teaspoons palm sugar
2 teaspoons fish sauce

2 teaspoons tamarind concentrate
pinch of salt

3 cloves garlic, finely sliced
3 small red chillies, seeded and sliced
1 tablespoon light soy sauce
1 cup (250 ml/8 fl oz) chicken stock
1 kg (2 lb) clams, scrubbed
1/2 cup (15 g/1/2 oz) Thai basil leaves

1 To make the roasted chilli paste, heat the oil in a wok and fry the spring onion, garlic, shrimps and chilli until golden brown. Remove with a slotted spoon and reserve the oil.
2 Place the spring onion, garlic, shrimps, chilli and sugar in a mortar and pestle or small food processor and grind until well blended. Add the fish sauce, tamarind and salt. Blend or grind to a finely textured paste.
3 Heat the reserved oil in a wok. Add the garlic, chilli, roasted chilli paste and soy sauce. Mix well, then add the chicken stock and bring just to the boil. Add the clams and cook over medium-high heat for 2–3 minutes. Discard any unopened clams. Stir in the basil and serve immediately.

NUTRITION PER SERVE
Protein 30 g; Fat 15 g; Carbohydrate 90 g;
Dietary Fibre 5 g; Cholesterol 280 mg;
2490 kJ (700 cal)

Use a slotted spoon to remove the onion, garlic, shrimps and chillies from the wok.

Blend or grind the mixture to obtain a finely textured paste.

Remove any clams that have not opened during the cooking time.

BLACK BEAN SCALLOPS IN GINGER CHILLI OIL

Preparation time: 10–15 minutes
Total cooking time: 8 minutes
Serves 4

GINGER CHILLI OIL
1/3 cup (80 ml/2 3/4 fl oz) peanut oil
3 dried red chillies, crushed
2.5 cm (1 inch) piece fresh ginger, grated
1 clove garlic, thinly sliced
1 tablespoon sesame oil
1 tablespoon soy sauce

2 tablespoons peanut oil
2.5 cm (1 inch) piece fresh ginger, cut into paper-thin strips
1 kg (2 lb) scallops, cleaned
2 tablespoons salted black beans, rinsed well
1/4 cup (60 ml/2 fl oz) dry sherry
1 red capsicum, cut into strips
90 g (3 oz) baby English spinach leaves

1 To make the ginger chilli oil, heat the peanut oil, chilli, ginger and garlic in a pan over medium heat, stirring constantly, for 2 minutes, or until the mixture begins to sizzle. Add the sesame oil and soy sauce and cook for

2 minutes. Cool slightly, then strain.
2 Heat the peanut oil in a wok over very high heat. Add the ginger; stir for a few seconds then cook the scallops in small batches, tossing frequently.
3 Stir-fry the black beans, sherry and capsicum for 1–2 minutes, then return the scallops to the pan to warm through. Remove from the heat and arrange the scallops on top of the spinach leaves. Drizzle with the ginger chilli oil and serve immediately.

NUTRITION PER SERVE
Protein 35 g; Fat 35 g; Carbohydrate 5 g;
Dietary Fibre 5 g; Cholesterol 80 mg;
2035 kJ (485 cal)

Allow the ginger chilli oil to cool slightly, then strain into a bowl and set aside.

Cook the scallops in batches over high heat, tossing them frequently.

Stir-fry the black beans, sherry and capsicum together for 1–2 minutes.

FRIED KOREAN NOODLES WITH PRAWNS

Preparation time: 30 minutes
Total cooking time: 25 minutes
Serves 4

3 tablespoons sesame seeds
2 tablespoons oil
2 teaspoons sesame oil
4 spring onions, chopped
2 cloves garlic, finely chopped
150 g (5 oz) peeled raw prawns
2 teaspoons finely chopped red
   chillies
150 g (5 oz) firm tofu, diced

100 g (3½ oz) button mushrooms,
   thinly sliced
1 red capsicum, cut into thin strips
2 tablespoons shoshoyu
2 teaspoons sugar
300 g (10 oz) packet Hokkien noodles

1 Dry-fry the sesame seeds over low heat for 3–4 minutes until golden. Cool and then grind in a mortar and pestle.
2 Combine the oils. Heat half the oil in the wok over medium-high heat. Stir-fry the spring onion, garlic and prawn meat for 1 minute. Add the chilli and cook for another minute. Remove from the wok.
3 Add the tofu to the wok and stir-fry until lightly golden, then remove. Add the remaining oil to the wok, add the mushrooms and capsicum and stir-fry for 3 minutes or until just crisp.
4 Add the shoshoyu, sugar, noodles and 2 tablespoons water to the wok. Toss gently to separate and coat the noodles in liquid. Cover and steam for 5 minutes. Add the prawn mixture and tofu and toss for 3 minutes over medium heat. Sprinkle with the crushed sesame seeds and serve.

NUTRITION PER SERVE
Protein 20 g; Fat 25 g; Carbohydrate 55 g;
Dietary Fibre 5 g; Cholesterol 70 mg;
2020 kJ (480 cal)

Stir-fry the onion, garlic and prawn meat for a minute and then add the chilli.

Stir-fry the tofu, tossing occasionally, until lightly golden. Remove and set aside.

Add the shoshoyu, sugar, noodles and water to the wok and toss gently.

VIETNAMESE PRAWNS WITH SNAKE BEANS

Preparation time: 25 minutes
Total cooking time: 15 minutes
Serves 4

2 tablespoons oil
2 onions, very finely sliced
5 cloves garlic, finely chopped
2 stems lemon grass, white part only, very finely sliced
3 red chillies, seeded and finely sliced
250 g (8 oz) snake beans, topped and tailed and cut into short pieces

300 g (10 oz) raw prawns, peeled and deveined
2 teaspoons sugar
1 tablespoon fish sauce
1 tablespoon rice wine vinegar
garlic chives, to garnish

1 Heat the oil in a large wok. Add the onion, garlic, lemon grass and chilli and stir-fry over medium-high heat for 4 minutes or until soft and golden.
2 Add the beans to the wok and stir-fry for 2–3 minutes or until bright green. Add the prawns and sugar and toss gently for 3 minutes.
3 Season with the fish sauce and rice wine vinegar, toss well and serve, sprinkled with garlic chives.

NUTRITION PER SERVE
Protein 18 g; Fat 10 g; Carbohydrate 4 g; Dietary Fibre 2.5 g; Cholesterol 112 mg; 765 kJ (183 cal)

NOTE: Snake beans are very long, dark green beans, about 30 cm (12 inches) long, with pointed tips. They are sold in bunches at speciality fruit and vegetable and Asian food stores. If they are not available, green beans can be used.

Top and tail the snake beans and then cut them into short pieces.

Stir-fry the onion, garlic, lemon grass and chilli in the wok.

Add the chopped snake beans to the wok and stir-fry until they are bright green.

BEAN VERMICELLI AND CRAB MEAT

Preparation time: 20 minutes
+ 20 minutes soaking
Total cooking time: 15 minutes
Serves 4

200 g (6¹/₂ oz) dried mung bean
   vermicelli (cellophane noodles)
2 tablespoons oil
10 Asian shallots, very finely sliced
3 cloves garlic, finely chopped
2 stems lemon grass, white part only,
   very finely sliced

1 red capsicum, cut into matchsticks
170 g (5¹/₂ oz) can crab meat, well-
   drained
2 tablespoons fish sauce
2 tablespoons lime juice
2 teaspoons sugar
3 spring onions, finely sliced

1 Soak the noodles in boiling water
for 20 minutes or until softened. Drain
and cut into shorter lengths.
2 Heat the oil in a wok over high
heat. Add the Asian shallots, garlic
and lemon grass and stir-fry for
2–3 minutes. Add the capsicum and
cook for 30 seconds, tossing well. Add

the noodles and toss. Cover and steam
for 1 minute, or until the noodles are
heated through.
3 Add the crab meat, fish sauce, lime
juice and sugar and toss well. Season
with salt and pepper, sprinkle with
spring onion and serve.

NUTRITION PER SERVE
Protein 8 g; Fat 10 g; Carbohydrate 16 g;
Dietary Fibre 1.5 g; Cholesterol 35 mg;
790 kJ (190 cal)

HINT: Fresh crab meat is excellent for
this recipe. Some fishmongers sell
fresh crab meat in vacuum packs.

Finely slice the white section of the fresh lemon
grass, using a sharp knife.

Snip the noodles several times with kitchen
scissors, to make them easier to eat.

Add the noodles to the wok, toss and steam,
covered, for 1 minute.

MALAY FISH CURRY

Preparation time: 25 minutes
Total cooking time: 25 minutes
Serves 4

3–6 red chillies, to taste
1 onion, chopped
4 cloves garlic
3 stems lemon grass, white part only, sliced
5 cm (2 inch) piece fresh ginger, sliced
2 teaspoons shrimp paste
1/4 cup (60 ml/2 fl oz) oil
1 tablespoon fish curry powder (see NOTE)
1 cup (250 ml/8 fl oz) coconut milk

1 tablespoon tamarind concentrate
1 tablespoon kecap manis
350 g (11 oz) firm white fish fillets, cut into bite-sized pieces
2 ripe tomatoes, chopped
1 tablespoon lemon juice

1 Combine the chillies, onion, garlic, lemon grass, ginger and shrimp paste in a small food processor and process until roughly chopped. Add 2 tablespoons of oil and process to a smooth paste.

2 Heat the remaining oil in a wok and add the paste. Cook for 3–4 minutes over low heat, stirring constantly until very fragrant. Add the curry powder and stir for another 2 minutes. Add the coconut milk, tamarind, kecap manis and 1 cup (250 ml/8 fl oz) water to the wok. Bring to the boil, stirring occasionally, then reduce the heat and simmer for 10 minutes.

3 Add the fish, tomato and lemon juice and season well. Simmer for 5 minutes or until the fish is just cooked. Serve immediately.

NUTRITION PER SERVE
Protein 22 g; Fat 30 g; Carbohydrate 6.5 g; Dietary Fibre 4 g; Cholesterol 65 mg; 1600 kJ (382 cal)

NOTE: Fish curry powder is a blend of spices suited to seafood flavours. It is available from Asian food stores.

Process the ingredients to make a smooth paste, then stir-fry over low heat for 3–4 minutes.

Add the coconut milk to the paste and simmer the sauce for 10 minutes, stirring occasionally.

Add the fish, tomato and lemon juice and season with salt and pepper.

CURRIED LOBSTER WITH CAPSICUM

Preparation time: 25 minutes
Total cooking time: 15 minutes
Serves 4

2 raw lobster tails
1 tablespoon oil
1–2 tablespoons red curry paste
  (use the recipe on page 246 or
  ready-made paste)
2 stems lemon grass, white part only,
  finely chopped
1 red capsicum, roughly chopped
1 cup (250 ml/8 fl oz) coconut milk
6 dried Chinese black dates
  (see NOTE)
1 tablespoon fish sauce
2 teaspoons soft brown sugar
1 teaspoon grated lime rind
1/2 cup (15 g/1/2 oz) coriander leaves

1 To remove the meat from the lobster, cut down the centre of each lobster tail on the underside. Pull away the shell, remove the flesh and cut into bite-sized pieces.

2 Heat the oil in a wok and swirl to coat the base and side. Add the curry paste and lemon grass and stir-fry for 1 minute over medium heat. Add the lobster pieces a few at a time and stir-fry each batch for 2 minutes, just until golden brown. Remove from the wok.

3 Add the capsicum to the wok and stir-fry for 30 seconds. Add the coconut milk and dates, bring to the boil and cook for 5 minutes or until the dates are plump.

4 Add the fish sauce, brown sugar and lime rind to the curry. Return the lobster to the wok to heat through. Serve immediately, sprinkled with coriander leaves.

NUTRITION PER SERVE
Protein 28 g; Fat 13 g; Carbohydrate 9 g;
Dietary Fibre 1.2 g; Cholesterol 136 mg;
1075 kJ (255 cal)

NOTE: You can buy dried dates from Chinese food stores.

Use kitchen scissors to cut down the centre of the lobster tails on the underside.

Stir-fry the lobster pieces in batches for 2 minutes or until golden brown.

Cook the mixture for about 5 minutes, until the dried Chinese dates have plumped up.

FISH FILLETS IN COCONUT MILK

Preparation time: 10 minutes
Total cooking time: 15 minutes
Serves 4

2 long green chillies
2 small red chillies
2 stems lemon grass, white part only
2 coriander roots
4 kaffir lime leaves
2.5 cm (1 inch) piece fresh ginger, thinly sliced
2 cloves garlic, crushed
3 spring onions, finely sliced
1 teaspoon soft brown sugar
1 cup (250 ml/8 fl oz) coconut milk
400 g (13 oz) firm white fish fillets, cut into bite-sized pieces
1/2 cup (125 ml/4 fl oz) coconut cream
1 tablespoon fish sauce
2–3 tablespoons lime juice

1 Heat a wok until hot, then add the whole chillies and roast until just beginning to brown. Remove from the wok, cool and slice.
2 Bruise the lemon grass and coriander roots by crushing them with the flat side of a knife.
3 Add the lemon grass, coriander roots, kaffir lime leaves, ginger, garlic, spring onion, sugar and coconut milk to the wok. Stir and bring to the boil. Reduce the heat and simmer for 2 minutes. Add the fish pieces and simmer gently for 2–3 minutes or until the fish is tender. Stir in the coconut cream.
4 Stir through the chopped green and red chillies, fish sauce, salt and lime juice, to taste and serve immediately.

NUTRITION PER SERVE
Protein 23 g; Fat 22 g; Carbohydrate 6.5 g; Dietary Fibre 2.5 g; Cholesterol 70 mg; 1323 kJ (316 cal)

Roast the whole chillies in a hot wok until they begin to brown.

Bruise the lemon grass and coriander roots by crushing them with the flat side of a knife.

Add the fish pieces to the wok and simmer gently for 2–3 minutes.

Just before serving, stir in the chillies, fish sauce, salt and lime juice.

FISH CUTLETS IN SPICY RED SAUCE

Preparation time: 10 minutes
Total cooking time: 35 minutes
Serves 4

1 tablespoon oil
2 onions, finely chopped
4 ripe tomatoes, peeled and chopped
1 tablespoon sambal oelek
1 tablespoon soft brown sugar
4 blue-eyed cod cutlets or other firm
  fish cutlets

2 tablespoons fish sauce
2 tablespoons rice vinegar or white
  vinegar
2 tablespooons chopped coriander

1 Heat the oil in a wok or large frying pan and add the onion. Cook over medium heat for 2 minutes or until soft but not browned. Add the tomatoes, sambal oelek, brown sugar and 3 tablespoons of water. Bring to the boil, then reduce the heat, cover the wok and simmer for 20 minutes or until the sauce is thick.

2 Add the fish cutlets to the wok and

spoon some sauce over them. Cover the wok and cook for 3–5 minutes. Turn the fish to cook the other side. (If the wok isn't big enough you can cook the fish in two batches.)

3 Remove the fish from the wok. Add the fish sauce, vinegar and chopped coriander to the sauce in the wok and stir well before spooning the sauce over the fish.

NUTRITION PER SERVE
Protein 20 g; Fat 7 g; Carbohydrate 9 g;
Dietary Fibre 2 g; Cholesterol 55 mg;
734 kJ (175 cal)

Add the chopped tomatoes, sambal oelek, brown sugar and water to the wok.

Place the fish cutlets in the wok, in batches if necessary, and spoon some sauce over.

Transfer the fish to serving plates and add the fish sauce, vinegar and coriander to the wok.

PRAWN OMELETTE

Preparation time: 15 minutes
Total cooking time: 15 minutes
Serves 2–4

2 tablespoons oil
3 cloves garlic, chopped
2 stems lemon grass, white part only,
    finely chopped
2 coriander roots, finely chopped
1–2 teaspoons chopped red chillies
500 g (1 lb) small raw prawns, peeled
3 spring onions, chopped
1/2 teaspoon black pepper
1 1/2 tablespoons fish sauce

2 teaspoons soft brown sugar
4 eggs
chilli sauce (see page 248), for serving

1 Heat half the oil in a wok. Add the garlic, lemon grass, coriander root and chilli and stir-fry for 20 seconds. Add the prawns and stir-fry until they change colour. Add the spring onions, pepper, 1 tablespoon fish sauce and brown sugar; toss well and remove.
2 Beat the eggs, remaining fish sauce and 2 tablespoons water until foamy. Add the remaining oil to the wok and swirl around to coat the side. Heat the wok and, when it is very hot, pour in the egg mixture and swirl around the

wok. Allow the mixture to set underneath, frequently lifting the edge once set, and tilting the wok a little to let the unset mixture run underneath. Repeat until the omelette is nearly set.
3 Place three-quarters of the prawn mixture in the centre of the omelette and fold in the sides to make a square (or simply fold the omelette in half). Slide onto a serving plate and place the remaining prawn mixture on top. Serve with chilli sauce.

NUTRITION PER SERVE (4)
Protein 30 g; Fat 10 g; Carbohydrate 3 g; Dietary Fibre 1 g; Cholesterol 320 mg; 925 kJ (220 cal)

Add the chopped spring onions, pepper, fish sauce and brown sugar to the prawns.

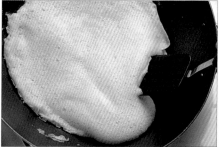
Tilt the wok and lift the edge of the omelette to let the unset mixture run underneath.

Fold the sides of the omelette over the filling to form a square.

PRAWNS IN SOURED LIME COCONUT SAUCE

Preparation time: 20 minutes
Total cooking time: 30 minutes
Serves 4

1 teaspoon shrimp paste
1 cup (250 ml/8 fl oz) coconut milk
2 stems lemon grass, white part only, finely chopped
2–4 kaffir lime leaves
2 teaspoons chopped red chillies
2 tablespoons tamarind purée
2 teaspoons fish sauce

1 teaspoon soft brown sugar
500 g (1 lb) raw prawns, peeled and deveined, tails intact
3 tablespoons shredded coconut, toasted
rind of 2 limes

1 Place the shrimp paste on a small piece of foil; fold one side over and then fold into a parcel. Cook under a hot grill for 2 minutes each side.
2 Mix the coconut milk with 1 cup (250 ml/8 fl oz) water in a wok and heat until just boiling. Add the lemon grass, kaffir lime leaves and chilli, reduce the heat and simmer for

7 minutes. Add the tamarind purée, fish sauce, shrimp paste and brown sugar and simmer for 8 minutes.
3 Add the prawns to the sauce and cook for 5 minutes or until pink. Sprinkle with coconut and shreds of lime rind just before serving.

NUTRITION PER SERVE
Protein 27 g; Fat 17 g; Carbohydrate 4 g;
Dietary Fibre 2 g; Cholesterol 188 mg;
1145 kJ (274 cal)

NOTE: Shrimp paste is roasted to develop the flavour, essential for this dish. The aroma may be unpleasant.

Place the shrimp paste on a small piece of foil and then fold to make a parcel.

Stir in the lemon grass, kaffir lime leaves and chilli, then reduce the heat and simmer.

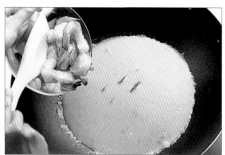
Add the prawns to the sauce and cook until the prawns turn pink.

SCALLOPS AND FISH IN GINGER AND LIME

Preparation time: 15 minutes
Total cooking time: 15 minutes
Serves 4

500 g (1 lb) firm white fish fillets
350 g (12 oz) scallops
2 tablespoons oil
5 cm (2 inch) piece fresh ginger, grated
3 spring onions, chopped
1 tablespoon lime juice
2 tablespoons chilli jam
2 teaspoons finely grated lime rind
3 tablespoons coriander leaves

1 Cut the fish into bite-sized pieces and remove any black veins from the scallops. Heat half the oil in a wok and stir-fry the ginger and spring onions for 30 seconds. Remove from the wok.
2 Reheat the wok and, when it is very hot, add the remaining oil. Add the fish and scallops in three batches and stir-fry for 2–3 minutes. Remove from the wok and set aside.
3 Add the lime juice, chilli jam, lime rind and 2 tablespoons water to the wok and bring to the boil, stirring. Return the fish, scallops, and onion mixture to the wok, tossing gently with the sauce. Serve immediately sprinkled with coriander leaves.

NUTRITION PER SERVE
Protein 37 g; Fat 14 g; Carbohydrate 3 g; Dietary Fibre 0 g; Cholesterol 116 mg; 1185 kJ (283 cal)

NOTE: Seafood should be stir-fried in a very hot wok, but don't cook it for too long or it will become tough.

Pull away any of the large black veins from the scallops.

Stir-fry the fish and scallops in three batches, then remove from the wok.

Return the seafood to the wok and toss gently through the sauce.

PRAWN FRIED RICE

Preparation time: 20 minutes
Total cooking time: 15 minutes
Serves 6

oil, for cooking
4 egg whites, lightly beaten
2 cloves garlic, crushed
350 g (12 oz) raw prawns, peeled,
    deveined and halved lengthways
100 g (3¹/₂ oz) cooked chicken,
    shredded
¹/₂ cup (80 g/2³/₄ oz) frozen peas
180 g (6 oz) sliced ham, cut into small
    strips
1 red capsicum, diced

4 spring onions, sliced
4 cups (750 g/1¹/₂ lb) cooked white
    and wild rice blend (see HINT)
1¹/₂ tablespoons soy sauce
3 teaspoons fish sauce
1¹/₂ teaspoons soft brown sugar

1 Heat 2 teaspoons of the oil in a wok
and pour in the egg white. Cook over
low heat, stirring until the egg is just
cooked and slightly scrambled, then
remove and set aside.
2 Reheat the wok, add a little more oil
and stir-fry the garlic, prawns,
chicken, peas, ham and capsicum for
3–4 minutes, or until the prawns are
cooked through.
3 Add the spring onion, rice, soy and

fish sauces and sugar and toss for
30 seconds, or until heated through.
Add the egg, toss lightly and serve.

NUTRITION PER SERVE
Protein 35 g; Fat 3 g; Carbohydrate 105 g;
Dietary Fibre 4 g; Cholesterol 120 mg;
2500 kJ (600 cal)

HINT: You will need to cook 1¹/₃ cups
(260 g/8 oz) rice to get 4 cupfuls. For
fried rice it is best to steam or boil your
rice a day in advance and leave it in
the fridge overnight. This allows the
grains to separate.

Stir the egg white over low heat until just cooked
and slightly scrambled.

When the prawns are cooked through, add the
spring onion, rice, sauces and sugar.

Stir-fry the garlic, prawns, chicken, peas, ham
and capsicum.

CHINESE NOODLES WITH PRAWNS AND PORK

Preparation time: 20 minutes
Total cooking time: 10 minutes
Serves 4

500 g (1 lb) Hokkien noodles,
    gently pulled apart
3 tablespoons peanut oil
2 teaspoons finely chopped garlic
10 large cooked prawns,
    peeled and deveined
200 g (6¹/₂ oz) roast or Chinese
    barbecued pork, thinly sliced
1 tablespoon black bean sauce
1 tablespoon soy sauce
1 tablespoon chilli and ginger sauce
1 tablespoon white vinegar
3 tablespoons chicken stock
125 g (4 oz) bean sprouts,
    tails removed
3 spring onions, finely sliced
¹/₄ cup (15 g/¹/₂ oz) chopped
    coriander

1 Cover the noodles with boiling water and stir with a fork to separate them. Leave for a couple of minutes to soften, then drain.

2 Heat a wok, add the oil and place over medium heat, swirling gently to coat the base and side of the wok with oil. Add the garlic and stir-fry until pale gold. Add the prawns and pork and stir-fry for 1 minute.

3 Add the noodles to the wok with the sauces, vinegar and stock. Stir-fry over high heat until the mixture has heated through and the sauce has been absorbed into the noodles.

4 Add the bean sprouts and the spring onion and cook for 1 minute. Serve immediately, sprinkled with coriander.

NUTRITION PER SERVE
Protein 26 g; Fat 18 g; Carbohydrate 30 g; Dietary Fibre 2 g; Cholesterol 82 mg; 1600 kJ (382 cal)

VARIATION: Fresh, thick, egg and wheat noodles (hokkien mee) are ideal for Chinese stir-fries. They require just a couple of minutes in boiling water to soften them before use. If Hokkien noodles are unavailable, you can use thick spaghetti, cooked first in plenty of boiling water until tender.

NOTE: Chinese barbecued pork can be bought from Chinese supermarkets and groceries.

The noodles need just a couple of minutes in hot water to soften them.

Stir-fry the garlic, then add the pork and prawns and cook for 1 minute.

Add the bean sprouts and spring onion to the wok and cook for 1 minute.

SICHUAN PRAWNS WITH HOKKIEN NOODLES

Preparation time: 20 minutes
Total cooking time: 15 minutes
Serves 4

500 g (1 lb) Hokkien noodles
2 tablespoons oil
2 cloves garlic, sliced
1 onion, cut into thin wedges
1 tablespoon Sichuan
    peppercorns, crushed
1 stem lemon grass, white part only,
    finely chopped
300 g (10 oz) green beans, cut into
    short lengths
750 g (1¹/₂ lb) large raw prawns,
    peeled, deveined, halved
    lengthways
2 tablespoons fish sauce
¹/₃ cup (80 ml/2³/₄ fl oz) oyster
    sauce
¹/₂ cup (125 ml/4 fl oz) chicken stock

1 Cover the noodles with boiling water and stir with a fork to separate them. Leave for a couple of minutes to soften, then drain.

2 Heat a wok until very hot, add 1 tablespoon oil and swirl to coat the base and side of the wok with oil. Add the garlic, onion, peppercorns and lemon grass and stir-fry for 2 minutes. Add the beans and stir-fry for 2–3 minutes, or until the beans are tender. Remove the bean and onion mixture from the wok.

3 Reheat the wok, add the remaining oil and swirl to coat the base and side of the wok. Add the prawns and stir-fry for 3–4 minutes, or until just cooked through. Add the bean and onion mixture and the noodles and stir-fry for 3 minutes, or until the noodles are heated through. Add the sauces and stock and bring to the boil. Toss well and serve.

NUTRITION PER SERVE
Protein 57 g; Fat 13 g; Carbohydrate 92 g; Dietary Fibre 6 g; Cholesterol 300 mg; 3013 kJ (720 cal)

NOTE: Hokkien noodles are also known as Fukkien or Singapore noodles. They are thick, yellow and rubbery in texture. Hokkien noodles are made from wheat flour and are cooked and lightly oiled before being packaged for sale.

Peel and devein the prawns, then cut them in half lengthways.

Cover the noodles with boiling water and stir them with a fork to separate them.

Add the beans and stir-fry for 2–3 minutes, or until they are tender.

SCALLOPS WITH BLACK BEAN SAUCE

Preparation time: 15 minutes
Total cooking time: 10 minutes
Serves 4–6

600 g (1¼ lb) large scallops, without roe
2 tablespoons cornflour
⅓ cup (80 ml/2¾ fl oz) peanut oil, plus 1 teaspoon, extra
3 spring onions, cut into short lengths
1 teaspoon finely chopped fresh ginger
2 cloves garlic, crushed
¼ cup (60 g/2 oz) salted black beans, rinsed, roughly chopped
2 tablespoons Chinese rice wine
1 tablespoon rice wine vinegar
1 tablespoon soy sauce
1 teaspoon soft brown sugar
½ teaspoon sesame oil

1 Remove and discard any veins, membrane or hard muscle from the scallops. Toss in the cornflour to coat. Shake off any excess.
2 Heat a wok until very hot, add 1 teaspoon peanut oil and swirl to coat. Add the spring onion and stir-fry for 30 seconds, then remove from the wok.
3 Add 1 tablespoon peanut oil to the hot wok and swirl to coat. Add one third of the scallops and stir-fry for 1–2 minutes, or until golden and well sealed—no liquid should be released.

Remove and set aside. Repeat twice more to seal the rest of the scallops.
4 Add the remaining tablespoon of peanut oil to the hot wok and swirl to coat. Add the ginger, garlic, black beans, rice wine, rice vinegar, soy sauce and brown sugar, and stir-fry for 1 minute, or until the sauce boils and thickens slightly.
5 Return the scallops to the wok and stir-fry for 1 minute, or until heated through and the sauce has thickened again. Stir in the spring onion and sesame oil and serve immediately.

NUTRITION PER SERVE (6)
Protein 15 g; Fat 15 g; Carbohydrate 7 g;
Dietary Fibre 2 g; Cholesterol 33 mg;
917 kJ (220 cal)

Rinse the black beans under running water, then roughly chop them.

Stir-fry the scallops for a couple of minutes until they are golden and well sealed.

Stir-fry the sauce for 1 minute, or until it comes to the boil and thickens slightly.

LEMON GRASS PRAWNS

Preparation time: 30 minutes
Total cooking time: 10 minutes
Serves 4

1 tablespoon peanut oil
2 cloves garlic, crushed
1 tablespoon finely grated fresh ginger
2 tablespoons finely chopped lemon
    grass, white part only
8 spring onions, cut into short lengths
1 kg (2 lb) raw prawns, peeled,
    deveined, tails intact

2 tablespoons lime juice
1 tablespoon soft brown sugar
2 teaspoons fish sauce
1/4 cup (60 ml/2 fl oz) chicken stock
1 teaspoon cornflour
500 g (1 lb) baby bok choy, cut in half
    lengthways
1/4 cup (15 g/1/2 oz) chopped mint

1 Heat a wok until very hot, add the oil and swirl to coat. Add the garlic, ginger, lemon grass and spring onion, and stir-fry for 1 minute, or until fragrant. Add the prawns and stir-fry for 2 minutes.

2 Place the lime juice, sugar, fish sauce, chicken stock and cornflour in a small bowl. Mix well, then add to the wok and stir until the sauce boils and thickens. Cook for a further 1–2 minutes, or until the prawns are pink and just tender.

3 Add the bok choy and stir-fry for 1 minute, or until wilted. Stir in the mint and serve.

NUTRITION PER SERVE
Protein 60 g; Fat 8.5 g; Carbohydrate 8 g;
Dietary Fibre 1.6 g; Cholesterol 373 mg;
1433 kJ (342 cal)

Peel the prawn bodies and heads, remove the dark veins, but leave the tail shells on.

Rinse the bok choy thoroughly and then slice in half down the middle.

Stir-fry the flavourings until they are fragrant, then add the prawns.

SWEET CHILLI SQUID

Preparation time: 20 minutes
Total cooking time: 10 minutes
Serves 4

750 g (1¹/₂ lb) squid tubes
1 tablespoon peanut oil
1 tablespoon finely grated fresh ginger
2 cloves garlic, crushed
8 spring onions, chopped
2 tablespoons sweet chilli sauce
2 tablespoons Chinese barbecue sauce

1 tablespoon soy sauce
550 g (1 lb 2 oz) bok choy, cut into short pieces
1 tablespoon chopped coriander leaves

1 Cut the squid tubes open, score diagonal slashes across the inside surface and cut into strips.
2 Heat a wok until very hot, add the oil and swirl to coat. Add the ginger, garlic, spring onion and squid and stir-fry for 3 minutes, or until browned.
3 Add the sauces and 2 tablespoons water to the wok and stir-fry for 2 minutes, or until the squid is just tender. Add the bok choy and coriander, and stir-fry for 1 minute, or until the bok choy is tender.

NUTRITION PER SERVE
Protein 40 g; Fat 8 g; Carbohydrate 4 g; Dietary Fibre 7.5 g; Cholesterol 375 mg; 1030 kJ (245 cal)

NOTE: Squid should be cooked at a very high temperature but quite quickly. If you cook it for too long it will toughen.

Rinse the bok choy thoroughly, then cut it into short pieces.

Score diagonal slashes across the inside surface of the squid tubes, then cut into strips.

Stir-fry the squid for 3 minutes. The score marks in the flesh will make it curl nicely.

PRAWN SALAD WITH KAFFIR LIME

Preparation time: 20 minutes
Total cooking time: 8 minutes
Serves 4

750 g (1½ lb) large raw prawns
1 tablespoon oil
4 spring onions, cut into short lengths
1 small red chilli, seeded, finely chopped
2 cloves garlic, sliced
2 kaffir lime leaves, finely shredded
3 teaspoons grated fresh ginger
3 teaspoons soft brown sugar
2 teaspoons soy sauce
2 tablespoons mirin
2 tablespoons lime juice
mixed lettuce leaves, to serve

1 Peel and devein the prawns, and cut in half lengthways. Heat a wok until very hot, add half the oil and swirl to coat. Add the prawns and stir-fry for 3 minutes, or until nearly cooked.
2 Add the spring onion, chilli, garlic, lime leaves and ginger. Stir-fry for 1–2 minutes, or until fragrant.
3 Combine the sugar, soy sauce, mirin and lime juice in a bowl, add to the wok and bring to the boil. Serve on the lettuce leaves.

NUTRITION PER SERVE
Protein 1 g; Fat 5 g; Carbohydrate 3.5 g;
Dietary Fibre 1 g; Cholesterol 2 mg;
263 kJ (63 cal)

Always shred kaffir lime leaves as finely as possible, or they can be tough.

Cut the prawns in half lengthways so they curl when you stir-fry them.

Mix together the sugar, soy sauce, mirin and lime juice and add to the wok.

CUCUMBER AND WHITE FISH STIR-FRY

Preparation time: 20 minutes
Total cooking time: 20 minutes
Serves 4

1/2 cup (60 g/2 oz) plain flour
1/2 cup (60 g/2 oz) cornflour
1/2 teaspoon Chinese five-spice
750 g (1 1/2 lb) firm white boneless fish
    fillets, such as ling, cut into cubes
2 egg whites, lightly beaten
oil, for deep-frying
1 tablespoon oil
1 onion, cut into wedges
1 telegraph cucumber, seeded, sliced

1 teaspoon cornflour, extra
3/4 teaspoon sesame oil
1 tablespoon soy sauce
1/3 cup (80 ml/2 3/4 fl oz) rice wine
    vinegar
1 1/2 tablespoons soft brown sugar
3 teaspoons fish sauce

1 Combine the flours and five-spice, and season. Dip the fish in the egg white, drain off any excess, then toss in the flour. Shake off any excess.
2 Fill a large saucepan one third full of oil and heat until a bread cube browns in 15 seconds. Cook the fish in batches for 6 minutes, or until golden brown. Drain and keep warm.
3 Heat a wok until very hot, add 1 tablespoon oil and swirl to coat. Add the onion and stir-fry for 1 minute. Add the cucumber and stir-fry for 30 seconds.
4 Blend the cornflour with 2 tablespoons water and add to the wok with the sesame oil, soy, vinegar, sugar and fish sauce. Stir-fry for 3 minutes, or until the mixture boils and thickens. Add the fish and toss to coat. Serve immediately.

NUTRITION PER SERVE
Protein 43 g; Fat 16 g; Carbohydrate 35 g; Dietary Fibre 1 g; Cholesterol 130 mg; 1990 kJ (475 cal)

Use boneless white fish fillets and cut them into bite-sized pieces.

Deep-fry the pieces of fish in oil, cooking in batches so the temperature stays high.

Stir-fry the mixture for 3 minutes, or until it boils and thickens, before adding the fish.

FISH WITH GINGER

Preparation time: 20 minutes
Total cooking time: 15 minutes
Serves 4

1 tablespoon peanut oil
1 small onion, finely sliced
3 teaspoons ground coriander
600 g (1¼ lb) boneless white fish
    fillets, such as perch, sliced

1 tablespoon julienned fresh ginger
1 teaspoon finely chopped and
    seeded green chilli
2 tablespoons lime juice
2 tablespoons coriander leaves

1 Heat a wok until very hot, add the oil and swirl to coat. Add the onion and stir-fry for 4 minutes, or until soft and golden. Add the ground coriander and cook for 1–2 minutes, or until the mixture is fragrant.

2 Add the fish, ginger and chilli, and stir-fry for 5–7 minutes, or until the fish is cooked through. Stir in the lime juice and season. Garnish with the coriander leaves and serve.

NUTRITION PER SERVE
Protein 30 g; Fat 9 g; Carbohydrate 1 g;
Dietary Fibre 0.4 g; Cholesterol 105 mg;
895 kJ (214 cal)

Peel the fresh ginger and then cut the flesh into julienne strips.

Stir-fry the onion for 4 minutes, or until it is soft and golden.

Add the fish, ginger and chilli to the wok and stir-fry until the fish is cooked through.

CALAMARI IN BLACK BEAN AND CHILLI SAUCE

Preparation time: 20 minutes
Total cooking time: 10 minutes
Serves 4

4 squid hoods
2 tablespoons oil
1 onion, cut into 8 wedges
1 red capsicum, sliced
115 g baby corn, halved
3 spring onions, cut into short lengths

BLACK BEAN SAUCE
3 teaspoons cornflour
2 tablespoons canned salted black
    beans, washed and drained
    (see NOTE)
2 small red chillies, chopped
2 cloves garlic, crushed
2 teaspoons grated fresh ginger
2 tablespoons oyster sauce
2 teaspoons soy sauce
1 teaspoons sugar

1 Open out each squid hood. Score the tender inner flesh into a diamond pattern. Then cut the squid into 5 cm (2 inch) squares.
2 To make the black bean sauce, mix the cornflour with 125 ml (4 fl oz) water until smooth. Mash the black beans with a fork, add the chilli, garlic, ginger, oyster and soy sauces, sugar and the cornflour mix and stir well.
3 Heat the oil in a wok and stir-fry the onion for 1 minute over high heat. Add the capsicum and corn and stir-fry for another 2 minutes.
4 Add the squid to the wok and stir-fry for 1–2 minutes, or until the flesh curls. Add the sauce and bring to the boil, stirring constantly until the sauce thickens. Stir in the spring onion.

NUTRITION PER SERVE
Protein 30 g; Fat 10 g; Carbohydrate 10 g;
Dietary Fibre 4 g; Cholesterol 180 mg;
1080 kJ (255 cal)

NOTE: Canned black beans can be bought from Asian food stores. Rinse them well before use.

Score a shallow diamond pattern over the tender squid flesh so that it curls when cooked.

Toss the squid in the wok with the capsicum and corn until the squid begins to curl.

Add the sauce to the wok and bring to the boil, stirring until the sauce thickens.

Tofu & Tempeh

TOFU WITH SHOSHOYU AND MIRIN

Preparation time: 20 minutes
  + 2 hours marinating
Total cooking time: 20 minutes
Serves 4

500 g (1 lb) firm tofu (see HINT), cut
  into small cubes
1/3 cup (80 ml/2 3/4 fl oz) shoshoyu
  (Japanese soy sauce)
1/4 cup (60 ml/2 fl oz) mirin
3 cloves garlic, finely chopped
2 tablespoons finely chopped fresh
  ginger
oil, for cooking
1 onion, thinly sliced
2 carrots, cut into batons
1 red capsicum, thinly sliced
150 g (5 oz) snow peas, thinly sliced

1 Combine the tofu with the
shoshoyu, mirin, garlic and ginger in a
glass or ceramic bowl. Cover and
refrigerate for 2 hours.
2 Heat the wok until very hot, add
1 tablespoon of the oil and swirl it
around to coat the side. Drain the tofu,
reserving the marinade. Stir-fry the
tofu in three batches over high heat
until it is golden brown. Heat
1 tablespoon of the oil between
batches. Remove all the tofu from the
wok and drain on paper towels.
3 Reheat the wok, add 1 tablespoon
of the oil and stir-fry the onion, carrot
and capsicum over medium-high
heat for 3–4 minutes, or until the
vegetables are tender. Add the snow
peas and cook for 3 minutes.
4 Increase the heat to high and add
the reserved marinade, tossing the
vegetables in the marinade until they
are thoroughly coated and the sauce
boils. Return the tofu to the wok and
toss until the mixture is well combined
and the tofu is heated through. Season
well with salt and pepper, and serve
immediately.

NUTRITION PER SERVE
Protein 15 g; Fat 15 g; Carbohydrate 9 g;
Dietary Fibre 4 g; Cholesterol 0 mg;
930 kJ (220 cal)

HINT: Tofu does not have a strong
flavour of its own but takes on flavour
from whatever it is mixed with.
Choose the firmest tofu you can find
for this recipe. Tempeh could
also be used.

Buy the firmest tofu you can find, drain it and cut
into bite-sized cubes.

Combine the tofu, shoshoyu, mirin, garlic and
ginger in a bowl and leave to marinate.

TOFU WITH ORANGE AND FRESH PINEAPPLE

Preparation time: 35 minutes
Total cooking time: 10 minutes
Serves 4

250 g (8 oz) firm tofu, cut into small
    cubes
5 cm (2 inch) piece fresh ginger,
    grated
2 teaspoons finely grated orange rind
oil, for cooking
2 large onions, cut into thin
    wedges
3 cloves garlic, finely chopped
2 teaspoons soft brown sugar
2 teaspoons white vinegar

250 g (8 oz) fresh pineapple, cut into
    bite-sized pieces
1 tablespoon orange juice

1 Combine the tofu, ginger, orange
rind and some freshly ground black
pepper in a glass or ceramic bowl,
mixing well. Cover and refrigerate.
2 Heat the wok until very hot, add
1¹/2 tablespoons of the oil and swirl it
around to coat the side. Stir-fry the
onion, garlic and brown sugar over
medium heat for 2–3 minutes, or until
the onion is soft and golden. Stir in the
vinegar and cook for 2 minutes.
Remove from the wok.
3 Reheat the wok and add the
pineapple pieces and orange juice.
Stir-fry for about 3 minutes over high

heat, or until the pineapple is just soft
and lightly golden. Stir in the onion
mixture, remove from the wok, cover
and set aside.
4 Reheat the wok until very hot and
add 1¹/2 tablespoons of the oil. Stir-fry
the tofu in two batches, tossing
regularly until it is lightly crisp and
golden. Drain on paper towels.
5 Return the tofu and the pineapple
mixture to the wok, and toss until well
combined and heated through. Season
well and serve immediately.

NUTRITION PER SERVE
Protein 6.5 g; Fat 3 g; Carbohydrate 15 g;
Dietary Fibre 3 g; Cholesterol 0 mg;
430 kJ (100 cal)

Drain the firm tofu and cut it into bite-sized pieces
for quick stir-frying.

Stir-fry the onion, garlic and brown sugar until the
onion is soft and golden.

Stir-fry the marinated tofu until it is lightly crisp
and golden.

CRISP TOFU IN HOT BEAN SAUCE

Preparation time: 35 minutes
  + 30 minutes marinating
Total cooking time: 15 minutes
Serves 4

500 g (1 lb) firm tofu,
    cut into small cubes
2 tablespoons peanut oil
1/4 cup (60 ml/2 fl oz) soy sauce
2 teaspoons finely grated fresh ginger
3/4 cup (130 g/4 1/2 oz) rice flour
oil, for cooking
2 onions, cut into thin wedges
2 cloves garlic, finely chopped
2 teaspoons soft brown sugar
1/2 red capsicum, cut into short,
    thin strips
5 spring onions, cut into short pieces
2 tablespoons dry sherry
2 teaspoons finely grated orange rind
2 tablespoons hot bean paste

1 Place the tofu in a glass or ceramic bowl with the peanut oil. Add the soy sauce and ginger, cover and refrigerate for 30 minutes.
2 Drain the tofu, reserving the marinade, and toss several pieces at a time in the rice flour to coat heavily. Heat the wok until very hot, add about 1/4 cup (60 ml/2 fl oz) of the oil and swirl it around to coat the side. Add the tofu to the hot oil and stir-fry over medium heat for 1 1/2 minutes, or until golden all over. Remove from the wok and drain on paper towels. Repeat with the remaining tofu. Keep warm. Drain any oil from the wok.
3 Reheat the wok and stir-fry the onion, garlic and sugar for 3 minutes, or until golden. Add the capsicum, spring onion, sherry, orange rind,

bean paste and the reserved tofu marinade. Stir and bring to the boil. Return the tofu to the wok, toss to heat through and serve.

NUTRITION PER SERVE
Protein 15 g; Fat 8 g; Carbohydrate 40 g; Dietary Fibre 3 g; Cholesterol 0 mg; 1215 kJ (290 cal)

Place the tofu in a bowl with the peanut oil and add the soy sauce.

Drain the tofu in a sieve, then toss it in the rice flour to coat heavily.

Stir-fry the tofu until it is golden on all sides, then drain on paper towels.

CHILLI TEMPEH

Preparation time: 15 minutes
Total cooking time: 10 minutes
Serves 4

250 g (8 oz) tempeh
oil, for cooking
1 onion, cut into thin slices
150 g (5 oz) asparagus,
    cut into short lengths
1 large carrot, cut into thick
    matchsticks
125 g (4 oz) snow peas, chopped

425 g (14 oz) can baby corn, drained
2 tablespoons sweet chilli sauce
2 tablespoons kecap manis
2 tablespoons dry sherry

1 Drain the tempeh, pat dry with paper towels and cut into bite-sized pieces for stir-frying.
2 Heat the wok until very hot, add 2 tablespoons of the oil and swirl it around to coat the side. Stir-fry the tempeh in batches until crisp. Remove from the wok and set aside.
3 Reheat the wok, add a little more oil if necessary and stir-fry the onion for

1 minute. Add the asparagus, carrot and snow peas, and stir-fry for 2–3 minutes, or until the vegetables are just tender.
4 Return the fried tempeh to the wok and add the baby corn, sweet chilli sauce, kecap manis and sherry. Bring to the boil, then reduce the heat and simmer for 2 minutes. Toss well until heated through and serve.

NUTRITION PER SERVE
Protein 5 g; Fat 15 g; Carbohydrate 10 g;
Dietary Fibre 8 g; Cholesterol 0 mg;
1270 kJ (300 cal)

Peel the carrot, cut it into short lengths and then into thick matchsticks.

Drain the tempeh, dry it on paper towels and cut it into bite-sized pieces.

Stir-fry the pieces of tempeh in the hot oil until they are crisp.

SESAME TOFU

Preparation time: 20 minutes
 + 30 minutes marinating
Total cooking time: 10 minutes
Serves 4

300 g (10 oz) firm tofu
2 teaspoons sesame oil
2 tablespoons soy sauce
1 tablespoon sesame seeds
2 tablespoons oil
3 zucchini, sliced
150 g (5 oz) button mushrooms,
    halved or quartered
1 large red capsicum, cubed
2 cloves garlic, crushed
3 cups (550 g/1 lb 2 oz) cold
    cooked brown rice
1–2 tablespoons soy sauce, for
    serving

1 Drain the tofu and pat dry with paper towels. Cut into cubes, place in a glass or ceramic bowl and add the sesame oil and soy sauce. Stir to combine and thoroughly coat the tofu. Cover and refrigerate for 30 minutes, stirring occasionally.

2 Heat the wok until very hot, add the sesame seeds and dry-fry until lightly golden. Leave on a plate to cool.

3 Reheat the wok, add the oil and swirl it around to coat the side. Remove the tofu from the dish with a slotted spoon and reserve the marinade. Stir-fry the tofu over high heat, turning occasionally, for about 3 minutes, or until browned. Remove from the wok and set aside.

4 Add the vegetables and garlic, and cook, stirring often, until they are just tender. Add the rice and tofu and stir-fry until heated through.

5 Add the toasted sesame seeds, the reserved marinade and the extra soy sauce, to taste. Toss through until the tofu and vegetables are well coated, then serve immediately.

NUTRITION PER SERVE
Protein 15 g; Fat 20 g; Carbohydrate 50 g;
Dietary Fibre 5.5 g; Cholesterol 0 mg;
1815 kJ (435 cal)

Dry-fry the sesame seeds until they are lightly golden brown.

DEEP-FRIED TOFU WITH HOKKIEN NOODLES

Preparation time: 10 minutes
Total cooking time: 5 minutes
Serves 4

100 g (3¹/₂ oz) deep-fried tofu puffs (see HINT)
2 tablespoons oil
1 onion, sliced
1 red capsicum, cut into squares
3 cloves garlic, crushed
2 teaspoons grated fresh ginger
³/₄ cup (120 g/4 oz) small chunks fresh pineapple

500 g (1 lb) thin Hokkien noodles, gently pulled apart
¹/₄ cup (60 ml/2 fl oz) pineapple juice
¹/₄ cup (60 ml/2 fl oz) hoisin sauce
¹/₄ cup (15 g/¹/₂ oz) roughly chopped fresh coriander

1 Slice the tofu puffs into three, then cut each slice into two or three pieces.
2 Heat the wok until very hot, add the oil and stir-fry the onion and capsicum for 1–2 minutes, or until beginning to soften. Add the garlic and ginger, stir-fry for 1 minute, then add the tofu and stir-fry for 2 minutes.
3 Add the pineapple chunks and noodles and toss until the mixture is

combined and heated through. Add the pineapple juice, hoisin sauce and chopped coriander and toss to combine. Serve immediately.

NUTRITION PER SERVE
Protein 10 g; Fat 15 g; Carbohydrate 65 g; Dietary Fibre 3.5 g; Cholesterol 0 mg; 1830 kJ (435 cal)

HINT: Deep-fried tofu puffs are available from the refrigerated section in Asian grocery stores and some supermarkets. They have a very different texture to ordinary tofu.

Use your fingers to gently separate the Hokkien noodles before cooking.

Slice the tofu puffs into three, then cut into smaller pieces.

Stir-fry the onion and capsicum until they are beginning to soften.

ASIAN GREENS WITH TERIYAKI TOFU DRESSING

Preparation time: 15 minutes
Total cooking time: 20 minutes
Serves 6

650 g (1 lb 5 oz) baby bok choy
500 g (1 lb) choy sum
440 g (14 oz) snake beans,
    topped and tailed
1/4 cup (60 ml/2 fl oz) oil
1 onion, thinly sliced
1/3 cup (60 g/2 oz) soft brown sugar
1/2 teaspoon ground chilli

2 tablespoons grated fresh ginger
1 cup (250 ml/8 fl oz) teriyaki sauce
1 tablespoon sesame oil
600 g (1 1/4 lb) silken firm tofu, drained

1 Cut the the baby bok choy and choy sum widthways into thirds. Chop the snake beans into shorter lengths.
2 Heat a wok over high heat, add 1 tablespoon of the oil and swirl to coat the side. Cook the onion for 3–5 minutes, or until crisp. Remove with a slotted spoon and drain on paper towels.
3 Heat 1 tablespoon of the oil in the wok, add half the greens and stir-fry for 2–3 minutes, or until wilted.

Remove and keep warm. Repeat with the remaining oil and greens. Remove. Drain any liquid from the wok.
4 Add the combined sugar, chilli, ginger and teriyaki sauce to the wok and bring to the boil. Simmer for 1 minute. Add the sesame oil and tofu and simmer for 2 minutes, turning once—the tofu will break up. Divide the greens among serving plates, then top with the dressing. Sprinkle with the fried onion to serve.

NUTRITION PER SERVE
Protein 19 g; Fat 11 g; Carbohydrate 20 g; Dietary Fibre 11 g; Cholesterol 1 mg; 1093 kJ (260 cal)

Cut the baby bok choy and choy sum widthways into thirds.

Cook the combined greens in two batches until the leaves are wilted.

Turn the tofu with an egg-flip halfway through the cooking time.

TEMPEH WITH CHINESE GREENS

Preparation time: 15 minutes
Total cooking time: 15 minutes
Serves 4

1 teaspoon sesame oil
1 tablespoon peanut oil
2 cloves garlic, crushed
1 tablespoon grated fresh ginger
1 red chilli, finely sliced
4 spring onions, sliced on the diagonal
300 g (10 oz) tempeh, cut into small
    cubes

500 g (1 lb) baby bok choy leaves
800 g (1 lb 10 oz) Chinese broccoli,
    chopped
1/2 cup (125 ml/4 fl oz) mushroom
    oyster sauce
2 tablespoons rice vinegar
2 tablespoons coriander leaves
1/4 cup (40 g/1 1/4 oz) toasted cashew
    nuts

1 Heat the oils in a wok over high
heat, add the garlic, ginger, chilli
and spring onion and cook for
1–2 minutes, or until the onion is soft.
Add the tempeh and cook for
5 minutes, or until golden. Remove

from the wok and keep warm.
2 Add half the greens and
1 tablespoon water to the wok and
cook, covered, for 3–4 minutes, or
until wilted. Remove and repeat with
the remaining greens and more water.
3 Return the greens and tempeh to
the wok, add the sauce and vinegar
and warm through. Top with the
coriander and nuts to serve.

NUTRITION PER SERVE
Protein 23 g; Fat 15 g; Carbohydrate 12 g;
Dietary Fibre 15 g; Cholesterol 0 mg;
2220 kJ (529 cal)

Stir-fry the garlic, ginger, chilli and spring onion for
1–2 minutes.

Add the tempeh and stir-fry for 5 minutes, or until
it has turned golden.

Add the greens to the wok in two batches and
cook until wilted.

VEGETARIAN PHAD THAI

Preparation time: 20 minutes
Total cooking time: 15 minutes
Serves 4

400 g (13 oz) flat rice-stick noodles
2 tablespoons peanut oil
2 eggs, lightly beaten
1 onion, cut into thin wedges
2 cloves garlic, crushed
1 small red capsicum, cut into thin
    strips
100 g (3½ oz) deep-fried tofu puffs,
    cut into thin strips
6 spring onions, thinly sliced on the
    diagonal

½ cup (30 g/1 oz) chopped coriander
    leaves
¼ cup (60 ml/2 fl oz) soy sauce
2 tablespoons lime juice
1 tablespoon soft brown sugar
2 teaspoons sambal oelek
1 cup (90 g/3 oz) bean sprouts
¼ cup (40 g/1¼ oz) chopped
    roasted unsalted peanuts

1 Cook the noodles in a saucepan of boiling water for 5–10 minutes, or until tender. Drain and set aside.
2 Heat a wok over high heat and add enough peanut oil to coat the bottom and side. When smoking, add the egg and swirl to form a thin omelette. Cook for 30 seconds, or until just set.

Roll up, remove and thinly slice.
3 Heat the remaining oil in the wok. Add the onion, garlic and capsicum and cook over high heat for 2–3 minutes, or until the onion softens. Add the noodles, tossing well. Stir in the omelette, tofu, spring onion and half the coriander.
4 Pour in the combined soy sauce, lime juice, sugar and sambal oelek and toss well. Sprinkle with the bean sprouts and top with roasted peanuts and the remaining coriander to serve.

NUTRITION PER SERVE
Protein 13 g; Fat 21 g; Carbohydrate 34 g;
Dietary Fibre 5 g; Cholesterol 90 mg;
1565 kJ (375 cal)

Using a sharp knife, slice the deep-fried tofu puffs into thin strips.

Once the omelette is golden and set, carefully roll it up, remove from the wok and thinly slice.

Stir in the omelette, tofu, spring onion and half of the coriander.

THAI NOODLES WITH BEAN CURD

Preparation time: 25 minutes
+ 20 minutes soaking
Total cooking time: 5–7 minutes
Serves 4–6

8 dried Chinese mushrooms
250 g (8 oz) rice vermicelli
2 tablespoons oil
3 cloves garlic, chopped
5 cm (2 inch) piece fresh ginger, grated
100 g (3¹/₂ oz) deep-fried tofu puffs,
    cut into small pieces
1 carrot, cut into matchsticks
100 g (3¹/₂ oz) green beans, cut into
    short lengths
¹/₂ red capsicum, cut into matchsticks
2 tablespoons Golden Mountain sauce
1 tablespoon fish sauce
2 teaspoons soft brown sugar
100 g (3¹/₂ oz) bean sprouts
1 cup (90 g/3 oz) finely shredded
    cabbage
60 g (2 oz) bean sprouts, extra,
    straggly ends removed, to garnish
chilli sauce (see page 248), for serving

1 Soak the dried Chinese mushrooms in hot water for 20 minutes. Drain and then slice.
2 In a heatproof bowl, pour boiling water over the vermicelli and soak for 1–4 minutes, or until soft. Drain.
3 Heat a wok, add the oil and, when very hot, add the garlic, ginger and tofu and stir-fry 1 minute. Add the carrot, beans, capsicum and mushrooms to the wok and stir-fry for 2 minutes. Add the sauces and sugar and toss well. Cover the wok and steam for 1 minute.
4 Add the vermicelli, bean sprouts and all but a few tablespoonsful of cabbage. Toss, cover and steam for 30 seconds. Arrange the noodles on a serving plate and garnish with the bean sprouts and remaining cabbage and serve with chilli sauce.

NUTRITION PER SERVE (6)
Protein 5 g; Fat 8.5 g; Carbohydrate 15 g; Dietary Fibre 5 g; Cholesterol 0 mg; 656 kJ (157 cal)

Cut the deep-fried tofu puffs into small cubes, using a sharp knife.

Place the vermicelli noodles in a heatproof bowl and pour boiling water over them.

Stir-fry the garlic, ginger and tofu in the hot oil for 1 minute.

Add the vermicelli, bean sprouts and cabbage to the wok, toss well and steam for 30 seconds.

HONEY-BRAISED VEGETABLES WITH BEAN CURD

Preparation time: 30 minutes
  + 30 minutes soaking
Cooking time: 20 minutes
Serves 6

8 dried Chinese mushrooms
20 dried lily buds (see NOTE)
2 tablespoons peanut oil
3 thin slices fresh ginger, cut into strips
250 g (8 oz) white sweet potato, halved and sliced
2 tablespoons soy sauce
1 tablespoon honey
2 teaspoons sesame oil
60 g (2 oz) deep-fried tofu puffs, cut into thin strips
2 teaspoons cornflour
4 spring onions, cut into short lengths
410 g (13 oz) can baby corn
230 g (7 1/2 oz) can water chestnuts, drained

1 Soak the mushrooms in hot water for 30 minutes. Drain, reserving 3/4 cup (185 ml/6 fl oz) of the liquid. Squeeze dry with your hands. Remove the stems and slice the mushrooms thinly. Soak the lily buds separately in warm water for 30 minutes, then drain.

2 Heat the oil in a wok. Add the ginger and stir-fry for 1 minute. Add the mushrooms and lily buds and stir-fry for 30 seconds. Add the sweet potato with the soy, honey, sesame oil, mushroom liquid and tofu. Simmer in the wok for 15 minutes.

3 Dissolve the cornflour in a little water and add to the wok. Stir until the liquid thickens. Add the spring onions, corn and water chestnuts and toss to heat through before serving.

NUTRITION PER SERVE
Protein 4 g; Fat 10 g; Carbohydrate 30 g;
Dietary Fibre 5 g; Cholesterol 0 mg;
920 kJ (220 cal)

NOTE: Dried lily buds are a Chinese speciality (see glossary of ingredients, pages 8–13). They can be left out without altering the flavour greatly.

Cut three thin slices of fresh ginger and then cut the slices into thin strips.

Add the sweet potato, soy, honey, sesame oil, mushroom liquid and tofu to the wok.

Stir until the sauce thickens, then add the spring onions, corn and water chestnuts.

FRIED TOFU, CHOY SUM AND BABY CORN IN OYSTER SAUCE

Preparation time: 5 minutes
Total cooking time: 6 minutes
Serves 4

2 tablespoons peanut oil
400 g (13 oz) deep-fried tofu puffs, halved
4 tablespoons oyster sauce
2 tablespoons light soy sauce
2 tablespoon sweet chilli sauce
2 tablespoon honey
2 cloves garlic, crushed
12 baby corn, halved lengthways
500 g (1 lb) choy sum leaves, cut into short lengths

1 Heat a wok over high heat, add the oil and swirl to coat the side. Add the tofu puffs and stir-fry for 2 minutes, or until crispy and golden.
2 Place the oyster sauce, soy sauce, sweet chilli sauce and honey in a small bowl and mix together well.
3 Add the garlic, baby corn and choy sum to the wok and pour in the combined sauce, along with 1/4 cup (60 ml/2 fl oz) water. Stir-fry for 3–4 minutes, or until the leaves have just wilted. Serve immediately.

NUTRITION PER SERVE
Protein 12 g; Fat 22 g; Carbohydrate 45 g;
Dietary Fibre 8 g; Cholesterol 0 mg;
1975 kJ (470 cal)

Stir-fry the tofu puffs for 2 minutes, or until crispy and golden.

Place the sauces and honey in a small bowl and mix together well.

Add the garlic, baby corn and choy sum to the wok and stir-fry.

CHINESE TOFU

Preparation time: 20 minutes
Total cooking time: 20 minutes
Serves 4–6

125 g (4 oz) rice vermicelli
oil, for cooking
1 tablespoon soy sauce
1 tablespoon sherry
1 tablespoon oyster sauce
1/2 cup (125 ml/4 fl oz) chicken stock
2 teaspoons cornflour
1 clove garlic, crushed
1 teaspoon grated fresh ginger
375 g (12 oz) firm tofu, cut into small
    pieces

2 carrots, cut into matchsticks
250 g (8 oz) snow peas, trimmed
4 spring onions, finely sliced
425 g (14 oz) can straw mushrooms,
    drained

1 Break the vermicelli into short
lengths. Heat 4 tablespoons of the oil
in a wok. Cook the vermicelli in
batches over medium heat until crisp,
adding more oil when necessary.
Drain on paper towels.
2 Combine the soy sauce, sherry,
oyster sauce and chicken stock. Blend
the cornflour with 2 teaspoons water.
3 Reheat the wok and heat a
tablespoon of oil. Add the garlic and
ginger and cook over high heat for

1 minute. Add the tofu and stir-fry for
3 minutes. Remove from the wok. Add
the carrot and snow peas and stir-fry
for 1 minute. Add the sauce and stock
mixture, cover and cook for another
3 minutes or until the vegetables are
just tender. Add the tofu.
4 Add the spring onion, mushrooms
and blended cornflour. Stir until the
sauce has thickened, then serve with
the rice vermicelli.

NUTRITION PER SERVE (6)
Protein 15 g; Fat 35 g; Carbohydrate 11 g;
Dietary Fibre 6 g; Cholesterol 0 mg;
1418 kJ (338 cal)

Fry the vermicelli in hot oil and then drain on
paper towels.

Combine the soy sauce, sherry, oyster sauce and
chicken stock.

Stir-fry the tofu cubes for 3 minutes or until they
are well browned. Remove from the wok.

TOFU WITH BOK CHOY

Preparation time: 20 minutes
  + 10 minutes marinating
Total cooking time: 10 minutes
Serves 4

600 g (1¼ lb) firm tofu, cut into small
  pieces
1 tablespoon grated fresh ginger
2 tablespoons soy sauce
2 tablespoons peanut oil
1 red onion, finely sliced
4 cloves garlic, crushed
500 g (1 lb) baby bok choy, cut into
  strips lengthways

2 teaspoons sesame oil
2 tablespoons kecap manis
¼ cup (60 ml/2 fl oz) sweet chilli
  sauce
1 tablespoon toasted sesame seeds

1 Put the tofu in a bowl with the
ginger. Pour in the soy sauce and leave
to marinate for 10 minutes. Drain.
2 Heat a wok until very hot, add half
the oil and swirl to coat the base and
side of the wok with oil. When the oil
is hot, add the onion and stir-fry for
3 minutes, or until soft. Add the tofu
and garlic and stir-fry for 3 minutes, or
until the tofu is golden. Remove and
keep warm.

3 Reheat the wok until very hot, add
the remaining oil and swirl to coat.
Add the bok choy and stir-fry for
2 minutes, or until wilted. Return the
tofu mixture to the wok.
4 Stir in the sesame oil, kecap manis
and chilli sauce and toss to heat
through. Scatter with the sesame seeds
and serve immediately.

NUTRITION PER SERVE
Protein 18.5 g; Fat 20 g; Carbohydrate 7 g;
Dietary Fibre 7 g; Cholesterol 0 mg;
1232 kJ (293 cal)

Put the tofu in a bowl with the ginger and soy
sauce and leave to marinate.

Add the marinated tofu and the garlic and stir-fry
for 3 minutes, or until golden.

Add the bok choy to the wok and stir-fry for
2 minutes, until it has wilted.

TOFU AND PEANUT NOODLES

Preparation time: 10 minutes
Total cooking time: 10 minutes
Serves 4

250 g (8 oz) firm tofu, cut into small
 pieces
2 cloves garlic, crushed
1 teaspoon grated fresh ginger
1/3 cup (80 ml/2³/4 fl oz) kecap manis
1/3 cup (90 g/3 oz) peanut butter
2 tablespoons peanut or vegetable oil
500 g (1 lb) Hokkien noodles
1 onion, chopped

1 red capsicum, chopped
125 g (4 oz) broccoli, cut into small
 florets

1 Combine the tofu with the garlic, ginger and half the kecap manis in a small bowl. Place the peanut butter, 1/2 cup (125 ml/4 fl oz) water and the remaining kecap manis in another bowl and mix well.
2 Heat the oil in a large wok. Drain the tofu and reserve the marinade. Cook the tofu in two batches in the hot oil until well browned. Remove from the wok.
3 Place the noodles in a large heatproof bowl. Cover with boiling

water and leave for 2 minutes. Drain and gently pull the noodles apart.
4 Add the vegetables to the wok and stir-fry until just tender. Add the tofu, reserved marinade and noodles. Add the peanut butter mixture and toss until heated through.

NUTRITION PER SERVE
Protein 32 g; Fat 30 g; Carbohydrate 96 g; Dietary Fibre 8 g; Cholesterol 20 mg; 3140 kJ (697 cal)

NOTE: Kecap manis is an Indonesian sweet soy sauce. If you are unable to find it, use soy sauce sweetened with a little soft brown sugar.

Mix together the tofu, garlic, ginger and half the kecap manis in a bowl.

Cook the tofu in two batches in the hot oil until it is well browned.

Soak the noodles in boiling water for a couple of minutes and then gently pull them apart.

211

Vegetables

POTATO NOODLES WITH VEGETABLES

Preparation time: 30 minutes + soaking
Total cooking time: 25 minutes
Serves 4

300 g (10 oz) dried potato starch
    noodles
30 g (1 oz) dried cloud-ear fungus
1/4 cup (60 ml/2 fl oz) sesame oil
2 tablespoons vegetable oil
3 cloves garlic, finely chopped
4 cm (11/2 inch) piece of fresh ginger,
    grated
2 spring onions, finely chopped
2 carrots, cut into short matchsticks
2 spring onions, extra, cut into short
    lengths
500 g (1 lb) baby bok choy or
    250 g (8 oz) English spinach,
    roughly chopped
1/4 cup (60 ml/2 fl oz) shoshoyu
    (Japanese soy sauce)
2 tablespoons mirin
1 teaspoon sugar
2 tablespoons sesame seed and
    seaweed sprinkle

1 Cook the dried potato noodles in boiling water for about 5 minutes or until translucent. Drain and then rinse under cold running water until cold. (Thoroughly rinsing the noodles will remove any excess starch.) Roughly chop the noodles into lengths of about 15 cm (6 inches), to make them easier to eat with chopsticks.

2 Pour boiling water over the fungus and soak for 10 minutes. Drain thoroughly and chop roughly. Heat 1 tablespoon of the sesame oil with the vegetable oil in a large, heavy-based pan or wok. Add the garlic, ginger and spring onion to the pan and cook for 3 minutes over medium heat, stirring regularly. Add the carrot sticks and stir-fry for 1 minute.

3 Add the noodles, extra spring onion, bok choy, remaining sesame oil, shoshoyu, mirin and sugar. Toss well, cover and cook over low heat for 2 minutes.

4 Add the drained fungus, cover the pan and cook for another 2 minutes. Sprinkle with the sesame seed and seaweed sprinkle. Serve immediately.

NUTRITION PER SERVE
Protein 5 g; Fat 11 g; Carbohydrate 20 g;
Dietary Fibre 3 g; Cholesterol 0 mg;
830 kJ (198 cal)

NOTE: Japanese soy sauce is lighter and sweeter than Chinese soy sauce. It is available from Asian speciality stores, along with potato starch noodles (Korean vermicelli) and cloud-ear fungus.

Make the noodles easier to eat by roughly chopping them with scissors.

Add the noodles, spring onion, bok choy, sesame oil, shoshoyu, mirin and sugar.

SPICY BROCCOLI AND CAULIFLOWER

Preparation time: 15 minutes
Total cooking time: 10 minutes
Serves 4

1 teaspoon ground cumin
1 teaspoon ground coriander
2 tablespoons oil
2 cloves garlic, crushed
1 teaspoon grated fresh ginger
1/2 teaspoon chilli powder

1 onion, cut into wedges
200 g (6¹/2 oz) cauliflower, cut into
   bite-sized florets
200 g (6¹/2 oz) broccoli, cut into bite-
   sized florets
200 g (6¹/2 oz) haloumi cheese, diced
1 tablespoon lemon juice

1 Heat the wok until very hot, add the cumin and coriander, and dry-fry the spices for 1 minute. Add the oil with the garlic, ginger and chilli powder, and stir-fry briefly. Add the onion and cook for 2–3 minutes, being careful not to burn the spices.

2 Add the cauliflower and broccoli, and stir-fry until they are cooked through but still crisp. Add the haloumi and toss well until the haloumi is coated with the spices and is just beginning to melt. Season well and serve sprinkled with lemon juice.

NUTRITION PER SERVE
Protein 12 g; Fat 15 g; Carbohydrate 3 g;
Dietary Fibre 4 g; Cholesterol 20 mg;
820 kJ (195 cal)

Haloumi cheese comes in a block—cut it into small cubes.

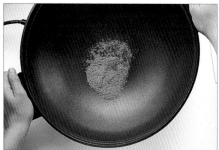

Dry-fry the ground cumin and coriander in a very hot wok.

Add the onion wedges to the spice mixture and toss to coat.

COLOURFUL CABBAGE STIR-FRY

Preparation time: 15 minutes
Total cooking time: 10 minutes
Serves 2

200 g (6½ oz) red cabbage
200 g (6½ oz) white cabbage
200 g (6½ oz) green cabbage
1 apple
oil, for cooking
1 teaspoon soft brown sugar
1 red onion, thinly sliced
1 red chilli, finely chopped
1 tablespoon chopped thyme
1 tablespoon cider vinegar
²/₃ cup (100 g/3½ oz) chopped blanched almonds

1 Finely shred the three different varieties of cabbage. Wash thoroughly, drain and dry well in a tea towel. Core and slice the apple.
2 Heat the wok until very hot, add 1 tablespoon of the oil and swirl it around to coat the side. Add the apple and brown sugar, and stir-fry for 1–2 minutes, or until the apple caramelizes. Remove the apple from the wok and set aside.
3 Reheat the wok, add a little oil if necessary and stir-fry the sliced red onion for 1 minute. Add the chopped chilli, shredded red cabbage and white cabbage, and stir-fry for 2–3 minutes. Add the shredded green cabbage and stir-fry for 1 minute. Stir in the thyme and the caramelized apple, and season well. Pour in the cider vinegar, cover

and steam for 1 minute. Add the almonds and toss well until evenly distributed. Serve immediately.

NUTRITION PER SERVE
Protein 15 g; Fat 40 g; Carbohydrate 20 g; Dietary Fibre 15 g; Cholesterol 0 mg; 2420 kJ (580 cal)

Finely shred the red, white and green cabbage before washing thoroughly.

STIR-FRIED ASIAN GREENS AND MUSHROOMS

Preparation time: 20 minutes
Total cooking time: 5 minutes
Serves 4

20 stems Chinese broccoli
4 baby bok choy
100 g (3½ oz) shimeji or
    enoki mushrooms
100 g (3½ oz) shiitake mushrooms
1 tablespoon soy sauce
2 teaspoons crushed palm sugar
1 tablespoon oil
4 spring onions, cut into short pieces
5 cm (2 inch) piece fresh ginger,
    cut into thin strips
1–2 small red chillies, seeded and
    finely chopped
2–3 cloves garlic, crushed
125 g (4 oz) snow peas, halved
1–2 teaspoons seasoning sauce

1 Remove any tough outer leaves from the Chinese broccoli and bok choy. Cut into 4 cm (1½ inch) pieces across the leaves, including the stems. Wash thoroughly, then drain and dry thoroughly. Wipe the mushrooms with a paper towel and trim the ends. Slice the shiitake mushrooms thickly.
2 Combine the soy sauce and palm sugar with ¼ cup (60 ml/2 fl oz) water. Set aside.
3 Heat the wok until very hot, add the oil and swirl it around to coat the side. Stir-fry the spring onion, ginger, chilli and garlic over low heat for 30 seconds, without browning. Increase the heat to high and add the Chinese broccoli, bok choy and snow peas. Stir-fry for 1–2 minutes, or until the vegetables are wilted.

4 Add the prepared mushrooms and soy sauce mixture. Stir-fry over high heat for 1–2 minutes, or until the mushrooms and sauce are heated through. Sprinkle with the seasoning sauce, to taste, and serve immediately.

NUTRITION PER SERVE
Protein 6.5 g; Fat 10 g; Carbohydrate 15 g;
Dietary Fibre 3 g; Cholesterol 0 mg;
780 kJ (185 cal)

You will need to gently separate the shimeji mushrooms from each other.

Trim the shiitake mushrooms and cut them into thick slices.

Peel the piece of ginger and cut it into thin strips with a very sharp knife.

THREE-BEAN STIR-FRY

Preparation time: 10 minutes
Total cooking time: 5 minutes
Serves 4

1 tablespoon oil
1 red onion, chopped
2 cloves garlic, crushed
1 tablespoon finely chopped thyme
200 g (6¹/₂ oz) green beans, cut into
    short lengths
300 g (10 oz) can cannellini beans,
    rinsed
1 cup (170 g/5¹/₂ oz) chickpeas,
    rinsed and drained

150 g (5 oz) rocket
2 tablespoons finely chopped parsley
3 tablespoons lemon juice

1 Heat the wok until very hot, add the oil and swirl it around to coat the side. Stir-fry the onion for 2 minutes. Add the garlic and stir-fry until soft. Stir in the thyme.
2 Add the green beans and stir-fry for 2–3 minutes, or until tender. Add the cannellini beans and chickpeas, and stir-fry until heated through. Season, and spoon the mixture onto the rocket on a platter. Sprinkle the parsley on top and drizzle with the lemon juice to serve.

NUTRITION PER SERVE
Protein 7 g; Fat 6 g; Carbohydrate 10 g;
Dietary Fibre 6.5 g; Cholesterol 0 mg;
530 kJ (125 cal)

Add the green beans to the onion, garlic and thyme and stir-fry until tender.

217

SPRING VEGETABLES WITH HERBED BUTTER

Preparation time: 20 minutes
Total cooking time: 10 minutes
Serves 6 as an accompaniment

2 tablespoons light olive oil
200 g (6¹/₂ oz) asparagus, cut into
    short lengths
115 g (4 oz) fresh baby corn spears,
    halved lengthways
250 g (8 oz) snow peas
250 g (8 oz) green beans, halved

300 g (10 oz) baby carrots, halved
    lengthways
2 cloves garlic, crushed
50 g (1³/₄ oz) butter
¹/₄ cup (15 g/¹/₂ oz) finely chopped
    parsley
¹/₄ cup (15 g/¹/₂ oz) finely chopped
    chives
¹/₄ cup (15 g/¹/₂ oz) finely chopped
    basil

1 Heat the wok until very hot, add the oil and swirl it around to coat the side. Stir-fry all the vegetables over high heat for 5 minutes. Cover and cook over low heat for 2 minutes, or until tender.
2 Add the crushed garlic, butter and all the fresh herbs, and toss until the butter has melted and the herbs have wilted slightly. Season well with salt and pepper and serve immediately as an accompaniment.

NUTRITION PER SERVE
Protein 3 g; Fat 12 g; Carbohydrate 8 g; Dietary Fibre 4 g; Cholesterol 20 mg; 695 kJ (165 cal)

Use a large sharp knife to finely chop the fresh parsley, chives and basil.

Stir-fry the asparagus, corn, snow peas, beans and carrot over high heat.

Add the garlic, butter and herbs to the tender vegetables and toss until the butter melts.

WILD MUSHROOMS WITH SPICES

Preparation time: 30 minutes
Total cooking time: 5 minutes
Serves 4

20 g (³/₄ oz) butter
1 tablespoon oil
2 cloves garlic, crushed
1 teaspoon ground cumin
1 teaspoon ground coriander
¹/₄ teaspoon sweet paprika
750 g (1¹/₂ lb) mixed mushrooms
    (see NOTE), cleaned and
    trimmed

2 tablespoons dry sherry
4 spring onions, sliced
¹/₄ cup (15 g/¹/₂ oz) finely chopped
    basil
2 tablespoons finely chopped flat-leaf
    parsley

1 Heat the wok until very hot, add the butter and oil and swirl it around the wok. Stir-fry the garlic, cumin, coriander and paprika for 1–2 minutes, or until fragrant. Add the mushrooms and stir-fry for 2 minutes, tossing well.
2 Add the sherry and bring to the boil. Cover and cook for 30 seconds. Toss the spring onion and herbs through the mushroom mixture.

NUTRITION PER SERVE
Protein 7 g; Fat 9.5 g; Carbohydrate 4 g; Dietary Fibre 5.5 g; Cholesterol 15 mg; 580 kJ (140 cal)

NOTE: Mushrooms such as shimeji, oyster, swiss brown, enoki and button can be used in this recipe. If using enoki mushrooms, add them when the sherry is added as they cook faster than the other mushrooms.

Clean and trim the mushrooms, cutting any larger ones in half.

Stir-fry the garlic, cumin, coriander and paprika until fragrant.

Add the sherry and enoki mushrooms, and cover and cook for 2 minutes.

GREEN BEANS WITH SHIITAKE MUSHROOMS

Preparation time: 15 minutes
Total cooking time: 12 minutes
Serves 4

2 tablespoons sesame seeds
1 tablespoon oil
1 teaspoon sesame oil
5 spring onions, sliced
800 g (1 lb 10 oz) green beans

200 g (6¹/₂ oz) shiitake mushrooms
2 teaspoons finely chopped fresh
  ginger
2 tablespoons mirin
2 tablespoons soy sauce
1 tablespoon sugar

1 Heat the wok until very hot, add the sesame seeds and stir-fry over high heat until they are golden. Remove from the wok and set aside.
2 Reheat the wok, add the oils and swirl to coat the side. Add the spring onion and beans, and stir-fry for 4 minutes. Add the mushrooms and ginger, and cook for 4 minutes.
3 Pour in the mirin, soy sauce and sugar, cover and cook for 2 minutes, or until the beans are tender. Sprinkle with the toasted sesame seeds and serve immediately.

NUTRITION PER SERVE
Protein 7.5 g; Fat 12 g; Carbohydrate 10 g;
Dietary Fibre 7 g; Cholesterol 0 mg;
885 kJ (210 cal)

Peel the fresh ginger and chop it finely to make up 2 teaspoons.

Dry-fry the sesame seeds over high heat until they are golden.

Stir-fry the spring onion and beans in the oil and sesame oil.

STIR-FRIED EGGPLANT WITH LEMON

Preparation time: 20 minutes
  + 30 minutes standing
Total cooking time: 12 minutes
Serves 4

1 kg (2 lb) small eggplants
1 tablespoon salt
olive oil, for cooking
8 spring onions, sliced
3 cloves garlic, crushed
2 teaspoons cumin seeds
1 tablespoon ground coriander
1 teaspoon grated lemon rind
1/3 cup (80 ml/2³/4 fl oz) lemon juice
2 teaspoons soft brown sugar
2 tablespoons coriander leaves

1 Peel the eggplants and cut into small cubes. Put in a colander and sprinkle with the salt. Leave for 30 minutes, then rinse under cold water and pat dry with paper towels.
2 Heat the wok until very hot, add 1¹/2 tablespoons of the oil and swirl it around to coat the side. Stir-fry the eggplant in two batches over high heat for 3–4 minutes, or until browned and cooked (use 1¹/2 tablespoons oil for each batch). Remove from the wok.
3 Return all the eggplant to the wok and add the spring onion. Stir-fry for 1 minute, or until the eggplant is soft. Add the garlic and cumin seeds, and cook for 1 minute. Stir in the ground coriander and cook for 30 seconds. Add the lemon rind, juice and sugar, and toss well. Season with salt and black pepper and sprinkle with coriander leaves before serving.

NUTRITION PER SERVE
Protein 3.5 g; Fat 10 g; Carbohydrate 10 g; Dietary Fibre 7 g; Cholesterol 0 mg; 640 kJ (155 cal)

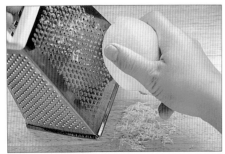
Grate the lemon rind on the fine side of a metal grater, avoiding the bitter pith underneath.

Put the eggplant cubes in a colander and sprinkle with the salt to draw out any bitter juices.

Stir-fry the eggplant in batches until it is browned and cooked through.

ASPARAGUS STIR-FRIED WITH MUSTARD

Preparation time: 10 minutes
Total cooking time: 10 minutes
Serves 2

480 g (15 oz) asparagus
1 tablespoon oil
1 red onion, sliced
1 clove garlic, crushed
1 tablespoon wholegrain mustard
1 teaspoon honey
1/2 cup (125 ml/4 fl oz) cream

1 Break the woody ends off the asparagus by holding both ends of the spear and bending gently until it snaps at its natural breaking point. Cut the asparagus into 5 cm (2 inch) lengths.
2 Heat the wok until very hot, add the oil and swirl to coat the side. Stir-fry the onion for 2–3 minutes, or until tender. Stir in the crushed garlic and cook for 1 minute. Add the asparagus to the wok and stir-fry for 3–4 minutes, or until tender, being careful not to overcook the asparagus.
3 Remove the asparagus from the wok, set it aside and keep it warm. Combine the wholegrain mustard, honey and cream. Add to the wok and bring to the boil, then reduce the heat and simmer for 2–3 minutes, or until the mixture reduces and thickens slightly. Return the asparagus to the wok and toss it through the cream mixture. Serve immediately.

NUTRITION PER SERVE
Protein 8.5 g; Fat 35 g; Carbohydrate 10 g;
Dietary Fibre 5 g; Cholesterol 85 mg;
1685 kJ (405 cal)

VARIATION: When asparagus is in season, white and purple asparagus are also available. Vary the recipe by using a mixture of the three colours. Do not overcook the purple asparagus or it will turn green as it cooks.

HINT: This dish can also be served on croutons, toasted ciabatta or toasted wholegrain bread as a smart starter or first course.

Gently bend the asparagus spear and the tough woody end will naturally snap off.

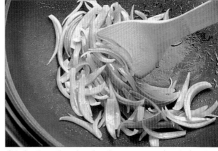

Stir-fry the sliced red onion over moderate heat for 2–3 minutes, or until tender.

PUMPKIN AND CASHEW STIR-FRY

Preparation time: 20 minutes
Total cooking time: 15 minutes
Serves 4–6

oil, for cooking
1 cup (155 g/5 oz) raw cashew nuts
1 leek, white part only, sliced
2 teaspoons ground coriander
2 teaspoons ground cumin
2 teaspoons brown mustard seeds
2 cloves garlic, crushed

1 kg (2 lb) butternut pumpkin, cubed
3/4 cup (185 ml/6 fl oz) orange juice
1 teaspoon soft brown sugar

1 Heat the wok until very hot, add 1 tablespoon of the oil and swirl to coat. Stir-fry the cashews until golden, then drain on paper towels. Stir-fry the leek for 2–3 minutes, or until softened. Remove from the wok.
2 Reheat the wok, add 1 tablespoon of the oil and stir-fry the coriander, cumin, mustard seeds and garlic for 2 minutes, or until the spices are fragrant and the mustard seeds begin

to pop. Add the pumpkin and stir to coat well. Stir-fry for 5 minutes, or until the pumpkin is brown and tender.
3 Add the orange juice and sugar. Bring to the boil and cook for 5 minutes. Add the leek and three-quarters of the cashews and toss well. Top with the remaining cashews to serve.

NUTRITION PER SERVE (6)
Protein 8 g; Fat 20 g; Carbohydrate 20 g;
Dietary Fibre 4 g; Cholesterol 0 mg;
1240 kJ (295 cal)

Stir-fry the cashews in 1 tablespoon of the oil until they are golden.

Reheat the wok and stir-fry the coriander, cumin, mustard seeds and garlic.

Add the pumpkin and stir to coat well in the spices. Stir-fry until brown and tender.

MIXED BEANS WITH BALSAMIC AND LIME

Preparation time: 15 minutes
Total cooking time: 10 minutes
Serves 6

1 tablespoon oil
2 cloves garlic, crushed
1 red onion, cut into thin wedges
1 red capsicum, cut into short thin strips
1 yellow capsicum, cut into short thin strips
400 g (13 oz) can chickpeas, drained
400 g (13 oz) can red kidney beans, drained

2 teaspoons soft brown sugar
2 tablespoons balsamic vinegar
1/4 cup (60 ml/2 fl oz) lime juice
250 g (8 oz) cherry tomatoes, halved
1 Lebanese cucumber, chopped
1/4 cup (15 g/1/2 oz) chopped coriander
butter lettuce leaves, to serve

1 Heat the wok until very hot, add the oil and swirl it around to coat the side. Stir-fry the garlic, onion and capsicum strips over moderate heat for 2–3 minutes, then remove from the wok and set aside.
2 Add the chickpeas and kidney beans to the wok, stir in the brown sugar and balsamic vinegar, and toss for 2–3 minutes, or until reduced by half. Add the lime juice and toss until well combined.
3 Using two wooden spoons, stir in the cherry tomatoes, chopped cucumber, coriander and the onion and capsicum mixture. Quickly stir-fry until heated through and thoroughly mixed. Put a couple of lettuce leaves on each plate and spoon the stir-fry into the leaves to serve.

NUTRITION PER SERVE
Protein 10 g; Fat 5 g; Carbohydrate 25 g;
Dietary Fibre 9 g; Cholesterol 0 mg;
750 kJ (180 cal)

Peel the red onion and then cut it into thin wedges for quick stir-frying.

Remove the seeds from the capsicum and cut the flesh into short, thin strips.

Cut the cucumber lengthways into strips, then cut the strips into small pieces.

WARM STIR-FRIED SALAD

Preparation time: 15 minutes
Total cooking time: 5 minutes
Serves 2

2 tablespoons olive oil
1 red onion, sliced
1 red capsicum, cut into small squares
2 cloves garlic, thinly sliced
250 g (8 oz) cherry tomatoes, halved

150 g (5 oz) baby English spinach leaves
1/2 cup (15 g/1/2 oz) basil leaves
125 g (4 oz) feta cheese, crumbled

1 Heat the wok until very hot, add the oil and swirl it around to coat the base and side of the wok. Add the onion, capsicum and garlic to the wok and stir-fry for 2 minutes, or until just beginning to soften. Add the tomatoes, spinach and basil and stir-fry until the leaves have just wilted.

2 Transfer the salad to a serving plate and top with the crumbled feta cheese. Serve immediately.

NUTRITION PER SERVE
Protein 15 g; Fat 35 g; Carbohydrate 7 g;
Dietary Fibre 6 g; Cholesterol 45 mg;
1635 kJ (390 cal)

NOTE: Serve as a main course with crusty bread or pasta or heap onto crostini as a starter.

Remove the seeds from the capsicum and cut the flesh into squares.

Peel the cloves of garlic, then cut each clove into thin slices.

Good-quality feta cheese should crumble easily between your fingers.

FRAGRANT GREENS

Preparation time: 15 minutes
Total cooking time: 8 minutes
Serves 4

2 tablespoons oil
300 g (10 oz) broccoli, cut into
    small florets
150 g (5 oz) snake beans, cut into
    short lengths
3 spring onions, sliced
250 g (8 oz) cabbage,
    finely shredded
1 green capsicum, cut into strips
2 tablespoons lime juice
1 tablespoon soft brown sugar
1/4 cup (15 g/1/2 oz) Thai basil,
    shredded (see NOTE)

1 Heat the wok until very hot, add the
oil and swirl it around to coat the side.
Stir-fry the broccoli and snake beans
for 3–4 minutes, or until the vegetables
are bright green and just tender. Add
the spring onion, cabbage and
capsicum, and continue stir-frying
until just softened.
2 Combine the lime juice and brown
sugar, stirring until the sugar has
dissolved. Add to the wok with the
basil. Toss to combine with the
vegetables and serve immediately.

NUTRITION PER SERVE
Protein 6 g; Fat 10 g; Carbohydrate 9 g;
Dietary Fibre 7 g; Cholesterol 0 mg;
630 kJ (150 cal)

NOTE: You can include any suitable
kind of green vegetable in this dish,
including Asian greens. If you can't
find Thai basil, use ordinary basil or
coriander—either will give fragrance
and flavour like Thai basil.

Top and tail the snake beans and cut them into
short lengths.

Using a large sharp knife, finely shred the
cabbage so that it will stir-fry quickly.

Shred the Thai basil just before you need it, or it
will turn black.

VEGETABLES PROVENCALE

Preparation time: 25 minutes
Total cooking time: 30 minutes
Serves 4

1 large eggplant, cut into thick
   batons
3/4 cup (90 g/3 oz) plain flour
oil, for cooking
2 onions, cut into wedges
2 cloves garlic, finely chopped
1/2 cup (125 ml/4 fl oz) white wine
150 g (5 oz) green beans
4 large zucchini, sliced

200 g (6 1/2 oz) button mushrooms
1/4 cup (15 g/1/2 oz) chopped basil
2 tomatoes, chopped
2 tablespoons tomato paste

1 Toss the eggplant in the flour until it is lightly coated. Heat the wok until very hot, add about 2 tablespoons of the oil and swirl it around to coat the side. Stir-fry the eggplant in three or four batches over medium-high heat, tossing regularly for about 3 minutes, or until it is golden and just cooked. Add more oil to the wok with each batch. Remove from the wok and drain on paper towels. Season with salt and freshly ground black pepper.

2 Add the onion and garlic to the wok and stir-fry for 3 minutes, or until softened. Add the wine, beans and zucchini. Cook for 2 minutes, tossing regularly. Add the mushrooms and cook, covered, for 2 minutes. Stir in the basil, tomato and tomato paste. Cook for 1 minute, then season well with salt and pepper.

3 Arrange the tomato mixture on a plate, top with the eggplant and serve.

NUTRITION PER SERVE
Protein 9 g; Fat 6 g; Carbohydrate 25 g;
Dietary Fibre 8.5 g; Cholesterol 0 mg;
910 kJ (215 cal)

Trim the top of the eggplant and cut the eggplant into short, thick batons.

Use two spoons to toss the eggplant in the flour until it is lightly coated.

Stir-fry the floured eggplant in batches until it is golden and just cooked.

CAULIFLOWER STIR-FRIED WITH CASHEWS AND WALNUTS

Preparation time: 30 minutes
Total cooking time: 20 minutes
Serves 4

2 tablespoons oil
2 tablespoons mild curry paste
1 tablespoon currants
1 tablespoon grated fresh ginger
4 spring onions, sliced on the
   diagonal

500 g (1 lb) cauliflower,
   cut into bite-sized florets
2 teaspoons sesame oil
150 g (5 oz) walnuts, toasted
150 g (5 oz) cashews, toasted
1 tablespoon sesame seeds

1 Heat the wok until very hot, add the oil and swirl it around to coat the side. Stir-fry the curry paste over medium heat for 3 minutes, or until fragrant. Add the currants, ginger, spring onion and cauliflower, and toss well. Stir-fry for 4–5 minutes, adding about $1/3$ cup (80 ml/$2^3/4$ fl oz) water to moisten the ingredients. Cover and steam for 1–2 minutes, or until the cauliflower is tender.

2 Season with salt and freshly ground black pepper, and drizzle with the sesame oil. Toss the toasted walnuts and cashews through the cauliflower mixture. Serve sprinkled with the sesame seeds.

NUTRITION PER SERVE
Protein 15 g; Fat 60 g; Carbohydrate 10 g;
Dietary Fibre 8 g; Cholesterol 0 mg;
2750 kJ (655 cal)

Toast the walnuts and cashews by dry-frying them in the wok.

Stir-fry the curry paste in the oil for about 3 minutes, or until it is fragrant.

Add the currants, ginger, spring onion and cauliflower and toss well.

CHILLI NOODLE AND NUT STIR-FRY

Preparation time: 20 minutes
Total cooking time: 12 minutes
Serves 4

1½ tablespoons oil
1 tablespoon sesame oil
2–3 small red chillies, finely chopped
1 large onion, cut into thin wedges
4 cloves garlic, very thinly sliced
1 red capsicum, cut into strips
1 green capsicum, cut into strips
2 large carrots, cut into batons
100 g (3½ oz) green beans
2 celery sticks, cut into batons

2 teaspoons honey
500 g (1 lb) Hokkien noodles, gently separated
100 g (3½ oz) dry-roasted peanuts
100 g (3½ oz) honey-roasted cashews
¼ cup (30 g/1 oz) chopped garlic chives, or 4 spring onions, chopped
sweet chilli sauce and sesame oil, to serve

1 Heat the wok over low heat, add the oils and swirl them to coat the side. When the oil is warm, add the chilli and heat until the oil is very hot.
2 Add the onion and garlic, and stir-fry for 1 minute, or until the onion just softens. Add the capsicum, carrot and beans, and stir-fry for 1 minute. Add the celery, honey and 1 tablespoon water, and season with salt and pepper. Toss well, then cover and cook for 1–2 minutes, or until the vegetables are just tender.
3 Add the noodles and nuts and toss well. Cook, covered, for 1–2 minutes, or until the noodles are heated through. Stir in the garlic chives and serve, drizzled with the sweet chilli sauce and sesame oil.

NUTRITION PER SERVE
Protein 20 g; Fat 45 g; Carbohydrate 75 g;
Dietary Fibre 7 g; Cholesterol 0 mg;
3330 kJ (795 cal)

Peel the cloves of garlic, then cut them into paper-thin slices.

Remove the seeds from the capsicum and cut the flesh into strips.

Heat the oil until warm, then add the chilli and heat until the oil is very hot.

UDON NOODLE STIR-FRY

Preparation time: 15 minutes
Total cooking time: 10 minutes
Serves 4

500 g (1 lb) fresh udon noodles
1 tablespoon oil
6 spring onions, cut into short lengths
3 cloves garlic, crushed
1 tablespoon grated fresh ginger
2 carrots, cut into short lengths
150 g (5 oz) snow peas, cut in half on
   the diagonal
100 g (3¹/2 oz) bean sprouts

500 g (1 lb) choy sum, cut into short
   lengths
2 tablespoons Japanese soy sauce
2 tablespoons mirin
2 tablespoons kecap manis
2 sheets roasted nori, cut into thin
   strips

1 Bring a saucepan of water to the boil, add the noodles and cook for 5 minutes, or until tender and not clumped together. Drain and rinse under hot water.

2 Heat the oil in a wok until hot, then add the spring onion, garlic and ginger. Stir-fry over high heat for 1–2 minutes, or until soft. Add the carrot, snow peas and 1 tablespoon water, toss well, cover and cook for 1–2 minutes, or until the vegetables are just tender.

3 Add the noodles, bean sprouts, choy sum, soy sauce, mirin and kecap manis, then toss until the choy sum is wilted and coated with the sauce. Stir in the nori just before serving.

NUTRITION PER SERVE
Protein 25 g; Fat 7.5 g; Carbohydrate 95 g;
Dietary Fibre 13 g; Cholesterol 0 mg;
2330 kJ (557 cal)

Cut the roasted nori sheets into very thin strips. It is available from Asian speciality shops.

Cook the udon noodles until they are tender and not clumped together.

Stir-fry the greens, noodles and sauces until the choy sum is wilted and coated with sauce.

TAMARI ALMONDS WITH SPICY GREEN BEANS

Preparation time: 10 minutes
Total cooking time: 25 minutes
Serves 4–6

1 tablespoon sesame oil
2 1/2 cups (500 g/1 lb) jasmine rice
2 tablespoons sesame oil, extra
1 long red chilli, seeded and finely chopped
2 cm (3/4 inch) piece of fresh ginger, peeled and grated
2 cloves garlic, crushed

375 g (12 oz) green beans, chopped
1/2 cup (125 ml/4 fl oz) hoisin sauce
1 tablespoon soft brown sugar
2 tablespoons mirin
250 g (8 oz) tamari roasted almonds, roughly chopped (see NOTE)

1 Preheat the oven to moderately hot 200°C (400°F/Gas 6). Heat the oil in a 1.5 litre (48 fl oz) ovenproof dish. Add the rice and stir to coat with oil. Stir in 1 litre (32 fl oz) boiling water. Cover and bake for 20 minutes, or until all the water is absorbed. Keep warm.
2 Meanwhile, heat the extra oil in a wok or large frying pan and cook the chilli, ginger and garlic for 1 minute, or until lightly browned. Add the beans, hoisin sauce and sugar and stir-fry for 2 minutes. Stir in the mirin and cook for 1 minute, or until the beans are tender but still crunchy.
3 Remove from the heat and stir in the almonds. Serve on a bed of the rice.

NUTRITION PER SERVE (6)
Protein 15 g; Fat 34 g; Carbohydrate 80 g; Dietary Fibre 9.5 g; Cholesterol 0 mg; 2874 kJ (687 cal)

NOTE: Tamari roasted almonds are available from health-food stores.

When chopping chillies, it's a good idea to wear rubber gloves to prevent chilli burns.

Cook the rice in the oven until all the water has been absorbed.

Stir-fry the beans for 2 minutes, tossing to coat them in the sauce.

VEGETABLES WITH HONEY AND SOY

Preparation time: 15 minutes
Total cooking time: 5 minutes
Serves 4

1 tablespoon sesame seeds
1 tablespoon oil
1 teaspoon sesame oil
1 clove garlic, crushed
2 teaspoons grated fresh ginger
2 spring onions, thinly sliced
250 g (8 oz) broccoli, cut into small
    florets

1 red capsicum, cut into thin strips
1 yellow capsicum, cut into thin strips
150 g (5 oz) button mushrooms,
    halved
¼ cup (30 g/1 oz) halved pitted black
    olives
1 tablespoon soy sauce
1 tablespoon honey
1 tablespoon sweet chilli sauce

1 Place the sesame seeds on an oven
tray and toast under a hot grill for a
couple of minutes, or until they are
golden. Heat a wok, add the oils and
swirl to coat the base and side of the
wok with oil. Add the garlic, ginger

and spring onions and stir-fry for
1 minute.
2 Add the broccoli, capsicum,
mushrooms and olives to the wok.
Stir-fry for a further 2 minutes or until
the vegetables are just tender.
3 Combine the soy sauce, honey and
chilli sauce in a bowl. Pour over the
vegetables and then toss lightly.
Sprinkle with the toasted sesame seeds
and serve immediately.

NUTRITION PER SERVE
Protein 6 g; Fat 8 g; Carbohydrate 9 g;
Dietary Fibre 5 g; Cholesterol 0 mg;
550 kJ (130 cal)

Remove the seeds and white membrane from
the capsicum before cutting into thin strips.

Stir-fry the vegetables until they are just tender
but keep their bright colours.

Mix together the soy sauce, honey and chilli
sauce and then pour over the vegetables.

SWEET AND SOUR NOODLES

Preparation time: 12 minutes
Total cooking time: 15 minutes
Serves 4–6

200 g (6½ oz) thin fresh egg noodles
3 tablespoons oil
1 green capsicum, sliced
1 red capsicum, sliced
2 sticks celery, sliced diagonally
1 carrot, sliced diagonally
250 g (8 oz) button mushrooms, sliced
4 fresh baby corn spears, sliced on the diagonal
3 teaspoons cornflour

2 tablespoons brown vinegar
1 teaspoon chopped fresh chilli
2 teaspoons tomato paste
2 chicken stock cubes, crumbled
1 teaspoon sesame oil
450 g (14 oz) can chopped pineapple pieces
3 spring onions, sliced diagonally

1 Cook the noodles in boiling water for 3 minutes; drain well. Heat the oil in a wok and stir-fry the capsicum, celery, carrot and mushrooms over high heat for 5 minutes.
2 Add the corn and noodles to the wok. Reduce the heat to low and cook for 2 minutes.
3 Blend the cornflour and vinegar into a smooth paste. Add the chilli, tomato paste, stock cubes, oil and undrained pineapple to the paste and stir well.
4 Pour the pineapple mixture into the wok. Stir over medium heat for 5 minutes or until the sauce has boiled and thickened. Add the spring onions and serve immediately.

NUTRITION PER SERVE (6)
Protein 8 g; Fat 12 g; Carbohydrate 36 g;
Dietary Fibre 5 g; Cholesterol 6 mg;
1182 kJ (282 cal)

VARIATION: Thinly sliced Chinese barbecued pork (*char siew*) can be added to this stir-fry.

Slice the celery, carrot and baby corn on the diagonal for an attractive stir-fry.

Cook the capsicum, celery, carrot and mushrooms, before adding the corn and noodles.

Stir in the spring onions just before serving, once the sauce has thickened.

THAI GOLDEN-FRIED EGGPLANT

Preparation time: 20 minutes
Total cooking time: 10 minutes
Serves 4

2 eggplants (see NOTE)
2 tablespoons oil
3 spring onions, chopped
3 cloves garlic, chopped
1 tablespoon soft brown sugar
2 teaspoons Golden Mountain sauce
1/4 Chinese or curly white cabbage, shredded
2 tablespoons lime juice
2 teaspoons fish sauce
1 chilli, finely sliced

1 Slice the eggplants and cut the slices into small wedges. Heat the oil in a wok. Add the onions and garlic and stir-fry for 1 minute over medium heat.
2 Add the sugar and eggplant to the wok and stir-fry for 3 minutes or until golden brown. Add the Golden Mountain sauce, cabbage and lime juice to the wok.
3 Toss well and then cover and steam for 30 seconds or until the cabbage softens slightly. Add the fish sauce, toss and serve immediately, sprinkled with the sliced chilli.

NUTRITION PER SERVE
Protein 2.5 g; Fat 10 g; Carbohydrate 10 g;
Dietary Fibre 4 g; Cholesterol 0 mg;
595 kJ (142 cal)

NOTE: You can use ordinary eggplant or Thai eggplant for this stir-fry. Thai eggplants are purple or striped purple and white and range from tiny pea-size to golf ball size, to small zucchini size. Any size may be used but the smaller ones may need less cooking.

Slice the eggplants and then cut the slices into small wedges.

Add the sugar and eggplant to the wok and stir-fry until golden brown.

Cover the wok and steam until the cabbage has softened. Then add the fish sauce.

THAI PEPPERED ASPARAGUS

Preparation time: 20 minutes
Total cooking time: 5 minutes
Serves 4

1 tablespoon green peppercorns
1/2 cup (30 g/1 oz) coriander leaves
    and stems
1 tablespoon oil
200 g (6 1/2 oz) snake beans, cut into
    short lengths
150 g (5 oz) asparagus, cut into short
    lengths

2 cloves garlic, chopped
1 teaspoon soft brown sugar
1 tablespoon fish sauce
1 teaspoon chopped red or green
    chillies

1 Finely crush the peppercorns and chop the coriander leaves and stems. Place in a bowl and mix well.
2 Heat the oil in a wok. Add the coriander and peppercorn mixture, snake beans, asparagus, garlic and sugar and stir-fry for 30 seconds over medium heat.
3 Add 2 teaspoons of water to the wok, cover and steam for 2 minutes or

until the vegetables are just tender. Season with fish sauce. Stir through the chilli just before serving.

NUTRITION PER SERVE
Protein 2 g; Fat 5 g; Carbohydrate 2 g;
Dietary Fibre 1.5 g; Cholesterol 0 mg;
252 kJ (60 cal)

VARIATION: Snake beans are particularly long, Asian green beans. If they are not readily available, you can use ordinary green beans or peeled broad beans.

Finely crush the peppercorns, using the flat side of a knife or a cleaver.

Add the coriander and peppercorn mixture, garlic, snake beans, asparagus and sugar to the wok.

Toss through the chopped chilli and stir in, just before serving.

THAI-SPICED CAULIFLOWER AND SNAKE BEANS

Preparation time: 10 minutes
Total cooking time: 10 minutes
Serves 4

4 coriander roots or 1 tablespoon
    chopped leaves and stems
1 teaspoon soft brown sugar
$1/2$ teaspoon ground turmeric
2 cloves garlic, crushed
2 tablespoons fish sauce
2 tablespoons oil
4 cloves garlic, extra, sliced
20 leaves English spinach, shredded
$1/2$ teaspoon cracked black pepper
400 g (13 oz) cauliflower, cut into
    florets
200 g ($6^{1}/2$ oz) snake beans, cut into
    short lengths
6 spring onions, cut into short lengths
1 tablespoon lime juice

1 Using a mortar and pestle or a blender, blend the coriander, sugar, turmeric, crushed garlic and 1 tablespoon fish sauce to make a smooth paste.
2 Heat half the oil in a wok, add the sliced garlic and stir-fry for 30 seconds or until just beginning to brown.
3 Add the spinach to the wok and stir-fry for another 30 seconds or until just wilted. Add the pepper and remaining fish sauce and mix well. Arrange on a serving plate and keep warm.
4 Heat the remaining oil in the wok, add the paste and cook over high heat for 1 minute or until aromatic. Add the cauliflower and stir-fry until well combined. Add 125 ml (4 fl oz) water and bring to the boil. Reduce the heat and simmer, covered, for 3 minutes. Add the beans; cover and cook for another 3 minutes. Add the spring onions and stir until just wilted. Spoon the vegetables over the spinach and drizzle with lime juice to serve.

NUTRITION PER SERVE
Protein 6 g; Fat 0 g; Carbohydrate 7 g;
Dietary Fibre 4.5 g; Cholesterol 0 mg;
232 kJ (55 cal)

Wash the snake beans, hold them in bunches and cut them into short lengths.

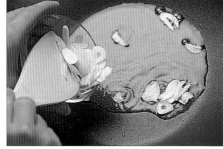

Add the extra sliced garlic to hot oil and stir-fry briefly until it starts to brown.

Stir in the remaining fish sauce and the pepper and then toss to combine.

When the paste is well combined with the cauliflower, add the beans to the wok.

THAI WOK-CURRIED VEGETABLES

Preparation time: 25 minutes
Total cooking time: 20 minutes
Serves 4–6

1 tablespoon oil
1 onion, finely chopped
1–2 tablespoons green curry paste
    (use the recipe on page 246 or
    ready-made paste)
1¹/₂ cups (375 ml/12 fl oz) coconut
    milk
100 g (3¹/₂ oz) snake beans, cut into
    short lengths
1 red capsicum, cut into strips

150 g (5 oz) broccoli, cut into florets
4 kaffir lime leaves
2 zucchini, sliced
2 cups (150 g/5 oz) shredded
    cabbage
2 tablespoons fish sauce
2 tablespoons lime juice
2 teaspoons finely grated lime rind
2 teaspoons soft brown sugar

1 Heat the oil in a large wok. Add the onion and curry paste and stir-fry for 3 minutes over medium heat. Add the coconut milk and 1 cup (250 ml/ 8 fl oz) water and bring to the boil, stirring. Reduce the heat and simmer for 5 minutes.
2 Add the snake beans, capsicum,

broccoli and kaffir lime leaves and simmer for 5 minutes. Add the zucchini and cabbage and simmer for 3 minutes, or until softened.
3 Add the fish sauce, lime juice and rind and brown sugar and toss together before serving.

NUTRITION PER SERVE (6)
Protein 4.5 g; Fat 14 g; Carbohydrate 6.5 g;
Dietary Fibre 4.5 g; Cholesterol 0 mg;
712 kJ (170 cal)

VARIATION: A Thai green curry can be made with just about any mix of vegetables. Celery or green beans could be used instead of snake beans.

Wash the snake beans, hold them in bunches and cut them into short lengths.

Add the sliced zucchini and the shredded cabbage to the wok. Cook for 3 minutes.

Use two spoons to toss the sauce, lime juice, rind and brown sugar through the curry.

VEGETABLES STIR-FRIED IN COCONUT MILK

Preparation time: 20 minutes
Total cooking time: 15 minutes
Serves 4

2 tablespoons oil
2 cloves garlic, chopped
5 cm (2 inch) piece fresh ginger, grated
2 teaspoons green peppercorns
1 eggplant, diced
1 small sweet potato, diced

100 g (3¹/₂ oz) green beans, cut into short lengths
200 g (6¹/₂ oz) asparagus, cut into short lengths
¹/₂ cup (125 ml/4 fl oz) coconut milk
2 teaspoons fish sauce
12 English spinach leaves, trimmed
¹/₂ cup (15 g/¹/₂ oz) Thai basil leaves

1 Heat the oil in a wok. Add the garlic, ginger and peppercorns and stir-fry for 30 seconds. Add the eggplant, sweet potato and 2 teaspoons water and stir-fry over medium heat for 5 minutes.

2 Add the beans to the wok, cover and steam for 4 minutes, shaking the wok occasionally to prevent the vegetables sticking.

3 Add the asparagus and coconut milk to the wok and stir-fry for 3 minutes or until the asparagus is just tender. Add the sauce, spinach and basil and toss until softened slightly. Serve immediately.

NUTRITION PER SERVE
Protein 3.5 g; Fat 16 g; Carbohydrate 10 g; Dietary Fibre 4 g; Cholesterol 0 mg; 826 kJ (197 cal)

Add the diced eggplant, sweet potato and water to the wok. Cook for 5 minutes.

Cover the wok after adding the beans and steam the vegetables for 4 minutes.

Use two spoons to toss briefly until the spinach and basil have softened slightly.

RED VEGETABLE CURRY

Preparation time: 25 minutes
Total cooking time: 30 minutes
Serves 4

1 tablespoon oil
1 onion, chopped
1–2 tablespoons red curry paste (use the recipe on page 246 or ready-made paste)
1¹/2 cups (375 ml/12 fl oz) coconut milk
2 potatoes, peeled and chopped
200 g (6¹/2 oz) cauliflower florets
6 kaffir lime leaves

150 g (5 oz) snake beans, cut into short lengths
¹/2 red capsicum, cut into strips
10 fresh baby corn spears, cut in half lengthways (see NOTE)
1 tablespoon green peppercorns, roughly chopped
¹/4 cup (7 g/¹/4 oz) Thai basil leaves, finely chopped
2 tablespoons fish sauce
1 tablespoon lime juice
2 teaspoons soft brown sugar

1 Heat the oil in a large wok and stir-fry the onion and curry paste for 4 minutes over medium heat.
2 Add the coconut milk and 1 cup (250 ml/8 fl oz) water, bring to the boil and simmer for 5 minutes. Add the potatoes, cauliflower and kaffir lime leaves and simmer for 7 minutes. Add the snake beans, capsicum, corn and peppercorns and cook for 5 minutes or until the vegetables are tender.
3 Add the basil, fish sauce, lime juice and sugar just before serving.

NUTRITION PER SERVE
Protein 7.5 g; Fat 24 g; Carbohydrate 23 g;
Dietary Fibre 6 g; Cholesterol 0 mg;
1414 kJ (338 cal)

NOTE: You could use canned corn spears—add just before serving.

Stir the chopped onion and curry paste in a wok for 4 minutes over medium heat.

Add the snake beans, capsicum, corn and peppercorns and cook until tender.

When the vegetables are tender, add the basil, fish sauce, lime juice and sugar.

THAI CURRIED SWEET POTATO

Preparation time: 25 minutes
Total cooking time: 30 minutes
Serves 4–6

1 tablespoon oil
1 onion, chopped
1–2 tablespoons green curry paste
    (use the recipe on page 246 or
    ready-made paste)
1¹/₂ cups (375 ml/12 fl oz) coconut
    milk
300 g (10 oz) sweet potato, peeled
    and cubed
1 eggplant, quartered and sliced
6 kaffir lime leaves
2 tablespoons fish sauce
2 tablespoons lime juice
2 teaspoons lime rind
2 teaspoons soft brown sugar
coriander leaves

1 Heat the oil in a large wok and stir-fry the onion and curry paste for 3 minutes over medium heat.
2 Add the coconut milk and 1 cup (250 ml/8 fl oz) water to the wok. Bring to the boil then reduce the heat and simmer for 5 minutes. Add the sweet potato and cook for 6 minutes.
3 Add the eggplant and kaffir lime leaves to the wok and cook for 10 minutes, or until the vegetables are very tender, stirring often.
4 Add the fish sauce, lime juice, rind and sugar and toss. Sprinkle with fresh coriander leaves to serve.

NUTRITION PER SERVE (6)
Protein 3 g; Fat 16 g; Carbohydrate 14 g;
Dietary Fibre 3 g; Cholesterol 0 mg;
862 kJ (205 cal)

NOTES: Traditional Thai, pea-sized eggplants can be used instead of the sliced eggplant. Add them to the curry about 6 minutes before serving. The pea-sized eggplants are available, when in season, from Asian fruit and vegetable speciality stores.

Peel the sweet potato and cut it into even-sized cubes for quick cooking.

When simmering the coconut milk, don't cover the wok or the milk will curdle.

Add the eggplant and kaffir lime leaves to the wok and cook until tender.

Toss the vegetables with the fish sauce, lime juice, rind and sugar.

MUSHROOMS WITH HOLY BASIL

Preparation time: 10 minutes
Total cooking time: 6 minutes
Serves 4

1 tablespoon oil
2.5 cm (1 inch) piece fresh galangal, finely sliced
2 cloves garlic, crushed
2 red chillies

200 g (6½ oz) button mushrooms, halved
100 g (3½ oz) oyster mushrooms, halved
1 tablespoon fish sauce
1 teaspoon Golden Mountain sauce
½ cup (30 g/1 oz) chopped Thai basil

1 Heat the oil in a wok and stir-fry the galangal, garlic and chillies for 2 minutes. Add the button mushrooms and stir-fry for 2 minutes. Add the oyster mushrooms and stir-fry for 30 seconds, until softened.

2 Add the fish sauce, Golden Mountain sauce and chopped basil and toss well. Serve immediately.

NUTRITION PER SERVE
Protein 3 g; Fat 5 g; Carbohydrate 2 g; Dietary Fibre 2 g; Cholesterol 0 mg; 275 kJ (65 cal)

VARIATION: You can use fresh shiitake, Swiss brown, straw or any other variety of fresh mushroom.

Fresh galangal is similar to fresh ginger. Peel it and then finely slice it.

Cook the oyster mushrooms briefly, until they begin to soften.

Toss in the fish sauce, Golden Mountain sauce and chopped basil.

MANY MUSHROOM NOODLES

Preparation time: 30 minutes
  + 20 minutes soaking
Total cooking time: 15 minutes
Serves 4–6

30 g (1 oz) dried Chinese mushrooms
1 tablespoon oil
1/2 teaspoon sesame oil
1 tablespoon grated fresh ginger
4 cloves garlic, crushed
100 g (3¹/2 oz) shiitake mushrooms, trimmed, sliced
150 g (5 oz) oyster mushrooms, sliced
150 g (5 oz) shimeji mushrooms, trimmed, pulled apart
3/4 cup (185 ml/6 fl oz) dashi (see NOTE)

1/4 cup (60 ml/2 fl oz) soy sauce
1/4 cup (60 ml/2 fl oz) mirin
30 g (1 oz) butter
2 tablespoons lemon juice
100 g (3¹/2 oz) enoki mushrooms, trimmed, pulled apart
500 g (1 lb) thin Hokkien noodles, separated
1 tablespoon chopped chives

1 Soak the Chinese mushrooms in 1¹/2 cups (375 ml/12 fl oz) boiling water for 20 minutes, or until soft. Drain, reserving the liquid. Discard the stems and slice the caps.
2 Heat a wok until very hot, add the oils and swirl to coat. Add the ginger, garlic, shiitake, oyster and shimeji mushrooms and stir-fry for 2 minutes, or until the mushrooms have wilted. Remove from the wok.

3 Combine the dashi, soy, mirin, 1/4 teaspoon white pepper and 3/4 cup (185 ml) reserved liquid, add to the wok and cook for 3 minutes. Add the butter, lemon juice and 1 teaspoon salt and cook for 1 minute, or until the sauce thickens. Return the mushrooms to the wok, cook for 2 minutes, then stir in the enoki and Chinese mushrooms.
4 Add the noodles and stir for 3 minutes, or until heated through. Sprinkle with chives to serve.

NUTRITION PER SERVE (6)
Protein 15 g; Fat 8.5 g; Carbohydrate 60 g; Dietary Fibre 5 g; Cholesterol 25 mg; 1610 kJ (385 cal)

NOTE: Dissolve 1¹/2 teaspoons dashi powder in 185 ml (6 fl oz) water.

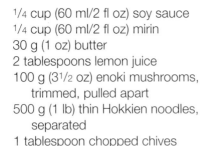

Soak the Chinese mushrooms in boiling water, then drain, reserving the liquid.

Stir-fry the mushrooms for 1–2 minutes, or until they have wilted.

Add the butter, lemon juice and 1 teaspoon salt to the wok and cook until thickened.

BRAISED BOK CHOY

Preparation time: 10 minutes
Total cooking time: 5 minutes
Serves 4 (as a side dish)

2 tablespoons peanut oil
1 clove garlic, crushed
1 tablespoon shredded fresh ginger

550 g (1 lb 2 oz) bok choy, separated, cut into 8 cm (3 inch) lengths
1 teaspoon sugar
1 teaspoon sesame oil
1 tablespoon oyster sauce

1 Heat a wok until very hot, add the oil, garlic and ginger and stir-fry for 1–2 minutes. Add the bok choy and stir-fry for 1 minute. Add the sugar, a pinch of salt, cracked black pepper

and 3 tablespoons water. Bring to the boil, then reduce the heat and simmer, covered, for 3 minutes, or until the stems are tender but crisp.
2 Stir in the sesame oil and oyster sauce and serve immediately.

NUTRITION PER SERVE
Protein 7 g; Fat 11 g; Carbohydrate 3 g; Dietary Fibre 6 g; Cholesterol 0 mg; 582 kJ (139 cal)

Separate the leaves of the bok choy and then cut them into shorter lengths.

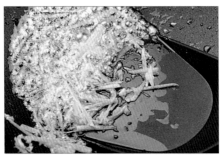
Heat the wok until very hot, then stir-fry the garlic and ginger in the oil.

Stir-fry the bok choy for 3 minutes, or until the stems are tender but still crisp.

SPICED CAULIFLOWER AND PEAS

Preparation time: 15 minutes
Total cooking time: 10 minutes
Serves 4–6

2 tablespoons oil
1 small onion, finely chopped
2 teaspoons yellow mustard seeds
3 cloves garlic, crushed
1 tablespoon finely chopped
    fresh ginger
1 tablespoon ground cumin
2 teaspoons ground coriander

2 teaspoons ground turmeric
1 small head (800 g/1 lb 10 oz)
    cauliflower, cut into florets
1 cup (150 g/5 oz) frozen peas
1/4 cup (15 g/1/2 oz) chopped
    coriander leaves

1 Heat a wok until very hot, add the oil and swirl to coat the base and side with oil. Add the onion and mustard seeds and stir-fry for 2 minutes, or until the mustard seeds pop.
2 Add the garlic, ginger, cumin, coriander, turmeric and 1 teaspoon salt, and stir-fry for 1 minute, or until the spices become fragrant. Add the

cauliflower and stir-fry to thoroughly coat with the spices.
3 Stir in 1 cup (250 ml/8 fl oz) water, cover and cook for 4 minutes. Add the peas and stir-fry for 2–3 minutes, or until the peas are cooked and the cauliflower is tender but still crisp. Remove from the heat and stir in the coriander before serving.

NUTRITION PER SERVE (6)
Protein 5 g; Fat 7 g; Carbohydrate 5 g;
Dietary Fibre 4.5 g; Cholesterol 0 mg;
418 kJ (100 cal)

Cut the head of cauliflower into small florets for quick and even stir-frying.

Stir-fry the onion and mustard seeds for 2 minutes, until the mustard seeds pop.

Add the cauliflower to the wok and toss to coat thoroughly with the spices.

EGGPLANT WITH HOT BEAN SAUCE

Preparation time: 20 minutes
Total cooking time: 15 minutes
Serves 4–6

1/4 cup (60 ml/2 fl oz) peanut oil
800 g (1 lb 10 oz) eggplant, cut into
  small cubes
4 spring onions, chopped
3 cloves garlic, crushed
1 tablespoon finely chopped fresh
  ginger
1 tablespoon hot bean paste

1/2 cup (125 ml/4 fl oz) vegetable
  stock
1/4 cup (60 ml/2 fl oz) Chinese rice
  wine
2 tablespoons rice vinegar
1 tablespoon tomato paste
2 teaspoons soft brown sugar
2 tablespoons soy sauce
1 teaspoon cornflour
2 tablespoons shredded basil

1 Heat a wok until very hot, add
1 tablespoon oil and swirl to coat.
Stir-fry the eggplant in batches for
3–4 minutes, or until browned.
Remove from the wok.

2 Reheat the wok, add the remaining
oil and stir-fry the spring onion, garlic,
ginger and bean paste for 30 seconds.
Add the stock, rice wine, rice vinegar,
tomato paste, sugar and soy and stir-
fry for 1 minute.

3 Mix the cornflour with 1 tablespoon
water, add to the wok and bring to the
boil. Return the eggplant to the wok
and stir-fry for 2–3 minutes to cook
through. Sprinkle with basil to serve.

NUTRITION PER SERVE (6)
Protein 2 g; Fat 10 g; Carbohydrate 5.5 g;
Dietary Fibre 3.5 g; Cholesterol 0 mg;
550 kJ (130 cal)

You don't need to peel eggplant before cooking
it. Simply cut it into cubes.

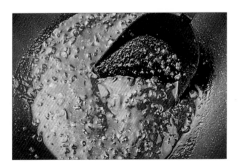

Stir-fry the spring onion, garlic, ginger and bean
paste for 30 seconds.

Add the stock, rice wine, rice vinegar, tomato
paste, sugar and soy and stir-fry for 1 minute.

Curry Pastes

Thai red and green curry pastes are those most commonly used for spicing up stir-fries, but the Panang curry paste is great for cooking chicken, and the musaman curry paste is traditionally used with beef.

RED CURRY PASTE

1 tablespoon coriander seeds
2 teaspoons cumin seeds
1 teaspoon black peppercorns
2 teaspoons dried shrimp paste
1 teaspoon ground nutmeg
12 dried or fresh red chillies, roughly chopped
4 French shallots, chopped
2 tablespoons oil
4 stems lemon grass (white part only), finely chopped
12 small cloves garlic, chopped
2 tablespoons coriander roots, chopped
2 tablespoons coriander stems, chopped
6 kaffir lime leaves, chopped
2 teaspoons grated lime rind
2 teaspoons salt
2 teaspoons turmeric
1 teaspoon paprika

Dry-fry the coriander and cumin seeds in a wok for 2–3 minutes, then finely grind in a mortar and pestle or spice grinder with the peppercorns. Wrap the shrimp paste in foil and cook under a hot grill for 3 minutes, turning twice. Process the ground spices, roasted shrimp paste, nutmeg and chillies for 5 seconds. Add the remaining ingredients and process for 20 seconds at a time until you have a smooth paste. Makes 1 cup

GREEN CURRY PASTE

1 tablespoon coriander seeds
2 teaspoons cumin seeds
1 teaspoon black peppercorns
2 teaspoons dried shrimp paste
8 large fresh green chillies, roughly chopped
4 French shallots, chopped
5 cm (2 inch) piece fresh galangal, pounded or chopped
12 small cloves garlic, chopped
60 g (2 oz) chopped coriander leaves, stems and roots
6 kaffir lime leaves, chopped
3 stems lemon grass (white part only), finely chopped
2 teaspoons grated lime rind
2 teaspoons salt
2 tablespoons oil

Dry-fry the coriander and cumin seeds in a wok for 2–3 minutes, then finely grind in a mortar and pestle or spice grinder with the peppercorns. Wrap the shrimp paste in foil and cook under a hot grill for 3 minutes, turning twice. Process the ground spices and shrimp paste for 5 seconds. Add the remaining ingredients and process for 20 seconds at a time until you have a smooth paste. Makes 1 cup

PANANG CURRY PASTE

8 large dried red chillies
2 teaspoons shrimp paste
3 French shallots, chopped
5 cm (2 inch) piece fresh galangal, pounded or chopped
12 small cloves garlic, chopped
4 coriander roots, chopped
3 stems lemon grass (white part only), finely chopped
1 tablespoon grated lime rind
1 teaspoon black peppercorns
2 tablespoons oil
1 tablespoon fish sauce
1 teaspoon salt
1/2 cup (125 g/4 oz) crunchy peanut butter

Trim the stems from the chillies and soak them in 125 ml
(4 fl oz) hot water for 30 minutes. Wrap the shrimp paste in
foil and cook under a hot grill for 2–3 minutes, turning the
package twice. Place the softened chillies and soaking
water, shrimp paste, shallots, galangal, garlic, coriander root,
lemon grass, lime rind, peppercorns and oil in a food
processor. Process for 20 seconds at a time, scraping down
the side of the bowl with a spatula each time, until the
mixture forms a smooth paste. Add the fish sauce, salt and
peanut butter; process for 10 seconds or until combined.
Makes approximately 1 cup

MUSAMAN CURRY PASTE

1 tablespoon coriander seeds
1 tablespoon cumin seeds
seeds from 4 cardamom pods
2 teaspoons black peppercorns
1 tablespoon shrimp paste
1 teaspoon grated nutmeg
1/2 teaspoon ground cloves
15 dried red chillies
3 French shallots, chopped
2 stems lemon grass (white part only), finely chopped
6 small cloves garlic, chopped
1 tablespoon oil

Dry-fry the coriander, cumin and cardamom seeds in a wok
for 2–3 minutes. Place the spices and peppercorns in a
mortar and pestle or spice grinder and finely grind. Place the
ground spices and remaining ingredients in a food
processor. Process for 20 seconds and scrape down the side
of the bowl with a spatula. Process for 5 seconds at a time
until the mixture forms a smooth paste.
Makes approximately 1 cup

Left to right: Red curry paste; Green curry paste; Panang curry paste;
Musaman curry paste

Sauces

As the majority of stir-fry recipes have Asian flavourings, many of them are enhanced by a chilli or dipping sauce for serving. You can also use the chilli sauces below as an ingredient when required in the recipe.

COOKED HOT CHILLI SAUCE

Chop 2 cloves of garlic and combine in a dry frying pan with 2 stems of finely chopped lemon grass, 6 chopped French shallots, 2–4 tablespoons of chopped, fresh red chillies and 2 chopped coriander roots. Stir for 5 minutes over low heat and then allow to cool. Place in a food processor with 2 teaspoons shrimp paste and 2 tablespoons soft brown sugar. Process for 20 seconds at a time, scraping down the side of the bowl each time, until the mixture forms a smooth paste. Add 2 tablespoons of fish sauce and 3 tablespoons of cold water and process until smooth. A little more water can be added if a thinner consistency is required. Refrigerate in an airtight container for up to 1 month.

QUICK CHILLI SAUCE

Trim the stems from 6 large, fresh red chillies. Cut the chillies open (remove the seeds for a milder flavour) and soak for 15 minutes in hot water. Place in a food processor with 3 tablespoons white vinegar, 1/3 cup (90 g/3 oz) caster sugar, 1 teaspoon of salt and 4 chopped cloves of garlic. Process until smooth. Transfer to a small pan and cook for 15 minutes over medium heat, stirring frequently until the sauce has thickened. Allow to cool and then stir in 2 teaspoons fish sauce. Note: To make sweet chilli sauce, increase the sugar to 1 cup (250 g/8 oz).

Clockwise, from top right: Green Mango Hot Sauce; Tamarind and Chilli Dipping Sauce; Sour Dipping Sauce; Basic Dipping Sauce (Nam Prik); Quick Chilli Sauce; Cooked Hot Chilli Sauce

BASIC DIPPING SAUCE (NAM PRIK)

In a bowl, combine 3 tablespoons fish sauce, 1 tablespoon of white vinegar, 2–3 teaspoons of finely chopped fresh red chillies, 1 teaspoon of sugar and 2 teaspoons of chopped fresh coriander stems and stir until the sugar dissolves.

HOT GREEN MANGO SAUCE

Combine 2 chopped cloves of garlic, 3 chopped French shallots, 1/4 teaspoon of freshly ground black pepper, 1 teaspoon of dried shrimp and 1 teaspoon of shrimp paste in a mortar and pestle or small-bowled food processor. Pound or process until finely chopped and then stir in 1 tablespoon of soft brown sugar, 1/2 finely grated green mango and 2 tablespoons of cold water. This sauce is best used within 12 hours.

SOUR DIPPING SAUCE

In a bowl, combine 3 tablespoons of fish sauce, 2 tablespoons of white vinegar and 2 tablespoons of lime juice. Chopped fresh coriander leaves can be added if you are serving a Thai dish.

TAMARIND AND CHILLI DIPPING SAUCE

Heat 1 tablespoon of oil in a wok; add 4 finely chopped French shallots and 2 chopped cloves of garlic and stir for 2 minutes over low heat. Add 1–2 teaspoons of chopped fresh red chillies and stir-fry for 30 seconds. Add 3 tablespoons of tamarind purée and 1 tablespoon of soft brown sugar. Bring to the boil, stirring, and then reduce the heat and simmer for 5 minutes. Allow to cool before serving. Can be seasoned with a little lime juice.

Flavoured Oils

Using flavoured oils in your stir-fries gives a delicious boost of flavour and, of course, you don't have to save them for cooking: you can use them for salad dressings as well. Use good-quality oil and do not heat above 120°C (250°F) or the ingredients may burn, affecting the flavour. Sterilize jars by washing thoroughly and drying in the oven on the lowest temperature for 20 minutes.

STAR ANISE AND ORANGE OIL

Heat 300 ml (10 fl oz) oil with 75 ml (2¹/₂ fl oz) good-quality peanut oil, 4 star anise and the zest of 4 large oranges in a wok to 105°C (220°F) and cook for 5 minutes. Pour into a sterilized glass jar, seal, cool and refrigerate for 2 days to infuse. Strain the solids and discard. Store in the fridge for up to 6 months. Makes 1¹/₂ cups (375 ml/12 fl oz).

SESAME AND CHILLI OIL

Heat 300 ml (10 fl oz) oil and 3 tablespoons chilli flakes in a wok to 105°C (220°F) and cook for 8 minutes. Remove from the heat and add 75 ml (2¹/₂ fl oz) sesame oil. Strain the chillies and discard. Pour into a sterilized glass jar, seal, cool and store in the fridge for up to 6 months.
Makes 1¹/₂ cups (375 ml/12 fl oz)

GINGER OIL

Heat 1 1/2 cups (375 ml/12 fl oz) oil and 400 g (13 oz) finely sliced fresh ginger in a wok to 105°C (220°F) and cook for 45 minutes, or until the ginger just starts to turn golden. Strain the oil and discard the ginger. Pour the oil into a sterilized glass jar, seal, cool and store in the fridge for up to 6 months. Makes 1 1/2 cups (375 ml/12 fl oz).

LIME AND LEMON GRASS OIL

Finely chop the white part of 2 stems of lemon grass (peel off the tough outer layer and chop away the tough, green end). Pour 1 1/2 cups (375 ml/12 fl oz) oil into a wok and add the lemon grass and the zest of 4 limes. Heat to 105°C (220°F) and cook for 5 minutes, then add 4 shredded kaffir lime leaves. Remove from the heat. Pour into a sterilized glass jar, seal, cool and refrigerate for 2 days then strain, discarding the solids. Store in a sterilized glass jar in the fridge for up to 6 months.
Makes 1 1/2 cups (375 ml/12 fl oz)

CORIANDER OIL

Blanch the leaves, stems and roots of 2 bunches (180 g/6 oz) coriander in simmering water for 10 seconds. Remove and plunge into iced water. Drain well and pat dry with paper towels. Chop the coriander roughly, then process with 1 1/2 cups (375 ml/12 fl oz) oil in a food processor. Seal in a sterilized glass jar and refrigerate overnight. Strain through a fine sieve and discard any solids. Store in a sterilized glass jar in the fridge for up to 2 weeks. Makes 1 1/2 cups (375 ml)

GARLIC OIL

Peel one whole head of garlic, place in a bowl and cover with white vinegar or lemon juice for 24 hours. Drain, discard the vinegar and dry the garlic on paper towels. Place the garlic in a wok with 1 1/2 cups (375 ml/12 fl oz) oil, heat to 105°C (220°F) and cook for 12 minutes, or until the garlic begins to turn golden. Pour into a sterilized glass jar, seal, cool and refrigerate overnight. Strain, discard the garlic and store in a sterilized glass jar in the fridge for up to 6 weeks. Makes 1 1/2 cups (375 ml/12 fl oz)

Left to right: Star anise and orange oil; Sesame and chilli oil; Ginger oil; Lime and lemon grass oil; Coriander oil; Garlic oil.

Index

USEFUL INFORMATION

The recipes in this book were developed using a tablespoon measure of 20 ml. In some other countries the tablespoon is 15 ml. For most recipes this difference will not be noticeable but, for recipes using baking powder, gelatine, bicarbonate of soda, small amounts of flour and cornflour, we suggest that, if you are using the smaller tablespoon, you add an extra teaspoon for each tablespoon.

The recipes in this book are written using convenient cup measurements. You can buy special measuring cups in the supermarket or use an ordinary household cup: first you need to check it holds 250 ml (8 fl oz) by filling it with water and measuring the water (pour it into a measuring jug or even an empty yoghurt carton). This cup can then be used for both liquid and dry cup measurements.

Liquid cup measures

1/4 cup	60 ml	2 fluid oz
1/3 cup	80 ml	2 1/2 fluid oz
1/2 cup	125 ml	4 fluid oz
3/4 cup	180 ml	6 fluid oz
1 cup	250 ml	8 fluid oz

Spoon measures

1/4 teaspoon	1.25 ml
1/2 teaspoon	2.5 ml
1 teaspoon	5 ml
1 tablespoon	20 ml

Nutritional Information

The nutritional information given for each recipe does not include any garnishes or accompaniments, such as rice or pasta, unless they are included in specific quantities in the ingredients list. The nutritional values are approximations and can be affected by biological and seasonal variations in foods, the unknown composition of some manufactured foods and uncertainty in the dietary database. Nutrient data given are derived primarily from the NUT-TAB95 database produced by the Australian New Zealand Food Authority.

Oven Temperatures

You may find cooking times vary depending on the oven you are using. For fan-forced ovens, as a general rule, set oven temperature to 20°C lower than indicated in the recipe.

Note: Those who might be at risk from the effects of salmonella food poisoning (the elderly, pregnant women, young children and those suffering from immune deficiency diseases) should consult their GP with any concerns about eating raw eggs.

Alternative names

bicarbonate of soda	—	baking soda
besan flour	—	chickpea flour
capsicum	—	red or green (bell) pepper
chickpeas	—	garbanzo beans
cornflour	—	cornstarch
fresh coriander	—	cilantro
cream	—	single cream
eggplant	—	aubergine
flat-leaf parsley	—	Italian parsley
hazelnut	—	filbert
minced beef	—	ground beef
plain flour	—	all-purpose flour
polenta	—	cornmeal
prawn	—	shrimp
sambal oelek	—	chilli paste
snow pea	—	mange tout
spring onion	—	scallion/shallot/green onion
thick cream	—	double/heavy cream
tomato paste (US)	—	tomato purée (UK)
zucchini	—	courgette

Weight

10 g	1/4 oz	220 g	7 oz	425 g	14 oz
30 g	1 oz	250 g	8 oz	475 g	15 oz
60 g	2 oz	275 g	9 oz	500 g	1 lb
90 g	3 oz	300 g	10 oz	600 g	1 1/4 lb
125 g	4 oz	330 g	11 oz	650 g	1 lb 5 oz
150 g	5 oz	375 g	12 oz	750 g	1 1/2 lb
185 g	6 oz	400 g	13 oz	1 kg	2 lb

This edition published in 2003 by Bay Books, an imprint of Murdoch Magazines Pty Limited, GPO BOX 1203, Sydney, NSW 1045, AUSTRALIA

Editor: Jane Price **Designer:** Annette Fitzgerald **Chief Executive:** Juliet Rogers **Publisher:** Kay Scarlett

ISBN 1 74045 271 2 Printed by Toppan Printing Hong Kong Co. Ltd. PRINTED IN CHINA.

Front cover, clockwise from top left: Chicken with lemon and capers; San choy bau; Garlic and ginger prawns; Honey and black pepper beef; Savoury rice and eggs; Three-bean stir-fry.